# CLARENDON STUDIES IN THE HISTORY OF ART

*General Editor*: Dennis Farr

*Roger II crowned by Christ:* Palermo, church of La Martorana.

# MESSAGES IN MOSAIC

## The Royal Programmes of
## Norman Sicily (1130–1187)

EVE BORSOOK

CLARENDON PRESS · OXFORD

1990

Oxford University Press, Walton Street, Oxford OX2 6DP
Oxford New York Toronto
Delhi Bombay Calcutta Madras Karachi
Petaling Jaya Singapore Hong Kong Tokyo
Nairobi Dar es Salaam Cape Town
Melbourne Auckland
and associated companies in
Berlin Ibadan

Oxford is a trade mark of Oxford University Press

Published in the United States
by Oxford University Press, New York

British Library Cataloguing in Publication Data
Borsook, Eve
Messages in mosaic: the royal programmes
of Norman Sicily (1130–1187)
1. Italy, Sicily. Mosaics, 1130–1187
I. Title
738.5'2'09458
ISBN 0–19–817504–3

Library of Congress Cataloging in Publication Data
Borsook, Eve.
Messages in mosaic: the royal programmes of Norman Sicily,
1130–1187 / Eve Borsook.
p.    cm.—(Clarendon studies in the history of art)
Bibliography: p.
Includes index.
1. Mosaics, Norman—Italy—Sicily—Themes, motives.   2. Normans—
Italy—Sicily.   I. Title.   II. Series.
NA3792.N67B67 1989
729'.7'09458—dc19    88–11779

ISBN 0–19–817504–3

Set and printed by Butler & Tanner Ltd, Frome and London

*for*
*Otto Demus*

# GENERAL EDITOR'S PREFACE

THIS is the third volume to appear in the Clarendon Studies in the History of Art, and the first to be devoted to a medieval topic. It is a pleasure to publish Eve Borsook's *Messages in Mosaic*, a study of the Norman mosaics of Sicily.

Dr Borsook examines these themes of mural decoration, their arrangement, and the inscriptions which form an integral part of them, and discusses their iconographic significance as a reflection of, and justification for, the new Norman monarchy's political aims. Her approach breaks new ground. She established her reputation with *Mural Painters of Tuscany, from Cimabue to Andrea del Sarto* (1960), the second edition of which was published by Oxford in 1981.

DENNIS FARR

# PREFACE

MORE than thirty years ago, thanks to Professor Harry Bober's memorable lectures on Byzantine art at the Institute of Fine Arts, New York University, I was introduced to Otto Demus's pioneering works, *Byzantine Mosaics in Greece* (written in collaboration with Ernst Diez) and *Byzantine Mosaic Decoration*. More than any others, these two books shaped my perception of the history of painting because they demonstrated how imagery functioned in, and developed from, specific sites. Today 'art in context' is taken for granted; but then it was something entirely new—especially for a young American whose only contact with murals was in the local post office, and who was accustomed to seeing objects in museums wrenched from their original settings, their uses forgotten or unknown. Demus's books, therefore, were a revelation. At that time, I believe he was alone in his approach, because even the most celebrated murals of the Italian Renaissance were seldom, if at all, considered in terms of their sites. During the last twenty-five years, this situation has been rectified to a great extent. Why then a return full circle, as it were, to the twelfth-century mosaics of Norman Sicily, which have been examined several times already by Demus, Ernst Kitzinger, Wolfgang Krönig, Ingamaj Beck, Benedetto Rocco, and others? Because these studies concentrated upon a few specific aspects—such as style, iconography, date, and condition—any message shared by all three of these royal mosaics—at Cefalù, the Cappella Palatina, and Monreale—has escaped notice. Several factors have contributed to this situation. Until now, photographs have given an inadequate view of how the mosaics are positioned, making study of their arrangement difficult. And the historical circumstances which might account for the unusual disposition of both imagery and texts have been neglected. In fact, these mosaics are full of inscriptions, whether on grounds of silver and gold or on the white scrolls of saints and prophets, and it comes as a surprise that the significance of these texts *in situ* as well as in their biblical contexts has been completely overlooked. All these elements—imagery, medium, text, and history—work together to deliver various messages in mosaic.

Taken by themselves, scene by scene and figure by figure, the Norman mosaics are of uneven quality. Demus and Kitzinger have pointed out that this is due to the variety of hands at work and countless restorations. Nevertheless, taken as a whole, these pictorial schemes are unique survivors; there are no other works of a comparable scale which so eloquently and so fully express the aspirations of their patrons.

The pretext for developing this study was offered by graduate seminars held between 1978 and 1986 at Williams College, the University of Virginia, La Trobe University (Australia), and the Scuola Normale Superiore at Pisa, as well as by the Regents' Lectures at the University of California at Santa Barbara in 1987. As an interloper to scholarship of the High Middle Ages, I am grateful to those specialists who shared their wide knowledge and did their best to save me from numerous pitfalls. Among these are Larry

Ayers, Joan Barclay-Lloyd, Hans Martin von Erffa, Anne Holmes, Chiara Frugoni, Julian Gardner, Valentino Pace, Margaret Riddle, Salvatore Settis, Randolph Starn, and Cäcelia Weyer-Davis. Beat Brenk was particularly generous in every way; his criticism and encouragement were of vital importance. To John Monfasani, Mason Hammond, John McManamon, and Ruggero Stefanini are due the beautiful English renderings of several Greek and Latin inscriptions which, thanks to them, now read as truly worthy of a king. Edward Tuttle kindly obtained rare printed matter for me. In carrying out the lengthy and sometimes arduous correspondence, I owe much to the interest and tact of the incomparable Fiorella Superbi Gioffredi. For assistance far beyond any call of duty, I thank Therese Gurski of the J. Paul Getty Museum Library. My warmest thanks to Ornella Francisci Osti who, as professional devil's advocate and friend, has once again cast her eagle eye on the text weeding out errors and contradictions.

Photography in Sicily was made possible by many individuals and institutions. The essential arrangements were made by Professor Oreste Ferrari (Soprintendente, Ufficio Centrale per il Catalogo e la Documentazione, Rome), the late Monsignor Giovanni Fallani (president, Pontificia commissione centrale per l'arte sacra in Italia), Gianna Cacòpardo Bruno of Palermo, and Professor Vincenzo Scuderi (superintendent of the Beni culturali, Palermo). Gracious permission to carry out the work in their churches was given by Monsignor Benedetto Rocco of the Cappella Palatina and the Curia Arcivescovile of Monreale. Sharing the information and expertise they had accumulated over years of looking after these buildings, as well as giving practical help of all kinds, our labour was eased and our knowledge greatly enhanced by the generosity and kindness of architects Lucio Trizzino, Girolamo Naselli-Flores, and Dr Luciano d'Agostino (the latter of Geosonda S.p.a.). Their collaboration turned the occasion into an unforgettable on-site seminar. The photographer, Luigi Artini, surpassed himself, often in circumstances of extreme difficulty, and I am much beholden to him and to the Kunsthistorisches Institut in Florence who lent him to the project. But his results, the pictures which illustrate the themes discussed here, could never have been realized without generous grants from the American Philosophical Society and the J. Paul Getty Trust.

The beautiful graphic renderings which contribute so much to a lucid understanding of the mosaics' situation and organization are the work of my old friends Gordon Morrill and Diane Zervas Hirst. To Professor Ernst Kitzinger and the Dumbarton Oaks Center for Byzantine Studies, I give my thanks for several photographs from their collections.

Finally, this study could not have been carried out without the help of the late Professor Rensselaer Lee of Princeton University, and the support and hospitality of the Harvard University Center for Italian Renaissance Studies at Villa 'I Tatti', and its former director, Professor Craig Hugh Smyth. My warm thanks to Françoise Pouncey Chiarini and her son Francesco for their infinite patience and attention to detail in typing several versions of the text including the final one.

Without the confidence and help of my editors, Frances Whistler and Anne Ashby, and the care of the Oxford University Press staff, the book simply would have been a much poorer effort. My thanks to all of them.

Lastly a few notes: for information concerning the condition of the mosaics, the reader should consult the works of Demus, Kitzinger, Naselli-Flores, and Andaloro, who have devoted many years to their study. As for the biblical texts: for all the Latin inscriptions the Vulgate numbering is used. With the numbering of the Psalms, the Vulgate (using the Greek numbering) precedes that of the modern Bible (following the Hebrew figure, which is usually one number greater than the Greek). For English renderings of biblical texts, I have relied almost entirely upon the *New Oxford Annotated Bible*, edited by H. G. May and B. M. Metzger. These have been used for the sake of convenience and are not intended as literal translations.

E.B.

*Florence*
*April 1986*

# CONTENTS

# LIST OF FIGURES

# LIST OF COLOUR PLATES

# LIST OF PLATES

# INTRODUCTION

SINCE early Christian times, mosaic has been the imperial pictorial medium *par excellence*. But after sixth-century Ravenna, it became a speciality of the Greek East. In the West there were a few scattered revivals on a relatively small scale: during the ninth and tenth centuries in Charlemagne's palace chapel at Aachen and in papal commissions in Rome (e.g. Santa Prassede and the Lateran). Towards the end of the eleventh century, in the narthex and apse of the new abbey church of Montecassino, work was carried out by Greek mosaicists imported for the purpose from Constantinople by Abbot Desiderius, and shortly afterwards another example of early Christian revival was carried out in the apse mosaic of S. Clemente in Rome.[1] But not a trace of the Montecassino mosaics has survived and all we have are some contemporary descriptions.[2] The next great mosaic projects were those of Venice and Norman Sicily. As for the Venetians, although Torcello's mosaics were well under way during the late eleventh century, the far larger project at St Mark's took centuries to complete.[3] In Sicily, however, all the Norman mosaics were probably carried out in less than sixty years.

The Normans surpassed all their medieval predecessors by using the mosaic medium on a scale seldom attempted either by the Byzantine emperors or the popes in Rome. Miraculously, despite countless restorations, these mosaic schemes have come down to us relatively intact. Even in their own day they were recognized as unrivalled since late antiquity.[4] Although the Norman mosaics used the same medium and even some of the same themes as Montecassino and palaeo-Christian Rome, the aesthetic and mystical ideas they express have much more in common with twelfth-century France, where there was a renewed interest in the metaphysics of light explored in the writings of an early Christian theologian whom we call Dionysius the pseudo-Aeropagite, but who was then known simply as St Denis. This saint was a protector of the Frankish monarchy, and the great new royal abbey church outside Paris was built in his honour under the Abbot Suger, who corresponded with King Roger II while the mosaics at Cefalù and Palermo were being set.[5]

The French component is also part of the monarchy itself, and is yet another factor which has been overlooked in the consideration of these royal monuments. As descendants of a Norman family (d'Hauteville), Roger II and his heirs were thoroughly aware of their French heritage. Although the d'Hautevilles had been in South Italy for over a century, they still relied on Frankish customs and ceremonial. We shall see how the Norman kings exploited various French royal traditions in order to justify and glorify their own new monarchy. In the glittering interiors of Cefalù cathedral, in the Cappella Palatina at Palermo, and in the great abbey church at Monreale overlooking the Norman capital, art, politics, theology, and ceremony merge.

The creation of the Sicilian kingdom in 1130 coincided with the recent Latin conquest of the Holy Land. In fact, the Norman conquest of Sicily in 1091 was regarded as a crusade *ante litteram*,[6] which lent the enterprise an aura of sanctity. This was reinforced by a dynastic event: the marriage in 1113 between Adelaide, widow of Sicily's first Norman ruler (Count Roger I), and Baldwin I, the second Latin king of Jerusalem. Part of the marriage agreement was that if the union proved barren, the crown would pass to Adelaide's son, the future Roger II of Sicily.[7] No child was born and in 1117 Baldwin repudiated his queen. Nevertheless, this gave Roger and the future kings of Sicily a claim on a glorious title which the mosaics helped to keep alive. It was the claim to the throne of Jerusalem which fortified the Norman monarchy's legitimacy. And eventually, in 1229, a successor—Frederick II—took actual possession of Jerusalem's crown. This link with the earthly Jerusalem coincided with French monarchical ideas and the pretensions of both haunt the mosaic programmes of the Norman kings of Sicily.

According to contemporary chroniclers, the institutions and trappings of other states were studied attentively by the new Sicilian monarchy.[8] Evidence of this will be considered in detail below. Modern observers have always been struck by how much the mosaics owe to Byzantium. And, indeed, among the artisans there may have been native Greeks who trained teams of local craftsmen to carry out these vast projects with remarkable speed.[9] Like the monarchy itself, the royal mosaics have been seen as hybrid, combining the longitudinal historical narratives characteristic of the Roman basilica with the liturgical cycle of feasts typical of the centralized churches of the Greek East.[10] Until very recently, however, little attention has been paid to the possibility that a comprehensive idea underlies all these mosaics. As far as the Cappella Palatina is concerned, Pasca (over a century ago) and Kitzinger suspected that the mosaics in the eastern end as well as those in the nave comprise a unity planned from the start, and Ingamaj Beck and others subsequently developed aspects of this hypothesis further.[11] Monsignor Rocco interprets the chapel programme as a combination of several themes: the royal-Christological, Christ as beginning and end—as light and life, as well as an exegesis on baptism. Nora Nersessian, on the other hand, sees the scheme as an anti-papal monument glorifying the king as head of a Sicilian Church.[12] As for Monreale, it has been regarded merely as a rhetorical enlargement of the Cappella Palatina: while 'extremely impressive stage decor', its scheme has been judged as 'emptied ... of much of its deeper significance'.[13] It has even been said of Monreale that 'The speculative element is almost completely lacking.'[14] Yet, in my view all the mosaics represent superbly articulated programmes which have been very carefully thought out and co-ordinated. While Cefalù, the Palatina, and Monreale all share the same basic theme, each has its own special message. I have not included the mosaics at La Martorana because they were not created for the king.

The repetition of several themes and images raises the question of whether this was due not to lack of ideas but rather to a deliberate reiteration of notions fundamental to these Norman foundations and their patrons. Why, for instance, is the Genesis cycle given such importance in the naves of both the Cappella Palatina and Monreale cathedral? And why, despite their considerable difference in length, do these biblical narratives conclude with the very same episodes—*Jacob's Dream* and his *Wrestling with the Angel*?[15] Although the possibility of an allegorical explanation for these and other features has been dismissed,[16] historical evidence points to just such a reading.

At this point, I must warn the reader that my understanding of the royal mosaics of Norman Sicily as cohesive arrangements turning upon a theme pertaining to the special status of the monarchy can be controversial. This is because the approach has always been to try to fit these mosaics into the Byzantine tradition. Yet the search for models and prototypes, whether Byzantine or Roman, has repeatedly come to a dead end, with the result that the Norman mosaics have been judged as disjointed and provincial. Certainly, the Normans exploited many traditions—Roman, Byzantine, and even French—and this applies not only to the mosaics but to the style of the monarchy itself. Nevertheless, both are original Norman formulations invented to suit the rulers' needs. In the mosaics, the special messages emerge if one simply takes the trouble to read the many inscriptions and to study the unusual arrangement of words and imagery in the context of their sites, the Bible, the nature of the monarchy, and contemporary events. Of course, the messages peculiar to the hopes and claims of the Norman monarchy are embedded within traditional biblical themes. Like all great monuments, especially those of the Middle Ages, the mosaics are polyvalent in meaning, adding to the universality of their appeal.

[1] O. Demus, *The Mosaics of Norman Sicily* (London, 1950), 371; H. Toubert, 'Le Renouveau paléochrétien à Rome au début du XIIᵉ siècle', *Cahiers archéologiques*, 20 (1970), 122 ff.; H. Bloch, *Monte Cassino in the Middle Ages* (Rome, 1986), i. 45, 123–5.

[2] Bloch, loc. cit., and id., 'Monte Cassino, Byzantium and the West in the Early Middle Ages', *Dumbarton Oaks Papers*, 3 (1946), 198–200.

[3] O. Demus, *The Mosaics of San Marco in Venice*, i. *The Eleventh and Twelfth Centuries* (Chicago and London, 1984), 278 ff.; I. Andreescu, 'Torcello, I: Le Christ inconnu; II: Anastasis et Jugement dernier: Têtes vraies, têtes fausses', *Dumbarton Oaks Papers*, 26 (1972), 192 f.; ead., 'Torcello, III: La Chronologie relative des mosaïques pariétales', *Dumbarton Oaks Papers*, 30 (1976), 257, fig. 1; M. Vecchi, *Torcello: Ricerche e contributi* and *Torcello: nuove ricerche* (Studia archaeologica, 25, 34; Rome, 1979, 1982).

[4] Pope Lucius III referring to Monreale in 1183; cited by T. White, *Latin Monasticism in Norman Sicily* (Cambridge, Mass., 1938), 142; B. Patera, *L'arte della Sicilia normanna nelle fonti medievali* (Palermo, 1980), 55: 'ut simile opus per aliquem regem factum non fuerit a diebus antiquis'; U. Falcando, *La historia o Liber de Regno Sicilie e la Epistola ad Petrum Panormitane Ecclesie Thessaurarium* (written in 1189), ed. G. B. Siragusa (Istituto storico italiano, fonti per la storia d'Italia; Rome, 1897), 180; Riccardus de S. Germano's *Chronica regni Siciliae*, written after 1243 (Demus, *The Mosaics of Norman Sicily*, 152 n. 60); and S. H. Steinberg, 'I ritratti dei re normanni di Sicilia', *Bibliofilia*, 39 (1937), 50.

[5] For the possible relation to the Montecassino cycles see Demus, *The Mosaics of Norman Sicily*, 206 ff., 252, 257; M. D'Onofrio and V. Pace, *Italia romanica: La Campania* (Milan, 1981), 43 ff.; for Roger II and France see E. Kitzinger, 'The Mosaics of the Cappella Palatina in Palermo: An Essay on the Choice and Arrangement of the Subjects', *Art Bulletin*, 31 (1949), 290–2. For St Denis, see E. Panofsky, *Abbot Suger on the Abbey Church of St. Denis and its Treasures*, 2nd edn (Princeton, 1979). For Roger II's letters to Suger in 1147–8 and his gift in 1140 of rock crystal which wound up in the treasury of St Denis, see J. P. Migne, *Patrologia Latina*, clxxxii, c. 640, cited by F. Chalandon,

*Histoire de la domination normande en Italie et en Sicile* (Paris, 1907), ii. 106 f.; H. M. Schwarz, 'Die Baukunst Kalabriens und Siziliens im Zeitalter der Normannen, i: Die lateinischen Kirchengründungen des 11. Jahrhunderts und der Dom in Cefalù', *Römisches Jahrbuch für Kunstgeschichte*, 6 (1942–4), 80; M. and C. Valenziano, 'La Supplique des chanoines de la cathédrale de Cefalù pour la sépulture du roi Roger', *Cahiers de civilisation médiévale*, 21 (1978), 21 f.

[6] White, *Latin Monasticism*, 38; E. Pontieri, 'I normanni d'Italia e la prima crociata', in *Tra i normanni nell'Italia meridionale*, 2nd edn (Naples, 1964), 363, 372.

[7] J. La Monte, *Feudal Monarchy in the Latin Kingdom of Jerusalem 1100 to 1291* (Cambridge, Mass., 1932), 7; E. Pontieri, 'La madre di re Ruggero: Adelaide del Vasto, contessa di Sicilia, regina di Gerusalemme (?–1118)', in *Atti del Convegno internazionale di studi ruggeriani, 21–25 aprile 1954* (Palermo, 1955), ii. 422–9.

[8] Falcando, *La historia*, 6: 'aliorum quoque regum ac gentium consuetudines diligentissime fecit inquiri, ut quod in eis pulcherrimum aut utile videbatur sibi transumeret'; E. Curtis, *Roger of Sicily and the Normans in Lower Italy 1016–1154* (New York and London, 1912), 298; As Safadi, cited in J. Deér, *The Dynastic Porphyry Tombs of the Norman Period in Sicily* (Cambridge, Mass., 1959), 125.

[9] Demus, *The Mosaics of Norman Sicily*, 57, 84, 148, 264 f., 369–72; E. Kitzinger, review of Demus, *The Mosaics of Norman Sicily*, in *Speculum*, 28/1 (1953), 144.

[10] Demus, *The Mosaics of Norman Sicily*, 27, 53, 197 ff., 225 ff., 234, 292 f.; Kitzinger, 'Mosaics of the Cappella Palatina', 270 f., 275 f., 288.

[11] C. Pasca, *Descrizione della imperiale e regal Cappella Palatina di Palermo* (Palermo, 1841), 34; Kitzinger, 'Mosaics of the Cappella Palatina', 270; id., review of Demus, 146 f.; V. Lazarev, *Storia della pittura bizantina* (Turin, 1967), 237; I. Beck, 'The First Mosaics of the Cappella Palatina in Palermo', *Byzantion*, 40 (1970), 119–64. Cf. Demus, *The Mosaics of Norman Sicily*, 58: 'The decoration never composed a unified whole, since it bears the imprint of three different personalities.'

[12] B. Rocco, 'I mosaici delle chiese normanne in Sicilia:

Sguardo teologico, biblico, liturgico', *Ho Theologos: Cultura cristiana di Sicilia*, 11–12 (1976), 121–212; 17 (1978), 10 ff.; 20 (1978),
77–110; N. N. Nersessian, *The Cappella Palatina of Roger II: The
Relationship of its Imagery to its Political Function*, Ph.D. diss. (University of California at Los Angeles, 1981).

[13] Kitzinger, review of Demus, 149; Demus (*The Mosaics of
Norman Sicily*, 228, 235, 250) qualifies this judgement by saying
that Monreale's mosaics 'did not follow the prototype of the
Palatina slavishly, because the apse programme is based on
Cefalù' (ibid. 228, 250, 312). While Demus concedes that Mon-
reale 'was planned as a whole' (ibid. 228 ff.), Kitzinger in 1981

saw no unity at Monreale and noted that its mosaic scheme
lacked focus ('... Monreale reflects a state of uncertainty and
exhaustion.'), E. Kitzinger, 'Art in Norman Sicily: Report on the
Dumbarton Oaks Symposium 1981', *Dumbarton Oaks Papers*, 37
(1983), 169.

[14] Demus, *The Mosaics of San Marco in Venice*, i. 259.

[15] The question has been raised without satisfactory answers:
Demus, *The Mosaics of Norman Sicily*, 245 f.; Kitzinger, 'Mosaics
of the Cappella Palatina', 282 n. 76; Rocco, 'I mosaici delle chiese
normanne', 17 (1978), 47 f., 51.

[16] Demus, *The Mosaics of Norman Sicily*, 245.

# 1

# THE ORIGIN OF THE NEW MONARCHY
# AND ITS STYLE

FROM the beginning, legend conferred the character of a sacred mission upon the Norman presence in South Italy. The site marking the origin of the Norman conquest is the Apulian shrine of Monte Sant'Angelo where, around 1015, Norman pilgrims stopped on their way home from the Holy Land. At this grotto, dedicated to the same saint revered by the Normans at Mont-Saint-Michel (then being built on the coast of the English Channel), a Lombard messenger begged the pilgrims to help drive out the Byzantines.[1] The Normans complied, first as mercenaries and soon afterwards as conquerors. By 1047, Dreux d'Hauteville, the ancestor of the rulers of Sicily, had become duke of Apulia, and by 1074, the remains of the Byzantine empire in the West had crumbled before another member of the same family—Robert Guiscard.

Since 1063, plenary indulgence had been promised by the papacy to anyone who would go to neighbouring Sicily to fight the infidel,[2] and in 1091 Sicily fell to Roger d'Hauteville (the Guiscard's brother). Seven years later Urban II rewarded Roger with the title of Count of Sicily and also granted him special authority relating to the apostolic legateship on the island.[3] All this was established by the papal bull of 5 July 1098, which acknowledged Roger I's successful crusade to regain Sicily for Christendom and the Roman Church. This came just a year before Jerusalem's recovery by the Latin Crusaders.

In the pope's eyes, Sicily was a fief of St Peter's, but this was not so in the view of its Norman conquerors.[4] Nevertheless, the pope charged Roger I with the reform of the Sicilian Church—i.e. replacing Byzantine with Latin clergy.[5] In the interests of religious conformity, the count was allowed to have the final say in establishing dioceses, choosing bishops, and approving papal legates.[6] And as a result of discord on the latter point, part of the bull of 1098 conceded that if no papal legate was available on the island, the Norman ruler could act as a substitute, called a *legati vicem*.[7] Of course, the Normans made sure that this substitute legate was always necessary. Difficulties ensued when the d'Hautevilles forbade any other papal legates on the island and insisted that the high clergy could only approach Rome through the Norman ruler.[8] Early chroniclers (Malaterra and Uguccione da Pisa) can hardly be blamed, therefore, for perpetuating the notion that the rulers of Sicily were, in fact, regular apostolic legates.[9] Moreover, this special authority was eventually reinforced by such visible signs as the use of the papal device—the red *Rota*, or wheel—which was used in lieu of a signature on Latin documents.[10]

When the Count of Sicily's son Roger II was allowed to inherit this surrogate apostolic legateship in 1117, a precedent was set for dynastic rule on the island which combined the highest ecclesiastical with the highest secular authority.[11] This happened in the very year that Roger II's mother, the luckless Queen Adelaide, was repudiated by her second husband Baldwin I, King of Jerusalem. Although it had been agreed that Roger would be the heir should the marriage prove childless, the young Count of Sicily did not fight for his rights, probably because he was busy consolidating his authority in Sicily and increasing his domains closer to home. Nevertheless, the claim on Jerusalem and what it stood for remained as a splendid ploy to be picked up later to enhance the prestige of the future Sicilian monarchy.

During the next eleven years, Roger expanded his territory by capturing the islands of Malta, Ozo, and Pantelleria and laying claim to Norman lands on the South Italian mainland.[12] At Benevento on 22 August 1128, Roger forced Pope Honorius II to invest him with the duchy of Apulia.[13] For some, this hegemony loomed as a menace. Confronted by growing imperial and papal hostility and the evident need to strengthen his authority and assert his independence, Roger sought the status of kingship. Opportunity allowed him to exploit rival papal factions in Rome, and in 1130 a king's crown was obtained for Sicily through a perfectly legitimate pope, Anacletus II. The pope was accommodating because he and Roger shared the same enemies, who subsequently declared Anacletus schismatic and Roger a usurper. Because Anacletus's papacy was not recognized by either the Holy Roman Emperor or the king of the Franks, and because relations with subsequent popes were turbulent, the Sicilian monarchy was challenged throughout the next twenty-six years.[14] It is in the light of this situation that the king's ceremonies, trappings, and decorations must be viewed.

The feasts marking the various steps in the creation of the Sicilian crown were very carefully chosen and they are reflected in the imagery of the royal mosaics. The papal bull proclaiming the new monarchy was made at Benevento on 27 September 1130, the Feast of SS Cosmas and Damian,[15] and, finally, it was celebrated according to traditional rites in Palermo cathedral. Remembering Charlemagne, William the Conqueror, and the first Latin King of Jerusalem, Roger II was crowned on Christmas Day.[16] Christmas and Easter were favourite coronation days; as commemorations of the Lord's Advent and the promise of salvation, they were appropriate for the beginning of a reign—for the advent of a new king.[17] Roger's coronation ceremony consisted of two parts: the unction and the crowning. The unction was performed by Anacletus II's nephew, Cardinal Conte, and the crown was presented by Roger's chief vassal, the prince of Capua (Robert II of Sorrento).[18]

Unction with a special holy chrism was a feature peculiar to the French, English, and Byzantine monarchies. Its formulas demonstrated the divine right to rule, and it conferred a Messianic character upon the king.[19] French legend attributed this chrism as a gift of the dove of the Holy Spirit no less, which descended on the occasion of Clovis's baptism.[20] Anointment with this balm gave the monarch a quasi-sacerdotal status, and endowed French kings with the power to absolve sins, save souls, and cure the sick.[21] The Franks saw themselves as a chosen people—instruments of divine providence—and their monarchy as a revival of the kingship of David.[22] With Roger II, the dynastic link with Jerusalem gave tangible form to the Davidic inheritance subsumed by the new Norman monarchy and appeared to be a fulfilment of biblical history. The sceptre of the realm was probably consigned to Roger II with these words: 'Accept this rod of virtue ... who is the key of David and the sceptre of the house of Israel.'[23] Evidently for the early Franks the exploits of Old Testament chiefs had a greater appeal than those of the pagan heroes of ancient Rome.[24] They even compared their armies to the columns of Israel leaving Egypt under the guidance of an angel who preceded them day and night.[25] The Franks used the biblical phrase 'Ecce mittam angelum meum' for the acclamation of kings—first in the Gallican liturgy and subsequently in the Roman pontifical.[26] And the very same phrase appears in two crucial locations in the mosaics at Monreale.[27] The fact that these words *Pls. 68, 69* were used by the Norman kings of Sicily together with elements of the Gallican liturgy[28] and parts of the Frankish coronation ceremony, shows how much the new monarchy relied upon French traditions—something that was recognized by Roger's contemporaries.[29] Anacletus II (1130–8) probably had an active role in all this. Not only was it he who granted the royal unction to Roger, but he also shared many French connections with him: he had been educated at Paris, had taken the habit of Cluny, and had later returned as papal legate to France.[30] Furthermore, the Gallican liturgy was enjoying a certain revival in Sicily as well as among Benedictines on the Italian mainland.[31]

But French traditions and ceremonial were not the only source of the style of the new Norman monarchy: Byzantium was another. With their absolute control over the Sicilian church, the Normans acknowledged the precedent set in the East.[32] Perhaps under the influence of Byzantines—long resident in Sicily—an edict of 1122 had described Roger as 'sun of justice' and 'light of wisdom'—words used for the Saviour as well as for Byzantine emperors.[33] The emperor of the East, like the Franks, clung to the idea of theocratic kingship, which also suited Roger during periods of difficulty with the papacy.[34] The Byzantine emperor was referred to as 'anointed of the Lord' and 'living icon of Christ',[35] while the coronation ritual acclaimed him as 'crowned by God' and 'crowned by Christ'.[36] This is exactly how Roger II was portrayed in the mosaic at La Martorana *frontis-* (S. Maria dell'Ammiraglio) in Palermo, an image which was particularly appropriate *piece* for an heir to the throne of Jerusalem who, it was then believed, owed his realm to God alone.[37]

As surrogate papal legate, Roger, from 1149 onwards, had the privilege of wearing the mitre, dalmatic, sandals, and other insignia of episcopal office.[38] At La Martorana he appears in priest-like garments, including the imperial *lorum* (or *loros*) of Byzantium, which is also worn by the four archangels in the apse of Cefalù (1148).[39] Moreover, the *Pls. 3–4* crown which Roger is wearing in the Palermo mosaic, as well as that worn by his grandson William II at Monreale, is that of an Eastern *basileus*.[40] In fact, to the outrage of *Pls. 104–5* contemporary Byzantine emperors, Roger allowed himself to be addressed as *basileus* and even appropriated Byzantine imperial imagery for some of his seals and coins.[41] But this may have been merely to preserve an appearance of continuity and legitimacy since the d'Hautevilles replaced Byzantine rule in South Italy.[42] The title was first used officially by Heraclius, who rescued the True Cross and brought it back to Jerusalem,[43] and it is not impossible that Roger's use of it alluded to Jerusalem too. Whatever the reason, the title was a deliberate choice of style—an imperial style for a new king who, not content with his vast Italian possessions, proceeded to invade the North African coast, to claim the principality of Antioch (after Bohemund II's death in 1131), and to make a serious attempt to take Byzantium itself.[44]

[1] Ordericus Vitalis, *The Ecclesiastical History of England and Normandy*, trans. and annot. by T. Forester, i (London, 1853), bk. III, ch. iii, 410 n. 2; F. Chalandon, *Histoire de la domination normande en Italie et en Sicile* (Paris, 1907), i. 27, 48 ff.

[2] E. Pontieri, 'I Normanni d'Italia e la prima crociata', in *Tra i Normanni nell'Italia meridionale*, 2nd edn. (Naples, 1964), 365.

[3] Chalandon, *Histoire de la domination normande*, ii. 620; Pontieri, 'I Normanni d'Italia', 372.

[4] P. Kehr, 'Die Belehnungen der süditalienischen Normannenfürsten durch die Päpste (1059–1192)', *Abhandlungen der preussischen Akademie der Wissenschaften*, Phil.-hist. Klasse (1934), 22–45; S. Podale, 'Il gran conte e la sede apostolica', in *Ruggero II gran conte e l'inizio dello stato normanno* (Relazioni e communicazioni nelle seconde giornate normanno-sveve, Bari, May 1975; Rome, 1977), 25–42; R. Elze, 'Ruggero II e i papi del suo tempo', in *Società, potere e popolo nell'età di Ruggero II* (Atti delle terze giornate normanno-sveve, Bari, 23–5 May 1977; Bari, 1979), 35 ff.; V. d'Alessandro, *Storiografia e politica nell'Italia normanna* (Naples, 1978); and D. C. Douglas, *The Norman Fate 1100–1154* (Berkeley and Los Angeles, 1976), 131.

[5] Podale, 'Il gran conte', 30 ff.

[6] Chalandon, *Histoire de la domination normande*, i. 304–7, ii. 595, 618 f.; E. Curtis, *Roger of Sicily and the Normans in Lower Italy 1016–1154* (New York and London, 1912), 97 ff.

[7] Podale, 'Il gran conte', 38–41.

[8] E. Jamison, *The Sicilian Norman Kingdom in the Mind of Anglo-Norman Contemporaries* (Annual Italian Lecture of the British Academy; London, 1938), 35; H. S. Fink, 'The Foundation of the Latin States, 1099–1118', in K. M. Setton and M. W. Baldwin (eds.), *A History of the Crusades* (Madison, Milwaukee, and London, 1969), i. 368–409.

[9] Podale, 'Il gran conte', 42; Fink, 'The Foundation of the Latin States', 406–9.

[10] The rota consisted of a circle divided by a cross including the king's name and motto. For its use by Roger II, see K. A. Kehr, *Die Urkunden der Normannisch-Sicilischen Könige* (Innsbruck, 1902), 169; H. Enzensberger, *Beiträge zum Kanzlei- und Urkundwesen der normannischen Herrscher Unteritaliens und Siziliens* (Kallmünz Opf., 1971), 78; C. Brühl, *Diplomi e cancelleria di Ruggero II* (Palermo, 1983), 58 ff.

[11] L. R. Ménager, 'L'Institution monarchique dans les états normands d'Italie: Contribution à l'étude du pouvoir royal dans les principautés occidentales aux XIᵉ–XIIᵉ siècles', *Cahiers de civilisation médiévale*, 2/4 (Oct.–Dec. 1959), 454. For the submission of the South Italian bishops, see Elze, 'Ruggero II e i papi del suo tempo', 37.

[12] H. Wieruszowski, 'The Norman Kingdom of Sicily and the Crusades', in Setton *et al.*, *History of the Crusades*, ii. 7 ff., 21.

[13] Chalandon, *Histoire de la domination normande*, i. 396 f.

[14] Ibid. ii. 6 f., 33 ff., 52 ff., 86, 110–22; Elze, 'Ruggero II e i papi del suo tempo', 27, 30–3; Curtis, *Roger of Sicily*, 132 f. At Roger II's death in 1154, Pope Hadrian IV still felt unable to recognize Roger's heir, William I as king: D. C. Douglas, *The Norman Fate 1100–1154*, 125, citing *Regesta pontificum*, viii, No. 177, p. 46.

[15] Chalandon, *Histoire de la domination normande*, ii. 7–9; E. Caspar, *Roger II. (1101–1154) und die Gründung der Normannisch-Sicilischen Monarchie* (Innsbruck, 1904), 93 f., 506 f.; M. Fuiano, 'La fondazione del *Regnum Siciliae* nella versione di Alessandro di

Telese', *Papers of the British School at Rome*, 24 (1956), 65–77.

[16] Caspar, *Roger II*, 96 f., 508 f.; K. A. Kehr, *Die Urkunden der Normannisch-Sicilischen Könige*, 307; P. Kehr, *Die Belehnungen der süditalienischen Normannenfürsten*, 42; R. Elze, 'Zum Königtum Rogers II. von Sizilien', *Festschrift Percy Ernst Schramm* (Wiesbaden, 1964), i. 106 ff.; H. Bloch, 'The Schism of Anacletus II and the Glanfeuil Forgeries of Peter the Deacon of Montecassino', *Traditio*, 8 (1952), 180 f.; id., *Monte Cassino in the Middle Ages* (Rome, 1986), ii. 967) gives the coronation day as 27 Dec. 1130, but this date refers to the papal bull confirming Roger as king and not to the coronation; Ménager, 'L'Institution monarchique', 447. For coronation days and their feasts, see A. Diemand, *Das Ceremoniell der Kaiserkrönungen von Otto I. bis Friedrich II.* (Munich, 1894), 51 n. 1; Orderic Vitalis, *The Ecclesiastical History*, ed. M. Chibnall, ii (Oxford, 1969), bk. III, 183, 185; H. E. Mayer, 'Das Pontifikale von Tyrus und die Krönung der lateinischen Könige von Jerusalem', *Dumbarton Oaks Papers*, 21 (1967), 160 f.; J. Prawer, *Colonialismo medievale: Il regno latino di Gerusalemme* (Rome, 1982), 544, for the crowning of Baldwin I in the church of the Nativity at Bethlehem; J. La Monte, *Feudal Monarchy in the Latin Kingdom of Jerusalem 1100 to 1291* (Cambridge, Mass., 1932), 6.

[17] E. M. Kantorowicz, 'The King's Advent and the Enigmatic Panels in the Doors of Santa Sabina', *Art Bulletin*, 26 (1944), reprinted in *Selected Studies* (Locust Valley, 1965), 45 n. 34; id., *Laudes regiae: A Study in Liturgical Acclamations and Medieval Ruler Worship*, 2nd edn. (Berkeley and Los Angeles, 1958), 166; O. von Simson, *The Gothic Cathedral* (London, 1956), 138.

[18] Chalandon, *Histoire de la domination normande*, i. 112 (chart), ii. 614; Caspar, *Roger II*, 96 f.; J. Deér, *The Dynastic Porphyry Tombs of the Norman Period in Sicily* (Cambridge, Mass., 1959), 11.

[19] M. Bloch, *The Royal Touch: Sacred Monarchy and Scrofula in England and France*, trans. J. E. Anderson (London, 1973), 36–8, 112–16, 131 f.; W. Ullmann, *The Carolingian Renaissance and the Idea of Kingship* (London, 1969), 71–7, 86, 91–3; id., *Principles of Government and Politics in the Middle Ages* (London and New York, 1974), 122 ff.; C. Walter, *Art and Ritual of the Byzantine Church* (London, 1982), 243; A. Marongiu, 'Concezione della sovranità di Ruggero II', in *Atti del Convegno internazionale di studi ruggeriani, 21–25 aprile, 1954* (Palermo, 1955), i. 217 ff.; S. Tramontana, *La monarchia normanna e sveva* (Turin, 1986), 138 f.

[20] Bloch, *The Royal Touch*, 131–2; P. E. Schramm, 'Das Alte und das Neue Testament in der Staatslehre und Staatssymbolik des Mittelalters', in *La bibbia nell'alto medioevo: Settimana di studio del Centro italiano di studi sull'alto medioevo*, 10, 26 Apr.–2 May 1962 (Spoleto, 1963), 236–42.

[21] Ménager, 'L'Institution monarchique', 319; E. O. James, *Christian Myth and Ritual* (London, 1933), 80.

[22] For the theoretical development of the idea of christian monarchs as either a new David or new Solomon, see F. Dvornik, *Early Christian and Byzantine Political Philosophy: Origins and Background*, ii (Washington, DC, 1966), 644 ff.; Schramm, 'Das Alte und das Neue Testament', 237; Kantorowicz, *Laudes regiae*, 56 ff. Pepin, Charlemagne, and Charles the Bald were all referred to as a new David by their contemporaries, as were such Byzantine emperors as Justinian: H. Steger, *David rex et propheta: König David als vorbildliche Verkörperung des Herrschers und Dichters im Mittelalter, nach Bilddarstellungen des achten bis zwölften Jahrhunderts* (Nuremberg, 1961), 126–30, 132–5; H. Fichtenau, 'Byzanz und

die Pfalz zu Aachen', *Mitteilungen des Instituts für Österreichische Geschichtsforschung*, 59 (1951), 28–35, 39. See also T. and D. Godefroy, *Le Cérémonial françois* (Paris, 1649), i. For the association of Byzantine emperors with Old Testament kings and patriarchs, see A. Cameron, 'Images of Authority: Élites and Icons in Late Sixth-Century Byzantium', *Past and Present*, 84 (Aug. 1979), 21 f.; M. Riddle, 'Illustration of the "Triumph" of Joseph the Patriarch', in E. and M. Jeffreys *et al.* (eds.), *Byzantine Papers: Proceedings of the First Australian Byzantine Studies Conference, Canberra, 17–19 May 1978* (Canberra, 1981), 71, 75; Walter, *Art and Ritual*, 242 f.

[23] R. Elze, 'Tre ordines per l'incoronazione di un re e di una regina del regno normanno di Sicilia', in *Atti del Congresso internazionale di studi della Sicilia normanna, Palermo, 4–8 dicembre 1972* (Palermo, 1973–4), 443, 449 f.; see also ch. 4 n. 147 below.

[24] Kantorowicz, Laudes regiae, 56 ff.

[25] Ibid. 56; id., 'The King's Advent', 55 f.

[26] Id., 'The King's Advent', 52 ff. For the use of the Gallican liturgy in the chapel, see L. Boglino, *Storia della Real Cappella di S. Pietro della reggia di Palermo* (Palermo, 1894), 72 n. 11.

[27] Also noted by E. Kitzinger ('The Mosaics of the Cappella Palatina in Palermo: An Essay on the Choice and Arrangement of the Subjects', *Art Bulletin*, 31 (1949), 282 f.), who discusses it in the context of Christ's infancy and the advent of kings.

[28] Kantorowicz, Laudes regiae, 157 ff. The Gallican liturgy was also used in Palermo because the first Sicilian bishops under the Normans were French clergy who preferred this rite: Boglino, *Storia della Real Cappella*, 72 n. 11; cf. I. Beck, 'The First Mosaics of the Cappella Palatina in Palermo', *Byzantion*, 40 (1970), 121.

[29] Odo of Deuil, *De profectione Ludovici VII in orientem*, ed. (with an English trans.) V. G. Berry (New York, 1948), 15: 'And it is not strange that Roger, a wise and powerful king ... one who came originally from our part of the world (and) cherished the Franks.' For neo-Carolingian ideas in both France and Sicily at this time, see von Simson, *The Gothic Cathedral*, 82. For the Gallican movement as an effort to achieve relative independence for the French clergy and monarchy, see Bloch, *The Royal Touch*, 125.

[30] Chalandon, *Histoire de la domination normande*, ii. 4; Bloch, *Monte Cassino in the Middle Ages*, ii. 948; R. Manselli, 'Anacleto II, papa', *Dizionario biografico degli Italiani*, iii (1961), 17 ff. For the Sicilian use of Norman liturgical song, see D. Hiley, 'The Norman Chant Traditions: Normandy, Britain, Sicily', *Proceedings of the Royal Musical Association*, 107 (1980–1), 5, 8, kindly brought to my attention by V. Pace.

[31] Kantorowicz, Laudes regiae, 9 ff.; Bloch, *The Royal Touch*, 125.

[32] M. Amari, *Storia dei musulmani di Sicilia*, iii (Florence, 1868), 303; Chalandon, *Histoire de la domination normande*, ii. 103 f.; Deér, *Dynastic Porphyry Tombs*, 160, 162 f.

[33] Ménager, 'L'Institution monarchique', 313; Dvornik, *Early Christian and Byzantine Political Philosophy*, ii. 620 f., 631; F. J. Dölger, *Antike und Christentum: Kultur und religionsgeschichtliche Studien*, v (Münster, 1936), 9; vi (Münster, 1950), 21—the pictorial image of Christ as the perpetual sun and eternal light became widespread from the 4th century onwards. For the monarch as a reflection of Christ's divine kingship, see H. Böhmer, *Kirche und Staat in England und in der Normandie im XI. und XII. Jahrhundert* (Wiesbaden, 1968; repr. of 1899 edn.), 227 f.

[34] Deér, *Dynastic Porphyry Tombs*, 162; H. de Lubac, *Esegesi medievale: I quattro sensi della scrittura*, i (Rome, 1971), 401.

[35] G. B. Ladner, *The Idea of Reform: Its Impact on Christian Thought and Action in the Age of the Fathers* (Cambridge, Mass., 1959), 110, 117 ff., 120 f.; D. J. Geanakoplos, *Byzantine East and Latin West: Two Worlds of Christendom in Middle Ages and Renaissance* (New York, 1966), 33, 59.

[36] Among the Norman king's titles were 'a deo coronatus': Chalandon, *Histoire de la domination normande*, ii. 612; Geanakoplos, *Byzantine East and Latin West*, 60.

[37] Ménager, 'L'Institution monarchique', 306 f.; A. Grabar, *L'Empereur dans l'art byzantin* (Paris, 1936), 120 and *passim*; O. Demus, *The Mosaics of Norman Sicily* (London, 1950), 303; E. Kitzinger, 'On the Portrait of Roger II in the Martorana in Palermo', *Proporzioni*, 2 (1950), 30–5. For the parallelism between Christ and king see Kantorowicz, Laudes regiae, 81; Deér, *Dynastic Porphyry Tombs*, 161 ff.; K. Corrigan, 'The Ivory Sceptre of Leo VI: A Statement of Post-iconoclastic Imperial Ideology', *Art Bulletin*, 60 (Sept. 1978), 410. For the dating of the Martorana mosaic, see Demus, *The Mosaics of Norman Sicily*, 82 f.

[38] Chalandon, *Histoire de la domination normande*, ii. 612; Caspar, *Roger II*, 402. The insignia granted to Roger by Eugenius III in 1149; Elze, 'Zum Königtum Rogers II.', 110 n. 50. Cf. Kantorowicz, Laudes regiae, 164; F. Pottino, 'Le vesti regali normanne dette dell'incoronazione', in *Atti del Convegno internazionale di studi ruggeriani, 21–25 aprile 1954* (Palermo, 1955), i. 291 ff.; S. H. Steinberg, 'I ritratti dei re normanni in Sicilia', *Bibliofilia*, 39 (1937), 48. The cape made for Roger II between 1132 and 1134, now in the Hofburg at Vienna, was later used as the coronation mantle of the Holy Roman emperors: see T. Al Samman, 'Arabische Inschriften auf den Krönungsgewändern des Heiligen Römischen Reiches', *Jahrbuch der kunsthistorischen Sammlungen in Wien*, 78 (1982), 7–34.

[39] Steinberg, 'I ritratti dei re normanni', 34; H. Norris, *Church Vestments: Their Origin and Development* (London, 1949), 26 f., 33; Pottino, 'Le vesti regali', 291 f. However, Roger's *lorum* (or *stola*) should not be confused with the *pallium*, which only priests could wear: P. E. Schramm, 'Die geistliche und die weltliche Mitra mit Seitenblicken auf die Geschichte der päpstlichen Tiara', in *Herrschaftszeichen und Staatssymbolik: Beiträge zu ihrer Geschichte vom dritten bis zum sechzehnten Jahrhundert*, i (Stuttgart, 1954), 80; id., 'Von der Trabea Triumphalis des römischen Kaisers über das byzantinische Lorum zur Stola der abendländischen Herrscher', 28–36. Schramm noted that Roger's *lorum* in the Martorana mosaic was not like the ecclesiastical *stola* ('Von der Trabea Trumphalis', 36). See also the important study of A. Pertusi, 'Insigne del potere sovrano e delegato a Bisanzio e nei paesi di influenza bizantina', in *Simboli e simbologia nell' alto medioevo, 3–9 Aprile 1957* (Atti: settimane di studio del centro Italiano di studi sull'alto medioevo XXIII) (Spoleto, 1976), 518 f.

[40] Steinberg, 'I ritratti dei re normanni', 33, 44 ff.; cf. Ménager, 'L'Institution monarchique', 455. The inscription in Greek says 'Rogerius Rex'. S. Settis pointed out to the author that although Roger's name is in Greek, his title is a transliteration of the Latin 'Rex'.

[41] Steinberg, 'I ritratti dei re normanni', 33 ff.; Kitzinger, 'On the Portrait of Roger II', 30; Kantorowicz, Laudes regiae, 9; A. A. Longo, 'Gli epitaffi giambici per Giorgio di Antiochia per la madre e per la moglie', *Quellen und Forschungen aus italienischen Archiven und Bibliotheken*, 61 (1981), 43.

[42] Chalandon, *Histoire de la domination normande*, ii. 611; cf. Deér, *Dynastic Porphyry Tombs*, 127 f., 160; C. Settis Frugoni, '*Historia Alexandri elevati per griphos ad aerem*: Origine, iconografia e fortuna di una tema', *Istituto storico italiano per il medio evo: Studi storici*, 80–2 (Rome, 1973), 310 ff.; ead., 'Il mosaico di Otranto: Modelli culturali e scelte iconografiche', *Bullettino dell'Istituto storico italiano per il Medio Evo e archivio muratoriano*, 82 (1970), 255 ff.

[43] Ladner, *The Idea of Reform*, 117 f. n. 32; H. Enzensberger, 'Basileus', *Lexikon des Mittelalters*, i (Munich and Zürich, 1980), col. 1523.

[44] Wieruszowski, 'The Norman Kingdom of Sicily', 10–26; Chalandon, *Histoire de la domination normande*, ii. 133; Demus, *The Mosaics of Norman Sicily*, 309; Deér, *Dynastic Porphyry Tombs*, 128 f.; S. Runciman, *A History of the Crusades: The Kingdom of Jerusalem and the Frankish East 1100–1187* (Cambridge, 1952), ii. 251 f.; Douglas, *The Norman Fate*, 190 f.

# CEFALÙ: ECHOES OF JERUSALEM
## (Plates 1–15)

*frontis-
piece*

*Pls. 1–2*
*Fig. 1*

LIKE the *Coronation* mosaic in the Martorana, Roger's assumption of Frankish ritual and Byzantine regalia signified that his monarchy was responsible to God alone; it was a declaration of independence from papal political interference.[1] The cathedral church of Cefalù was an expression of the same stance.[2] It was the king's first ecclesiastical creation and, as on other occasions, great care was taken with the ceremonial and the significance of the feast-days connected with its founding. The dedication day chosen for laying the corner-stone was Pentecost Sunday, 7 June 1131. The feast commemorated the Holy Spirit's descent to Mary and Christ's disciples empowering them to carry out their evangelical mission. It was also used by the Byzantine emperors to reaffirm their divine right to rule. Originally, Cefalù was dedicated to the Saviour alone; the names of Peter and Paul were added later.[3] Pope Anacletus II decreed it a cathedral on 14 September 1131.[4] This was the Feast of the Exaltation of the True Cross commemorating Constantine the Great's dedication of the church of the Holy Sepulchre in Jerusalem, which in Roger's time was being rebuilt by the Crusaders, who intended to use it as the burial site for the new dynasty of the Latin kings.[5] Roger planned to use Cefalù in a similar way: to commemorate his own burial as well as to perpetuate his name.[6]

Cefalù's joint dedication to the Saviour and subsequently to the founders of the Latin Church reveals the king's concept of the sources of royal power. Franco-Byzantine ideas of theocratic kingship came first, the Roman connection via the Apostles came afterwards. According to Byzantine theory, God was the universal source of all authority, both religious and secular; Christ as the Divine Logos was the supreme priest and king on earth united.[7] But after Christ's departure from this world, the power was divided between the spiritual sphere assigned to the Apostles and the civil authority granted to Caesar. For the Byzantines and also for the Frankish kings (because of unction with the holy chrism), the king's authority came directly from God, while that of the Church was only derived from Christ through the Apostles.[8] In the East, the emperor was God's minister on earth and he ruled in imitation of the Almighty, hence the likeness of Roger to Christ

*frontis-
piece*

*Pl. 3*

in the Martorana *Coronation* mosaic.[9] However, the emperor was also compared to an Apostle sharing in the evangelical mission.[10] As an acting apostolic legate, Roger II fulfilled this mission by returning Sicily to the Roman Church—faithful to the charge of 1063 when the pope gave the Normans a flag of St Peter after the victory of Cerami.[11] Nevertheless, the dedicatory inscription in the apse of Cefalù mentions only the Saviour and not Peter and Paul. Altogether, they—as well as Roman saints generally—occupy minor roles at Cefalù, even though Alexander of Telese, a Benedictine contemporary of

FIG. 1 Cefalù cathedral: view from the south-west

Roger's, reported a dream in which Peter and Paul figure as the king's guides and protectors.[12] Another legend, perhaps related to the dream, claimed that Cefalù was built in thanksgiving for Roger's survival from a stormy sea-crossing when the king begged the Saviour to rescue him as he had saved Peter and Paul.[13] But there may have been still other factors which accounted for the inclusion of these Apostles. One of them had a special relationship with the name of Cefalù itself. Since the seventh century before Christ, the rocky headland upon which the town is situated was called Cephalaedium—related *Pl. 2* to the Greek transliteration of Peter's name in Aramaic.[14] Like Peter, Roger built his first church upon a rock. Furthermore, Peter and Paul were important to Roger's status because in the Bible they invoke the king's authority as God's minister.[15] At Cefalù this meaning is less than obvious, but the theme subsequently became explicit in the mosaics at Monreale.

Although Augustinians were frequently chosen to serve as cathedral canons, those invited to come to Cefalù had close ties with the Holy Land.[16] They were known as canons of the Holy Sepulchre of Jerusalem and they were probably French.[17] Roger brought them to Cefalù from their monastery at Bagnara, which had been founded by his father on the Calabrian coast in 1085. These Augustinians had been entrusted with the care of many holy sites in Jerusalem and owned properties in Sicily, some of which came from Roger's mother Queen Adelaide.[18]

*Pl. 1*

Intended as a royal mausoleum, Cefalù's construction must have been sufficiently advanced by 1145 to accommodate two precious porphyry sarcophagi sent there by the king. Somehow, Roger must have acquired the porphyry as spoils which were then carved for him in imitation of classical examples.[19] One of the sarcophagi was intended for the king's body, but the second was deliberately left empty as a cenotaph honouring his name.[20] They were situated somewhere in the transept, but whether they were close to the presbytery or in the arms of the transept is unclear.[21]

The unique Egyptian quarry which supplied porphyry was already exhausted in ancient times. Porphyry was a stone traditionally reserved for emperors, who in the Christian era resorted to spoils. Although Byzantine emperors used porphyry for the room in which the imperial children were born (hence the phrase 'born to the purple') and for ceremonial pavement-markers and revetments, the stone had not been used for imperial sarcophagi since the mid-fifth century.[22] However, just two years before Roger II sent his porphyry sarcophagi to Cefalù, the king's antagonist Pope Innocent II had taken the unprecedented step of appropriating the ancient porphyry sarcophagus in Hadrian's mausoleum in Rome for his own use in the basilica of St John in the Lateran.[23] Roger's decision to use porphyry sarcophagi therefore appears as a deliberate riposte because the material was a sign of sovereignty. Originally, these sarcophagi may have been furnished with the canopies to be seen over them now in Palermo cathedral. The matter has been disputed, but recently a neglected event has been brought to light: a century ago the remains were discovered of a canopy, some parts of which were made of porphyry from the tomb of Roger's father.[24] This lends support to the idea that such structures were also part of Roger II's intentions. Because such arrangements resemble altar ciboria, these free-standing canopied tombs allude to the sacred nature of the rulers buried beneath them.

*Pls. 1, 3*

Because of an ecclesiastical dispute, Cefalù cathedral, which was begun the year after Roger's coronation, was not consecrated until 1166, and the building itself may have been completed then or not long afterwards.[25] The basilican plan of the church with its transept, choir, apses, and engaged colonettes belongs to a type already found in Calabria and eastern Sicily (particularly Catania and Mazara cathedrals).[26] By 1148, the eastern end of the building was finished up to the crossing, and the inscription in the lower border of the apse mosaics states that they were completed in that year:

ROGERIVS REX EGREGIVS PLENIS [sic] PIETATIS
HOC STATVIT TEMPLVM MOTVS ZELO DEITATIS
HOC OPIBVS DITAT VARIIS VARIOQVE DECORE

ORNAT MAGNIFICAT IN SALVATORIS HONORE
ERGO STRVCTORI TANTO SALVATOR ADESTO
VT SIBI SVBMISSOS CONSERVET CORDE MODESTO:
ANNO AB INCARNACIONE DMI MILLESIMO CENTESIMO
XLVIII INDICTIONE XI ANNO V°[VERO] REGNI EIVS XVIII
HOC OPVS MVSEI FACTVM EST

[Roger, the illustrious king, full of piety, built this temple, moved by zeal for the deity. He endows it with various riches and adorns it with various embellishments. He glorifies it in the honour of the Saviour. Therefore, for so great a builder, let the Saviour be present [or: be of help] in order that he may retain for himself [the affection] of his subjects by his modest, unassuming heart. In the year from the Incarnation of [our] Lord, the one thousand, one hundred and forty-eighth year in the eleventh indiction in the eighteenth year, indeed, of his reign, this mosaic was executed.]

The style and scheme of the mosaics partly reflect Greek examples: the Byzantine Ascension devised for a cupola and its supporting arches was here recast in abbreviated form into a basilican apse and presbytery.[27] The dominating image, in the apse conch, is *Pls. 3–5* the\ bust of Christ as the omnipotent, or Pantocrator, holding the open book with the Greek and Latin texts from John 8:12: 'I am the Light of the World, he who follows me will not walk in darkness.'

The half-length Pantocrator with a closed Gospel-book had already appeared in late seventh-century Byzantine coinage.[28] Examples with the open book seem to be a Western variation. The mosaic Pantocrators in the domes of Constantinople have all been lost: in the palatine chapel of Our Lady of Pharos (ninth century), in the Apostoleion, and in Hagia Sophia (before 1345).[29] In the early twelfth century, there was a mosaic of the risen or ascendent Christ with Mary and attendant Apostles in the sanctuary area of the church of the Holy Sepulchre in Jerusalem.[30] Intertwined with the Ascension theme is the mystery of salvation: Christ's reunion with the Father and his return at the end of time.[31] This eschatological aspect is taken up by the inscription around the Saviour's bust at Cefalù and is particularly appropriate to royalty either living or dead:

FACTVS HOMO FACTOR HOMINIS FACTIQVE REDEMPTO[R]
IVDICO CORPOREVS CORPORA DEVS

[Made man, I the maker and redeemer of the made, I judge bodies [i.e. humans] as an embodied God'.]

On the curved apse wall below the Saviour are three tiers of figures including Mary, *Pls. 3–4* angels, and twelve Apostles in an arrangement which in several respects resembles paleo-Christian pictorial schemes for the Ascension.[32] The uppermost tier has as its centre the *Col. Pl. I* orant Virgin flanked by four archangels in imperial vestments. Then there are two tiers of Apostles arranged on either side of a central window: *Mark, Matthew, Peter, Paul, John,* and *Luke* (above); and *Philip, James, Andrew, Simon, Bartholomew,* and *Thomas* (below). Appropriately, the higher tier was reserved for the evangelists and the founders of the *Pls. 6–7,* Church of Rome. In the vault there are angels and seraphim. *Col. Pl. II*

*Pls. 8–13*
On either side of the apse, more mosaics fill the lunettes and three tiers on the walls below them. Each figure is identified by an inscription and many carry scrolls with abbreviated messages appropriate to the site and its function. For instance, five of the six Old Testament prophets who occupy the lunettes are rulers. The single exception, Hosea, *Pl. 10* has the same name as the last biblical king of Israel. The lunette on the liturgical right (our left) includes a medallion of *Melchizedek*, the priest-king of Salem, and below him on either side are *Moses* (the recipient of the sacred law) and *Hosea*. These three are all *Pl. 11* prophets of the Messiah, while those opposite them are ancestors of Christ. In the lunette on our right, *Abraham* occupies the medallion as father of the faithful who made a covenant with God, and beside him are the two kings of Jerusalem *David* and *Solomon*. The surviving scrolls[33] held by Hosea, David, and Solomon bear messages alluding to the Resurrection and the Last Judgement, and admonish the beholder to hearken unto the Lord.[34]

Beneath the lunettes stand further prophets—three on either wall. From left to right, *Pls. 8–9* they are: *Joel, Amos, Obadiah, Jonah, Micah,* and *Nahum*. Joel's scroll refers to Pentecost, Cefalù's foundation day, while Amos's concerns the restoration of the Davidic monarchy.[35] Obadiah's scroll is a nineteenth-century reconstruction, probably based on bits of the heavily damaged original.[36] The message on his scroll refers to the house of Jacob—an important theme at both the Cappella Palatina and Monreale.[37] Opposite, Jonah's message may be a reminder of Roger's miraculous survival from a stormy crossing to Sicily, while Micah and Nahum's scrolls refer to eschatological matters.[38]

Below these prophets are two tiers of saints arranged according to certain categories. For instance, most of the saints on our left (which is the liturgical right and therefore a place of precedence) are Latin saints, while those on the opposite wall are all Greek, appropriately identified by inscriptions in Greek.[39] In the upper tier, most of the figures on our left are deacon martyrs: *Peter of Alexandria, Vincent of Saragossa* (also an army saint), *Lawrence,* and *Stephen*. Opposite them is a row of Eastern warrior saints: *Theodore, George, Demetrius,* and *Nestor,* several of whom had special Norman associations.[40] For instance, George, Stephen, Vincent, and Theodore (along with Denis in the lower tier) were invoked for the king in the Gallo-Frankish royal laudes.[41] In 1147, the year before the apse inscription, Theodore's relics were brought to the West by Norman sailors.[42] The same thing happened in 1087, when the bones of St Nicholas were brought to Bari, where he became the patron saint of the duchy of Apulia.[43] Several of the other warrior saints were seen by the Normans in legendary visions during great moments in their history: in 1063 St George appeared at the battle of Cerami, and in 1099 he reappeared with Demetrius and Mercurius to rescue the Norman Crusaders at Antioch.[44] Finally, George was said to have come again to protect Roger II during a perilous crossing to Sicily.[45]

The lowermost tier is reserved for bishop saints with, once again, a separation between the Latins and the Greeks. On our left are: *Gregory, Augustine, Sylvester,* and *Denis* (Dionysius); with *Nicholas of Myra, Basil, John Chrysostom,* and *Gregory the Theologian* (Nazianzenus) on the right. These saints are so arranged that appropriate types face each other symmetrically. *Pope Gregory the Great* faces *Gregory the Theologian*—fathers of the Western and Eastern Churches—and, similarly, *Augustine* faces *John Chrysostom*. Then *Sylvester,* the bishop of Rome, faces *Basil,* a Doctor of the Church and archbishop of Caesarea. The places of honour, on either side of the apse, are occupied by *Denis* and *Nicholas*. Instead of being grouped with the other Eastern saints, Denis is set among the Latins. This is because he was a patron of the French monarchy as well as a legendary Apostle of Gaul. At Cefalù he has the place of precedence on the liturgical right, while *Nicholas*—the recently installed patron saint of Apulia—is the pendant figure on the opposite side.

As to the Augustinians who officiated at Cefalù, their patron saint is included among the Latin church fathers, while the titulars of their home monastery at Bagnara are represented by Mary and the Apostles—the witnesses of the ascended Saviour in the apse.

*Pls. 3, 8, 12*

Due to lack of archaeological evidence, the question of where the king and archbishop sat at Cefalù has not been resolved. This is important, because the arrangement of the mosaics was undoubtedly determined by this factor. Because so many of the royal allusions in both imagery and inscriptions are situated on the liturgical right (our left), which is also the side of all the Latin saints, there is good reason to suppose that this was also the side of the Norman king—i.e. that originally either Roger's sarcophagus or some kind of royal seat (or both) were located in or near this side of the presbytery.[46] In fact, a royal throne was built on to the left side of the presbytery entrance, but unfortunately this throne, as well as that of the bishop facing it, were pseudo-medieval concoctions and were dismantled in March 1985.[47] The prototype for these pastiches (as well as for the bishop's throne still in Palermo cathedral) is clearly that of the authentic royal throne located in an analogous position in Monreale cathedral.

*Pl. 14*

*Pl. 15*

*Pls. 64, 103*
*Col. Pl. VIII*

There is further iconographical as well as historical evidence to support the idea that the royal side at Cefalù was on the left—called the liturgical right because the officiating cleric faced the faithful from behind the altar. We know that the church was intended as a royal burial site and that the *Pantocrator* and several inscriptions in the apse appropriately included eschatological messages. As Christ's apotheosis,[47] the Ascension was particularly well suited to the royal mausoleum of an anointed ruler linked to Jerusalem's throne and Christ's kingship. The idea that after his Ascension Christ shared the throne of Heaven on the right of the Father was a beloved feature of benediction formulas for medieval rulers who aspired to a place close to the celestial throne in the hereafter.[49] In this spirit, Roger II used this motto on all his diplomas from at least 1136 onwards:

DEXTERA DOMINI FECIT VIRTUTEM, DEXTERA DOMINI EXALTAVIT ME.

[The right hand of the Lord made me strong, the right hand of the Lord exalted me.]

This is part of Vulgate Psalm 117—a psalm of thanksgiving for deliverance in battle.[50] Since the position of the royal throne at Monreale, as well as the inscription in the mosaic above it, accord perfectly with this motto, it seems very likely that the royal side at Cefalù was planned to conform to the same idea.

*Pls. 103–4*
*Col. Pl. VIII*

Because there was hostility between the papacy and Roger for most of his reign, it is hardly surprising that Rome's role at Cefalù was not conspicuous. In fact, Rome did not formally recognize the Sicilian monarchy with all its claims until 1156—two years after Roger's death.[51] Therefore, Cefalù was planned and administered as a not so remote reflection of the church of the Holy Sepulchre in Palestine, and the messages of the mosaics had a double meaning, alluding to the Messiah as well as to the king of Sicily's link to both the terrestrial and the celestial Jerusalem.[52]

*Pls. 8–13*

As for the execution of the mosaics, recent scholarship seems to agree that the apse, the vault, and possibly the lunettes as well were completed by Greeks called to the site during Roger's lifetime.[53] The saints on the side walls, however, are recognized as being of different workmanship, and they have been dated later than the others—even a decade or so after Roger's death in 1154.[54] Whether by Greek or local artisans, the statuesque figures have been compared to Byzantine ivories and to contemporary French sculpture—specifically to the *Porte royale* of Chartres cathedral, with its sentry-like figures standing

*Pl. 3*

beneath an Ascension.[55] In their own way, the apse mosaics of Cefalù also comprise a royal gate to the celestial kingdom, both visually and thematically.

While the apse mosaics were being carried out, Roger's kingdom expanded and his military exploits ranged from one end of the Mediterranean to the other. In 1146 Tripoli was added to the North African possessions.[56] Meanwhile, the Second Crusade was under way. At first, Roger was a willing collaborator; in February 1148 he offered his great fleet to bring the Crusaders to Syria, where he hoped to realize his claim to the principality of Antioch.[57] But when it was decided to take the land route, Roger lost all interest in the enterprise, which was being promoted by King Louis VII of France, Bernard of Clairvaux, and Pope Eugenius III.[58] Instead, Roger sent his admiral and minister of state George of Antioch to raid Greece and the shores of the Bosphorus,[59] and it is possible that part of the booty, besides the relics of St Theodore, included Greek mosaicists and tesserae subsequently used for work at Cefalù and Palermo. But not a single document or account tells us anything about who the mosaicists were or even where their materials came from. There must have been a lot of Greek artisans about in those years, for their workmanship has been detected not only at Cefalù but throughout Admiral George's church of La Martorana in Palermo (1143–51), and possibly in the earliest mosaics of the Cappella Palatina as well.[60]

During this same period, Roger's relations with France reached new peaks. In the spring of 1149, as the disappointed Louis VII was sailing back from the Holy Land, he was rescued from a sea battle by a Sicilian ship and taken to Calabria. There he was joined by Roger II and Louis's wife Eleanor of Aquitaine who had been a guest at the court of Palermo.[61] At this point, Roger was at the height of his power: he was master of South Italy and the North African coast; he had gained the sympathy of the French king; and he had momentarily humiliated the Byzantine emperor. In the same year, therefore, he attempted a *rapprochement* with the papacy.[62] Eugenius III needed money and troops to regain Rome and Roger supplied him with both. Although the pope renewed Roger's surrogate apostolic legateship, he wavered in recognizing all his territorial claims and even left privileges of the Sicilian monarchy in doubt.[63] Nevertheless, a contemporary French poem praises Roger as one of the glories of Rouen, the capital of Normandy: 'Tu Rogere potens, tu maxima gloria regum, ruler of Italy and Sicily, Africa, Greece and Syria; even Persia trembles, even the bright skies of Ethiopia and the dark gloom of Germany seek protection. Rouen alone is worthy of the empire of the world.'[64]

That the mosaics at Cefalù were restricted to a limited area in the presbytery was due to Roger II's diminishing interest in the church.[65] Its status as a cathedral was disputed throughout his lifetime,[66] and Cefalù never fulfilled its intended purpose as a royal mausoleum. At Roger's death in 1154, the unfinished church was still unconsecrated, so the king's body remained in the capital and never entered the cathedral down the coast.[67] After years of haggling, the two empty porphyry sarcophagi were eventually taken to Palermo by Frederick II.

[1] J. Deér, *The Dynastic Porphyry Tombs of the Norman Period in Sicily* (Cambridge, Mass., 1959), 160 f.

[2] O. Demus, *The Mosaics of Norman Sicily* (London, 1950), 195.

[3] L. T. White, *Latin Monasticism in Norman Sicily* (Cambridge, Mass., 1938), 189; K. Corrigan, 'The Ivory Sceptre of Leo VI: A Statement of Post-Iconoclastic Imperial Ideology', *Art Bulletin*, 60 (Sept. 1978), 413, 415. For the text of the foundation document, see M. and C. Valenziano, 'La Supplique des chanoines de la cathédrale de Cefalù pour la sépulture du roi Roger', *Cahiers de civilisation médiévale*, 21 (1978), 10 f. Pentecost was linked mystically with the giving of the law to Moses on Mt Sinai and, therefore, was also used sometimes as a coronation day; e.g. Frederick II: E. Kantorowicz, *Laudes regiae: A Study in Liturgical Acclamations and Medieval Ruler Worship*, 2nd edn. (Berkeley and Los Angeles, 1958), 166; O. Treitinger, *Die oströmische Kaiser- und Reichsidee nach ihrer Gestaltung im höfischen Zeremoniell* (Jena, 1938), 37; O. von Simson, *Sacred Fortress: Byzantine Art and Statecraft in Ravenna* (Chicago, 1948), 34. Although an archbishop named Ugone is said to have added the Apostles' names in 1145, neither Roger nor the bishop of Cefalù (between 1150 and 1156) ever referred to the church as anything other than S. Salvatore. The addition of Peter and Paul seems to have been an effort to romanize Roger's church. In fact, the 14th-century *Rollus rubeus* (a series of putative copies of earlier, lost documents which is now in the Archivio di Stato, Palermo) introduced the legend that Cefalù was founded as a votive offering after Peter and Paul had saved Roger from shipwreck before his safe landing at Cefalù on the Feast of the Transfiguration (6 Aug. 1130): C. Valenziano, 'La basilica cattedrale di Cefalù nel periodo normanno', *Ho Theologos*, 19 (1978), 86, 96 ff., 100; cf. B. Rocco, 'I mosaici delle chiese normanne in Sicilia: Sguardo teologico, biblico, liturgico', *Ho Theologos*, 20 (1978), 79.

[4] White, *Latin Monasticism*, 189; M. and C. Valenziano, 'La Supplique des chanoines', 10 f.

[5] For the consecration of Constantine's church of the Holy Sepulchre and Eusebius of Caesarea's comparison of the occasion to a second Pentecost, see A. Heisenberg, *Grabeskirche und Apostelkirche: Zwei Basiliken Konstantins: Untersuchungen zur Kunst und Literatur des ausgehenden Altertums* (Leipzig, 1908), i. 1, 16. The Crusaders rebuilt the church between 1099 and 1161 and it was consecrated on the 50th anniversary of their capture of Jerusalem on 15 July 1149: R. G. Ousterhout, 'The Church of Santo Stefano: A "Jerusalem" in Bologna', *Gesta*, 20/2 (1981), 312; H. E. Mayer, 'Das Pontifikale von Tyrus und die Krönung der lateinischen Könige von Jerusalem', *Dumbarton Oaks Papers*, 21 (1967), 183 f.; B. Hamilton, 'Rebuilding Zion: The Holy Places of Jerusalem in the Twelfth Century', in *Renaissance and Renewal in Christian History* (Studies in Church History, 14; Oxford, 1977), 107; N. Kenaan-Kedar, 'Symbolic Meaning in Crusader Architecture: The Twelfth-century Dome of the Holy Sepulchre Church in Jerusalem', *Cahiers archéologiques*, 34 (1986), 109–17. Cefalù's treasury includes a reliquary made from wood of the True Cross: C. Valenziano, 'La basilica cattedrale di Cefalù', 117 f.; ead., 'Reliquario della croce e frammenti di abiti ruggeriani', in *Materiali per la conoscenza storica e il restauro di una cattedrale: Mostra di documenti e testimonianze figurative della basilica ruggeriana di Cefalù* (Palermo, 1982), 159 f.

[6] Another possible prototype for Cefalù may have been Justinian's church of the Holy Apostles in Constantinople, which was used as an imperial burial site until the early 11th century. Empty sarcophagi were also used as cenotaphs there, but they commemorated the Apostles: T. Thieme and I. Beck, *La cattedrale normanna di Cefalù* (Analecta Romana Instituti Danici 8, Supplementum; Odense, 1977), 42.

[7] G. B. Ladner, *The Idea of Reform: Its Impact on Christian Thought and Action in the Age of the Fathers* (Cambridge, Mass., 1959), 120 f.; F. Dvornik, *Early Christian and Byzantine Political Philosophy: Origins and Background* (Washington, DC, 1966) ii. 617 ff.; D. J. Geanakoplos, *Byzantine East and Latin West: Two Worlds of Christendom in Middle Ages and Renaissance* (New York, 1966), 60.

[8] Geanakoplos, loc. cit.

[9] Treitinger, *Die oströmische Kaiser*, 125; Ladner, *The Idea of Reform*, 111, 118, 120 f.; E. Kitzinger, 'On the Portrait of Roger II in the Martorana in Palermo', *Proporzioni*, 2 (1950), 31.

[10] Treitinger, *Die oströmische Kaiser*, 130.

[11] V. d'Alessandro, *Storiografia e politica nell'Italia normanna* (Naples, 1978), 68 ff., 163–6. See also Chapter I, nn. 2–3 above.

[12] M. Reichenmiller, 'Bisher unbekannte Traumerzählungen Alexanders von Telese', *Deutsches Archiv für Erforschung des Mittelalters*, 19 (1963), 343; cf. N. Nersessian, 'The Cappella Palatina of Roger II: The Relationship of its Imagery to its Political Function', Ph.D. diss. (University of California at Los Angeles, 1981), 212 ff. This legend was probably fabricated to demonstrate the king's dependence upon Rome.

[13] White, *Latin Monasticism*, 189; V. Lazareff, 'The Mosaics of Cefalù', *Art Bulletin*, 17 (1935), 184 f. See also n. 3 above.

[14] R. Salvo di Pietraganzili, *Cefalù: La sua origine e i suoi monumenti* (Palermo, 1888), 23.

[15] Ladner, *The Idea of Reform*, 108 f.; 1 Peter 2: 13–15; Romans 13: 3–5.

[16] Hamilton, 'Rebuilding Zion', 107 ff.; see also n. 18 below.

[17] White, *Latin Monasticism*, 48 f., 184, 186, 229; Thieme and Beck, *La cattedrale normanna* 12 f. n. 18. For the documents of the priorate of S. Maria di Bagnara, see H. Enzensberger, *Beiträge zum Kanzlei- und Urkundwesen der normannischen Herrscher Unteritaliens und Siziliens* (Kallmünz Opf., 1971), 18. For French clergy in South Italy, see also C. S. Frugoni, '*Historia Alexandri elevati per griphos ad aerem*: Origine, iconografia e fortuna di un tema' (Rome, 1973), 310.

[18] White, *Latin Monasticism*, 229–33. In the Holy Land, the Augustinians (also known as Austin canons) were entrusted with Mt Zion, the Shrine of the Ascension on the Mt of Olives, the Dome of the Rock (converted by the Crusaders into a church honouring Christ's Presentation in the Temple); Hamilton, 'Rebuilding Zion', 107 ff.

[19] Deér, *Dynastic Porphyry Tombs*, 117 ff.

[20] Ibid. 1 f., with the text of the royal donation: 'Sarcophagos vero duos porphyriticos ad decessus mei signum perpetuum conspicuous in praefata ecclesia stabilimus fore permansuros, in quorum altero iuxta canonicorum psallentium chorum post diei mei obitum conditus requiescam, alterum vero tam ad insignem memoriam mei nominis, quam ad ipsius ecclesiae gloriam stabilimus.'

[21] White, *Latin Monasticism*, 194; Deér, *Dynastic Porphyry Tombs*, 9, 25, 71; M. and C. Valenziano, 'La Supplique des chanoines', 28; C. Valenziano, 'La basilica cattedrale di Cefalù', 115 f.; W. Krönig, 'Vecchie e nuove prospettive sull'arte della Sicilia normanna', in *Atti del Congresso internazionale di studi sulla Sicilia normanna, Palermo, 4–8 dicembre 1972* (Palermo, 1973–4), 134 ff.; Thieme and Beck, *La cattedrale normanna*, 29.

[22] Deér, *Dynastic Porphyry Tombs*, 126, 142–55; R. Gnoli, *Marmora romana* (Rome, 1971), 98–107.

[23] Deér, *Dynastic Porphyry Tombs*, 149 ff.; Treitinger, *Die oströmische Kaiser*, 58 ff. Porphyry was also used in tombs of the first Latin kings of Jerusalem which were also furnished with baldachins destroyed in the 19th century; I. Herklotz, 'Sepulcra' e 'Monumenta' *del medioevo: studi sull'arte sepolcrale in Italia* (Rome, 1985), p. 135 n. 107. For use of porphyry in earlier tombs, see ibid. 110–14.

[24] Deér (*Dynastic Porphyry Tombs*, 34 f., 40) believed the ciboria were Norman, while L. C. Pratesi ('In margine ad alcuni recenti studi sulla scultura medievale dell'Italia meridionale', *Commentari*, 16 [1965] 186ff.), did not. For the earlier use of porphyry in the baldachin sheltering the tomb of Count Roger I, see L. Faedo, review of G. Occhiato, 'La SS. Trinità di Mileto e l'architettura normanna meridionale', in *Prospettiva*, 19 (1979), 70 f.; ead., 'La sepoltura di Ruggero, conte di Calabria', in *Aparchai: Nuove ricerche e studi sulla Magna Grecia e la Sicilia antica in onore di Paolo Enrico Arias* (Pisa, 1982), ii. 693–706, kindly brought to my attention by Salvatore Settis. Cf. Herklotz, 'Sepulcra', 83 n. 133, 169, 205 n. 84.

[25] H. M. Schwarz, 'Die Baukunst Kalabriens und Siziliens im Zeitalter der Normannen, I: Die lateinische Kirchengründungen des 11. Jahrhunderts und der Dom in Cefalù', *Römisches Jahrbuch für Kunstgeschichte*, 6 (1942–4), 87; Demus, *The Mosaics of Norman Sicily*, 5–9; W. Krönig, *Cefalù: der sizilische normannendom* (Kassel, 1963). All believe the church was completed towards the end of the century, whereas recent examinations of the masonry on the façade by Trizzino and Brenk suggest an earlier date.

[26] Thieme and Beck, *La cattedrale normanna*, 25, 35 f., 54–61. Among those who have perceived Anglo-Norman elements in the building, see Schwarz, 'Die Baukunst Kalabriens', 60, 69, 80 ff., 85; Demus, *The Mosaics of Norman Sicily*, 9; G. Di Stefano, *Monumenti della Sicilia normanna*, ed. W. Krönig (2nd edn., Palermo, 1979), pp. xxxi, 10, 45 ff., 49 f., 53 ff.; V. Pace, 'Le componenti inglesi nell'architettura normanna di Sicilia nella storia della critica', *Studi medievali*, 3rd ser., 16 (1975), 399 ff.; J. Sumption, *Monaci, santuari, pellegrini: La religione nel medioevo* (Rome, 1981), 279.

[27] For an earlier example of what also seems to be an abbreviated Ascension with a bust of the Pantocrator in the apse conch, see the mid-7th-century mural in the chapel of S. Venanzio, Lateran Palace, Rome (C. Ihm, *Die Programme der christlichen Apsismalerei vom vierten Jahrhundert bis zur Mitte des achten Jahrhunderts* (Wiesbaden, 1960), plate XXIII. 2; J. Beckwith, *Early Christian and Byzantine Art* (Harmondsworth, 1970), fig. 125). See also Demus, *The Mosaics of Norman Sicily*, 220; id., *The Mosaics of San Marco in Venice*, 4 vols. (Chicago and London, 1984), i. 244 f.; H. Gutberlet, *Die Himmelfahrt Christi in der bildenden Kunst von den Anfängen bis ins hohen Mittelalter*, 2nd edn. (Strasburg, 1935), 119 f.

[28] The coinage of Justinian II (685–95, 705–11). See also J. Osborne, 'The Christological Scenes in the Nave of the Lower Church of San Clemente, Rome', in *Medieval Lazio: Studies in Architecture, Painting, and Ceramics* (Papers in Italian Archaeology, 3, *British Archaeological Reports*; International Series, 125 (1982)), 245 ff.; J. J. G. Alexander, *Norman Illumination at Mont St. Michel, 966–1100* (Oxford, 1970), 105 ff.; Nersessian, *The Cappella Palatina of Roger II*, 27 ff.

[29] Demus, *The Mosaics of San Marco*, i. 244 f.; and R. J. H.

Jenkins and C. Mango, 'The Date and Significance of the Tenth Homily of Photius', *Dumbarton Oaks Papers*, 9–10 (1956), 132 f.

[30] Demus, *The Mosaics of San Marco*, i. 174. The Jerusalem mosaic is mentioned but, alas, not described by the Russian pilgrim Daniel. See also M. L. Bulst-Thiele, 'Die Mosaiken der "Auferstehungskirche" in Jerusalem und die Bauten der "Franken" im 12. Jahrhundert', *Frühmittelalterliche Studien*, 13 (1979), 447: the mosaic was on the soffit of the triumphal arch with Mary and the Apostles watching below.

[31] Y. Christe, *Les Grands Portails romans: Études sur l'iconologie des théophanies romanes* (Geneva, 1969), 62, 95; Gutberlet, *Die Himmelfahrt Christi*, 14 f., 231–4, who, after citing Honorius of Autun and Hrabanus Maurus, remarks that it is often difficult, if not impossible, to distinguish the Ascension from images of the Second Coming; see also B. Brenk, *Tradition und Neuerung in der christlichen Kunst des ersten Jahrtausends: Studien zur Geschichte des Weltgerichtsbildes* (Vienna, 1966), 57 ff.; Demus, *The Mosaics of San Marco*, i. 369 n. 62.

[32] See, for instance, the Ascensions illustrated in: the Rabula Gospels, Florence, Bib. Laurenziana, MS Pl. 1. 56, fo. 13ʳ; on the painted box cover in the Museo Sacro of the Vatican Library; and in the 12th-century Comnenian illumination in Paris, Bib. Nat., Cod. Gr. 1208, fo. 3ᵛ.

[33] For the restorations and condition of the mosaics, see Demus, *The Mosaics of Norman Sicily*, 9 ff.; M. Andaloro, 'La decorazione del presbiterio prima del Seicento: I mosaici', in *Mostra di documenti e testimonianze figurative della basilica ruggeriana di Cefalù* (Cefalù, 1982), 96–101; ead., 'I mosaici di Cefalù dopo il restauro', in *III° Colloquio internazionale sul mosaico antico, Ravenna 6–10 settembre 1980* (Ravenna, 1984), 105–16.

[34] *Hosea* (Hosea 6: 2):
*Vivificabit nos d[omi]n[u]s d[eu]s post duos dies in die tercia suscitabit nos et veni* [sic: *vivemus*].
(After two days he will revive us, on the third he will raise us up, that we may live.)

*David* (Psalm 44/45: 10):
*Audi filia et vide et inclina aurem tuam.*
(Hear, O daughter, consider and incline your ear.)

*Solomon* (Prov. 1: 8):
*Audi filii in* [sic: *fili mi*] *precepta patris tui.*
(Hear, my son, your father's instruction.)

[35] *Joel* (Acts 2: 17):
*Effundam de spiritu[m] | [sic] meo sup[er] o[mnem] carnem.*
(I will pour out my spirit upon all flesh.)
From Peter's sermon at Pentecost, which is based on Joel 2: 28.

*Amos* (Amos 9: 13–14):
*Ecce dies veniu[n]t dicit d[omi]n[u]s et co[m]prehendet ... [et convertam captivitatem populi mei Israhel ...].*
('Behold, the days are coming,' says the Lord, ['and I will restore the fortunes of my people Israel ...'].)

[36] Entirely remade by Riolo: Demus, *The Mosaics of Norman Sicily*, 23 n. 86.

[37] *Obadiah* (Obadiah 1: 17):
*In moam* [sic: *monte*] *sio[n] erit salvatio et erit s[an]c[tu]s et posside[bit] [domus Jacob eos qui se possederant].*
(But in Mount Zion there shall be those that escape, and it shall be holy and [the house of Jacob] shall possess [their own possessions].)

[38] *Jonah* (Jonah 1: 1):
*Factum e[st] verbum d[om]in[i] ad Iona[m] filiu[m] Am[a]thi dicens.*
(Now the word of the Lord came unto Jonah, the son of Amittai, saying ...)

Whether this refers to Jonah's adventure with the whale or to his name, which in Hebrew means 'dove' (another possible allusion to the dove of the Holy Spirit at Pentecost), is uncertain.

*Micah* (Micah 1: 2):

*Audite populi omnes et att[end]at[?] tura [sic: terra] e[t] plenitudo.*
(Hear, you peoples, all of you; hearken, O earth, and all that is in it ... [for behold, the Lord is coming].)

*Nahum* (Nahum 1: 4):

*Infirmatus e[st] Basa[n] et Carmel[us] et flos Libani.*
(Bashan and Carmel wither, the bloom of Lebanon fades.)

[39] It could be argued that *Peter of Alexandria* and *St Denis* are interlopers in this group. However, Peter sided with Rome in the controversy with the Eastern church fathers, and St Denis's patronage of the Frankish monarchy justifies his place among the Latin saints: M. J. Johnson, 'The Royal View at Cefalù: A Note on the Choice of Subjects and their Arrangement in the Mosaics of Norman Sicily', Abstract from the Ninth Byzantine Studies Conference, 4–6 Nov. 1983, Duke University, North Carolina 112 f. This was kindly given to me by Professor Margaret Riddle.

[40] Of this group, Theodore, Demetrius, and Nestor also appear among the group of holy warriors in the Cappella Palatina at Palermo.

[41] In an oversight, Demus (*The Mosaics of Norman Sicily*, 13 f.) reversed the locations of the saints on the right and left. For the invocation of these saints in the royal laudes, together with George and Theodore, see Kantorowicz, Laudes regiae, 29, 44, 52.

[42] Johnson, 'The Royal View at Cefalù', 112 f. Theodore is a patron saint of Brindisi.

[43] E. Jamison, *The Sicilian Norman Kingdom in the Mind of Anglo-Norman Contemporaries* (Annual Italian Lecture of the British Academy; London, 1938), 12; C. W. Jones, *San Nicola: Biografia di una leggenda* (Bari, 1983), 167–229. Roger II's particular devotion to this saint is illustrated by an enamel in Bari cathedral which shows Nicholas either blessing or crowning the king. S. H. Steinberg ('I ritratti dei re normanni di Sicilia', *Bibliofilia*, 39 [1937], 38–41) dates the enamel between 1139 and 1149, explaining that thereafter Roger's likeness on coins and seals no longer display him as a *basileus* but as an apostolic legate. Others interpret the enamel as a crowning: H. Pierce and R. Tyler, 'Three Byzantine Works of Art', *Dumbarton Oaks Papers*, 2 (1941), 7 pl. 13; Kitzinger, 'On the Portrait of Roger II', 34 n. 16; L. R. Ménager, 'L'Institution monarchique dans les états normands d'Italie: Contribution à l'étude du pouvoir royal dans les principautés occidentales aux xie–xiie siècles', *Cahiers de civilisation médiévale*, 2/2, 4 (1959), 306; I. Beck, 'The First Mosaics of the Cappella Palatina in Palermo', *Byzantion*, 40 (1970), 123.

[44] I. La Lumia, *Storie siciliane*, i (Palermo, 1882), 182, citing Malaterra, bk. II, ch. 33, 192. In 1137, SS George, Theodore, Demetrius, and Sebastian were invoked by the bishop of Jerusalem before a fight with Zengi: Orderic Vitalis, *The Ecclesiastical History ...*, ed. M. Chibnall, 6 vols. (Oxford, 1969–80), v, bk. IX, 115, 155; ibid., vi, bk. XIII, 499.

[45] C. Valenziano, 'La basilica cattedrale di Cefalù', 100.

[46] E. Kitzinger, *The Art of Byzantium and the Medieval West: Selected Studies*, ed. W. E. Kleinbauer (Bloomington and London, 1976), 306, n. 92. This royal distribution of subjects was also noted by Johnson, 'The Royal View at Cefalù', 112 f. For discussion of the intended placement of the sarcophagi, see R. Elze, 'Zum Königtum Rogers II. von Sizilien', *Festschrift Percy Ernst Schramm*, i (Wiesbaden, 1964), 111 n. 51: '... in quorum altero iuxta canonicorum psallentium chorum ...' see n. 20 above; C. Valenziano, 'La basilica cattedrale di Cefalù', 115 f.; Thieme and Beck, *La cattedrale normanna*, 29.

[47] Documentation for these thrones is totally lacking so far, and little has been written about them: see F. Gandolfo, 'Scultori e lapicidi nell'architettura normanno-sveva della chiesa e del chiostro', in *Mostra di documenti e testimonianze figurative della basilica ruggeriana di Cefalù* (Palermo, 1982), 83 f. According to R. Calandra (in the same volume, 129), they were already in place by the second half of the 16th century; cf. O. Demus, *The Church of San Marco in Venice: History, Architecture, Sculpture* (Washington, DC, 1960), 43, 48. The epigraphy is certainly not medieval. For thrones in Palermo cathedral and their modifications from the 15th century onwards, see G. Bellafiore, 'Iconografia della cattedrale di Palermo anteriore al 1781', *Bollettino d'arte*, 57 (1972), 102–4, 111 nn. 84–6.

[48] For the *Ascension* as Christ's apotheosis, see A. A. Schmid, 'Himmelfahrt Christi', *Lexikon der christlichen Ikonographie*, ii (Rome, Freiburg, Basle, and Vienna, 1970), col. 268 f.

[49] E. Kantorowicz, 'The King's Advent and the enigmatic Panels in the Doors of Santa Sabina', *Art Bulletin*, 26 (1944), repr. in *Selected Studies* (Locust Valley, 1965), 46 f.; id., Laudes regiae, 50; Treitinger, *Die oströmische Kaiser*, 32 f.

[50] H. G. May and B. M. Metzger, *The New Oxford Annotated Bible: The Holy Bible*, 2nd edn. (New York and Oxford, 1971), 747; Enzensberger, *Beiträge zum Kanzlei- und Urkundwesen*, 78; Deér, *Dynastic Porphyry Tombs*, 157. See also Exodus 15: 6: 'Thy right hand, O Lord, glorious in power, thy right hand, O Lord, shatters the enemy.' The motto may already have been introduced by 1136: C. Brühl, *Diplomi e cancelleria di Ruggero II* (Palermo, 1983), 60 f.

[51] D'Alessandro, *Storiografia e politica*, 210.

[52] Another of the many links between Cefalù and the Holy Land is the fact that the timber beams in the nave are of Lebanon cedar—a recent discovery communicated through the kindness of Dr Giulia Aurigemma of the Palermo Soprintendenza. For a discussion of the Islamic paintings on these beams, see now: M. Gelfer-Jørgensen, *Medieval Islamic Symbolism and the Paintings in the Cefalù Cathedral* (Leiden, 1986).

[53] M. Andaloro, 'I mosaici di Cefalù', 109 ff., 115 n. 39.

[54] Ibid. 112, 115 n. 39.

[55] E. Kitzinger, 'The Mosaics of the Cappella Palatina in Palermo: An Essay on the Choice and Arrangement of the Subjects', *Art Bulletin*, 31 (1949), 291 f.; O. von Simson, *The Gothic Cathedral* (London, 1956), 151.

[56] F. Chalandon, *Histoire de la domination normande en Italie et en Sicile*, 2 vols. (Paris, 1907), ii. 161.

[57] Ibid. 133 f.

[58] Ibid.; S. Runciman, *A History of the Crusades: The Kingdom of Jerusalem and the Frankish East 1100–1187*, ii (Cambridge, 1952), 252, 259.

[59] Chalandon, *Histoire de la domination normande*, ii. 136 f., 143.

[60] E. Kitzinger, 'Two Mosaic Ateliers in Palermo in the 1140's', Abstract from *Artistes, artisans et production artistique au Moyen Âge* (Colloque international, Université de Rennes, 2–6 mai 1983), i (Paris, 1986), 278 ff., discerns three distinct Greek teams working contemporaneously at La Martorana, the Cappella Palatina, and Cefalù.

[61] Chalandon, *Histoire de la domination normande*, ii. 143 f., 147 f.; E. Caspar, *Roger II (1101–1154) und die Gründung der normannisch-sicilischen Monarchie* (Innsbruck, 1904), 404; Kitzinger, 'The Mosaics of the Cappella Palatina', 289 f.

[62] Chalandon, *Histoire de la domination normande*, ii. 118 f.

[63] Ibid. 119 ff.

[64] Jamison, *The Sicilian Norman Kingdom*, 15 f., 45 n. 28, citing C. Richard, *Notice sur l'ancienne bibliothèque des Échevins de la ville de Rouen* (Rouen, 1845), 37. For the entire Latin passage, see Kantorowicz, Laudes regiae, 157–8 n. 8.

[65] Demus, *The Mosaics of Norman Sicily*, 4, 9 f. Five large mosaics of uncertain date with donation scenes in the façade porch were demolished in the 15th century.

[66] J. Deér, 'Das Grab Friedrichs II.', in J. Fleckenstein (ed.), *Probleme um Friedrich II.* (Sigmaringen, 1974), 365; id., *Dynastic Porphyry Tombs*, 4 ff., 10.

[67] Schwarz, 'Die Baukunst Kalabriens', 86 f. n. 200; White, *Latin Monasticism*, 197; Di Stefano, *Monumenti della Sicilia*, 48.

# 3

# THE CAPPELLA PALATINA AT PALERMO:
# A CORONATION COMMEMORATED
## (Plates 16–56)

BECAUSE Cefalù was far from the capital and its status as a cathedral was so uncertain, the focus of the king's interest in ecclesiastical decoration shifted to his new palace chapel at Palermo. Yet many of the same ideas, nascent at Cefalù, were developed and enlarged in the mosaics of the Cappella Palatina which were planned under Roger but completed by his son William I.[1] There were two earlier chapels within the precincts of the royal palace about which almost nothing is known. One of these was a richly endowed sanctuary with the name of S. Maria di Gerusalemme, said to have been built by the conquerors of Sicily—Robert Guiscard and Count Roger I.[2] Later, Roger II built a chapel dedicated to St Andrew.[3] Why he subsequently built another dedicated to St Peter, the present Cappella Palatina, is a matter of conjecture.[4] In 1132, a parish of St Peter's had been created in the area.[5] Despite hostile relations with the papacy, the chapel's dedication to the prince of the Apostles may have been intended as an acknowledgement of the royal mission to return the Sicilian populace to the Roman rite. This was fortified by the belief that anointed rulers were successors to the Apostles.[6] The dedicatory inscription which encircles the crossing, and the date of which corresponds to the year 1143,[7] reads:

> Other kings of old erected sanctuaries to other saints but I, King Roger, sceptred ruler [dedicate this church] to the foremost of the Lord's disciples, the leader and archpriest Peter, to whom Christ entrusted his church which he himself consecrated by the sacrifice of his blood ... the third Indiction ... the fifty first year in correct measurement after 6000 and 600 years had elapsed in an ever moving circle.[8]

Three years earlier, on 28 April 1140, in the tenth year of his reign, Roger had granted the chapel a charter of endowment. Written on purple parchment, the charter was a declaration of the king's gratitude to the Lord for the creation of the Sicilian kingdom and a commemoration of all his family.[9] Whether the charter's date was also the chapel's consecration day is uncertain. The Feast-day of Peter and Paul (29 June) has been suggested as its foundation or dedication day because of a homily devoted to these Apostles which was delivered in the chapel by Philagathos of Cerami, a famous preacher.[10] Unfortunately, the year of the homily is just as vague as the dedication year which it may only have commemorated.[11] There are still three altars in the chapel apparently dedicated to Peter, Paul, and Andrew. The known relics preserved there included those of the Baptist, SS Julian, Gervase, Protase, Barnabas, Sebastian, and Philip.[12]

The so-called chapel is really a small church located along the southern flank of the

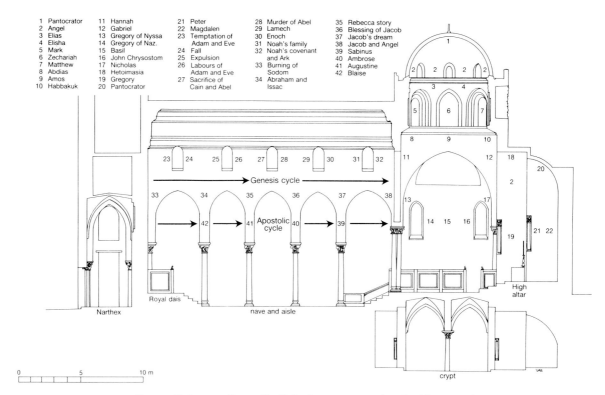

| | | | | |
|---|---|---|---|---|
| 1 Pantocrator | 11 Hannah | 21 Peter | 28 Murder of Abel | 35 Rebecca story |
| 2 Angel | 12 Gabriel | 22 Magdalen | 29 Lamech | 36 Blessing of Jacob |
| 3 Elias | 13 Gregory of Nyssa | 23 Temptation of | 30 Enoch | 37 Jacob's dream |
| 4 Elisha | 14 Gregory of Naz. | Adam and Eve | 31 Noah's family | 38 Jacob and Angel |
| 5 Mark | 15 Basil | 24 Fall | 32 Noah's covenant | 39 Sabinus |
| 6 Zechariah | 16 John Chrysostom | 25 Expulsion | and Ark | 40 Ambrose |
| 7 Matthew | 17 Nicholas | 26 Labours of | 33 Burning of | 41 Augustine |
| 8 Abdias | 18 Hetoimasia | Adam and Eve | Sodom | 42 Blaise |
| 9 Amos | 19 Gregory | 27 Sacrifice of | 34 Abraham and | |
| 10 Habbakuk | 20 Pantocrator | Cain and Abel | Issac | |

FIG. 2 Palermo, Cappella Palatina: cross-section looking north

royal palace. It was built on top of an earlier church or chapel (possibly S. Maria di Gerusalemme), part of which today serves as the crypt. This earlier structure had a centralized plan, an altar in the middle, and a mural of a very Greek *Madonna* painted on one of the walls—this has been detached and is now displayed in the narthex upstairs.[13] At one point this lower church, or crypt, served as a temporary burial site for Roger II's son William I.[14]

Although Roger's chapel has often been described as a combination of a Roman basilican nave and aisles with a sanctuary and domed crossing reminiscent of Byzantium,[15] its plan is actually closer to earlier Basilian churches on the island such as those at Itàla and Agrò.[16] Elaborate Islamic woodwork covers the nave and aisles, while the eastern end is entirely vaulted. A dome on squinches is set over the central square, which is flanked by two quasi-barrel-vaulted chapels. There may have been an unsuccessful attempt to vault the nave as well, because the walls at the top of the arcade splay outwards and the wooden ceiling cuts off some of the original windows of the once higher walls.[17]

The Greek element is stronger in the sanctuary area—in its ground plan, vaulting, and inscriptions. The text of the dedication is not only Greek in script but also in style, because its model was devised for Justinian's sixth-century church of SS Sergius and Bacchus in Constantinople.[18] The Byzantine imperial style was also in Philagathos's mind when he composed the homily for Roger's chapel; his text was based on a descriptive poem written by Paul the Silentiary for Hagia Sophia, also in Constantinople.[19] These were literary 'spoils' used to exalt the chapel. But actual classical spoils were used in the structure of the nave arcade.[20] The arches rise and fall to compensate for the uneven height of the shafts and capitals, while the irregular size of the columns and their various colours were

*Fig. 2*

*Pl. 16*
*Pls. 17–18*

*Pls. 16, 25*

organized in symmetrical pairs—such as the two matching spiral shafts which support
the western side of the triumphal arch. Pink granite alternates with greyish-white columns,
while paired ancient Corinthian capitals face each other beneath the mosaic renderings
of *SS Ambrose* and *Cataldus*, and *Athanasius* and *Blaise*. As for the apse, actual porphyry
columns support the arches instead of the mosaic shafts at Cefalù, which only simulate
porphyry and verde antico.

    At first, the chapel was served by eight canons (this was later increased to twelve).[21]
For a time, the chief cleric was Roger's father-confessor, who was also abbot of the nearby
Benedictine monastery of St John of the Hermits—another Rogerian foundation dating
from 1142 to 1148.[22] Many of the canons were members of the king's Privy Council, and
the royal chancellor was, on occasion, also the *magister cappellanus*.[23] Otherwise, the chapter
was exempt from all ecclesiastical authority save that of the king.[24] Some of the clergy
seem to have been non-Italian, and both Gallican and Greek rites were used in the
chapel.[25] According to his chroniclers, Roger carefully adopted 'what was most useful
and sound' from the customs and institutions of other kings,[26] and this explains not only

*Pls. 55–6*
*Pls. 20, 49,*
*54, 50, 53*

FIG. 3 Bern, Burger Bibliothek, MS 120, c. 4 (97): View of
the high altar of the Cappella Palatina in Pietro da Eboli's
*Liber ad honorem Augusti*, late twelfth century

the mixed character of the chapel's design, structure, ceremonial, and decoration, but also the style of the monarchy itself.

*Pls. 17–18*      The palace chapel had various functions: it was a private chapel used by the royal household as well as a public audience hall. The high altar was probably in the apse just
*Fig. 3*      as it is today, although it has been transformed by several remodelling campaigns.[27] According to Lucio Trizzino, the pulpit at the foot of the stairs, at the south-east corner, was enlarged in the sixteenth century to accommodate musicians. A porphyry slab from the original pulpit is now immured next to the passage-way leading down to the crypt. This slab indicates the width of the first pulpit, which may have had a baptismal font nearby. The clergy sat in the presbytery in front of the altar behind a high walled enclosure which was dismantled in the seventeenth century.[28] Early in the same century,
*Pl. 28*      there was a royal loge with access to the palace in the northern chapel.[29] All that remains of it today is the blind arched recess. This structure, however, is a late modification of
*Pl. 37*      the original pair of Norman windows (like those in the southern chapel opposite) which were widened and incorporated into a lunette-shaped aperture.[30] Although there is a tradition of elevated royal loges going back to sixth-century Byzantium and eighth-century Oviedo,[31] it is difficult to prove that there was also one in Roger's chapel. He may have had only a portable wooden seat, and it is possible that the king's only access to his chapel was through the front doors, as it was at the Zisa (another royal palace in Palermo).[32] Nevertheless, we will see that the distribution of the mosaics and their
*Pl. 16*      inscriptions indicate that one of the king's viewing-places was in the northern chapel which opens on to the crossing, but that he also had a fixed public seat at the western end of the nave. However, before examining the mosaics' arrangement, more needs to be said about the building's public and private functions and the structural and decorative traditions associated with them, because these elements stood behind the formulation of the mosaics for Roger's chapel.

## THE CHAPEL AS AN AUDIENCE HALL

Structurally, the Cappella Palatina has little or nothing in common with earlier imperial chapels and audience halls in either Byzantium or the West (e.g. the Chrysotriclinium and chapel of Our Lady of Pharos inside the Great Palace of Constantinople,[33] or the triclinia of Charlemagne at Ingelheim and of the pope in the Lateran at Rome[34]). Pictorially, however, several of the mosaics in the Cappella Palatina are clearly related to some of these earlier royal audience halls.[35] In the Chrysotriclinium (or 'golden triclinium') at Constantinople, there was a royal throne beneath a mosaic of the enthroned Saviour in the central apse, and directly opposite, at the other end of the room, there was a mosaic of the Virgin among Apostles, saints, and a portrait of an imperial donor.[36] At Palermo, probably because it was a chapel, the location of the imagery was simply
*Pls. 17–18*      reversed: the *Enthroned Christ flanked by Peter and Paul* appears above a royal seat on the entrance wall, and the saints and Apostles surmounted by the *Pantocrator* fill the apse (the *Virgin* is an eighteenth-century addition replacing a window).[37]

As well as the imperial Byzantine precedent for juxtaposing celestial and terrestrial thrones in a palace audience hall, there are several other reasons for supposing that in his public capacity the Norman king sat beneath the *Enthroned Saviour* at the western end of the nave—in a place normally occupied by a central entrance door. At the Cappella *Pl. 19* Palatina, two imposing bronze doors give access to the aisles on either side of a gabled, inlaid marble, throne dais.[38] This dais is a pastiche partly made up of materials from the original sanctuary enclosure dismantled late in the seventeenth century.[39] However, the big shiny octagon inlaid just beneath the gable of the throne dais is probably part of the original arrangement, because it caught the eye of Nompar de Caumont, an early fifteenth-century traveller.[40] Although not altogether an original Norman structure, the dais occupies an appropriate site for a royal seat from which to exalt the king's status as God's minister for the good of mankind (Romans 13: 1–6). The situation of the two thrones may allude to the theme of judgement—a subject traditionally found on the western walls of chapels and churches, whether at late eleventh-century Torcello or in sixteenth-century Rome (the Sistine chapel). Although it has been argued on stylistic grounds that the Cappella Palatina mosaic of the *Enthroned Saviour*, as well as the royal dais beneath it, were among the last parts of the chapel to be completed,[41] the inscription of 1143 in the crossing-dome suggests that neither of them were, in fact, afterthoughts, namely, the Greek words of Isaiah (66: 1) and Acts (7: 49): ' "Heaven is my throne and the earth is my footstool" saieth the Lord Pantocrator' (the final phrase is an addition).[42] On the entrance wall, the seat of the Sicilian king would have appeared as the footstool of the *Saviour in Majesty*.[43] Paradoxically, in the Bible, the eschatological inscription in the cupola is connected with the idea that no house made by mortal hands can contain the Creator, the Lord of heaven and earth—in apparent contradiction to Roger's chapel and its mosaics. Yet, the concept of the Christian basilica as the *aula dei* was an ancient one,[44] and Roger's palace chapel, like its Byzantine predecessor, was the audience hall of the King of kings as well as of an earthly ruler.

The cupola mosaic with its medallion of the *Pantocrator* accompanied by angels in *Pl. 25* Byzantine court dress recalls Photius's account of a ninth-century mosaic in the vault of the palace chapel of Our Lady of Pharos in Constantinople, also situated near a throne-room:[45] 'On the very ceiling is painted in coloured mosaic cubes a man-like figure bearing the traits of Christ … In the concave segments next to the summit of the hemisphere a throng of angels … escorting our common Lord …'[46]

In Roger's chapel the image of the *Enthroned Christ* is flanked by Peter and Paul. Such *Pl. 19* a composition was also understood as a vision of the future kingdom of the just, with the Apostles' presence signifying the unity of the Church—the concord between the sovereign and his vicars.[47] Furthermore, according to Roger II's biographer Alexander of Telese, Peter and Paul were the king's special guardians, to whose intervention the monarchy owed its existence;[48] later in the century, when the kingdom was in jeopardy, Pietro da Eboli's manuscript shows the queen in another chapel imploring their help.[49]

There is a royal axis between the entrance wall and the apse.[50] From their respective *Pls. 16–18* thrones, the heavenly and earthly rulers faced the apse with its ranks of holy intercessors standing beneath the large bust of the Saviour whose open book displays the same text *Pls. 3, 18,* as at Cefalù in both Greek and Latin (John 8: 12): 'I am the Light of the World; he who *21–2* follows me will not walk in darkness, but will have the light of life.' Even in the use of materials there seems to be a conscious use of royal red; but whereas the columns of the nave arcade on either side of the throne are only pink granite, those in the apse are of actual porphyry. In line with this axis, on the eastern face of the triumphal arch supporting the cupola, is the figure of *King Solomon* (to whom Roger was compared),[51] and it is hardly fortuitous that a pair of columns chosen to support this arch are carved with spirals, which in the medieval mind were associated with those in Solomon's Temple.[52] The figure of *David* which faces *Solomon*, however, is probably an eighteenth-century restorer's substitute for what was originally a window set directly over the *Annunciation*.[53]

*Pl. 17*

*Pls. 16–18*

All three of the royal mosaic schemes commissioned by the Normans display the same image of the Saviour in the main apse conch regardless of the building's dedication: at Cefalù it was to the Saviour, at the Cappella Palatina it was to Peter, and at Monreale it was to the Assumption of Mary. Despite arguments to the contrary—that originally Peter (and not the Saviour) must have occupied this position in Roger's chapel—there is no precedent for such imagery in a main apse.[54] Rather, this repeated image of the Pantocrator in the context of the Ascension and the Second Coming was a deliberate choice, a way not only of representing the heavenly kingdom, but of establishing a link between divine apotheosis and the status of the Sicilian kings, whose motto declared that they too sat at the Lord's right hand in this world and, hopefully, in the next also.

*Pls. 3, 18, 64*

## THE PRIVATE ROYAL VIEW

The coincidence between Roger's royal motto, *Dextera Domini fecit virtutem, dextera Domini exaltavit me*, and the *Pantocrator* represented in the main apse of all three of the mosaic programmes commissioned by the Norman kings justified a royal viewing-place on the liturgical right (our left). The imagery at Cefalù implied that such was the situation there, and at Monreale we know this was in fact the case. At the Cappella Palatina the choice of subjects in the northern chapel suggests that the same was true here. The idea of the Ascension as Christ's apotheosis to which the king's destiny was linked is reiterated in the long, narrow vault of the northern chapel.[55] Here the *Ascension* appears in its full, non-abbreviated form as a scene. Below it, on the eastern end wall, is the traditional Byzantine image for the protector of kings, the standing figure of the Virgin and Child known as the *Hodegetria*.[56] Their off-centre position, as well as that of the three female saints facing them at the opposite end of the chapel, is difficult to explain, however.[57] To the left of the Virgin stands another intercessor—*John the Baptist*. The Greek inscription on the Baptist's scroll ('Behold the Lamb of God') has relevance not only to Jesus but also to *St Andrew* who is represented in the apse conch below,[58] because the same phrase was used when Andrew introduced his younger brother Peter to the Saviour (John 1: 35–42). In the chapel, the smaller *Baptist* and the large *Andrew* face the northern aisle where the Peter sequence ends at the foot of the chamber. Finally, the Baptist's text and the figure of the Virgin were appropriate to the Greek rite of the *Proskomide* (or preparation of the Eucharist), which in Byzantine churches was usually carried out in a chamber (prothesis) to the left of the presbytery just as it is here.[59]

*Pl. 31*

*Pl. 34*

*Pl. 33*

*Pls. 16, 56*

Between the altar and *St Andrew* there are three standing saints. *Joseph* in the centre is *Pl. 34* a late eighteenth-century replacement for a window.[60] But *Barnabas* and *Stephen*, his companions on either side, are particularly appropriate to the site; not only are there relics in the altar, but Stephen's name in Greek means 'crown'.[61]

Beneath the arch separating the northern chapel from the aisle below are *SS Cosmas* *Pls. 29–30* and *Damian*, on whose feast-day the Sicilian monarchy was created. Above them, on the western end wall facing the *Hodegetria*, are three female martyrs: *Agatha*, *Catherine*, and possibly *Parasceve/Veneranda*, with peacocks (symbols of immortality) at their feet and *Pl. 33* orange trees overhead.[62] Agatha, although born in Palermo, was the protectress of Catania, while Catherine of Alexandria, though a royal personage like Agatha, has no other known relevance here. Parasceve was the allegorical figure of Good Friday in Byzantium and is sometimes shown carrying symbols of the Passion; here she carries a cross.[63]

As at Cefalù, there are warrior saints on the wide wall above the arch framing the view *Pls. 9, 35–6* to the south: *Theodore Tiro, Demetrius, Nestor*, and *Mercurius*.[64] The last figure, *St Nicholas of Bari*, does not seem to belong to the group. Nevertheless, all these saints had special associations for the Normans, either through visions or relics.[65] They face the walled-up lunette above the eighteenth-century scenes of the *Baptist*. Below these are original mosaics *Pl. 28* representing five more Greek saints: *Gregory of Nyssa, Gregory Nazianzenus, Basil, John Chrysostom* (all theologians), and another *St Nicholas*. They are each of them shown giving *Col. Pl. V* a blessing in a different manner and each has a different kind of cross on his pallium. These are among the best-preserved mosaics in the building. With the exception of Gregory of Nyssa, all these holy men either were associated with the Greek liturgy for the *Proskomide*[66] or appear in psalter illustrations connected with it—further evidence that the north-east chapel in the Cappella Palatina was used as a prothesis.

St Nicholas of Bari's double appearance in the chapel—at either end and on opposite sides—seems awkward unless a diversity of contexts was intended: on the southern wall he appears as the guardian of Norman Apulia, while at the north-eastern end, close to the altar, he is a liturgical participant in the pre-eucharistic rite.

Whether he sat in this chapel in a lowly or an elevated position, the king would have *Pl. 37* beheld further messages and scenes appropriate to the monarchy. Looking up into the central square, he could see two prophets (*Jeremiah* and *Jonah*) on the southern section of the drum. The Greek text on *Jeremiah*'s scroll is taken from Ezekiel 44: 2, which in its entirety reads thus (the italicized passage is what appears in abbreviated form in the mosaic):

[Then he brought me back to the outer gate of the sanctuary, which faces east; and it was shut. And he said to me '*This gate shall remain shut;* it shall not be opened, and *no one shall enter by it;* for the LORD, the God of Israel, has entered by it; therefore it will remain shut. Only the prince may sit in it to eat bread before the LORD; he shall enter by way of the vestibule of the gate, and shall go out by the same way.'[67]]

Either the northern chapel or the northern side of the crossing would correspond to such a vestibule, and it hardly seems coincidental that a closed gate is represented there in the *Pl. 29* mosaic beneath the feet of *St Cosmas*.[68] Although Jeremiah's message is frequently associated with the virgin birth, one is reminded here of the Byzantine emperor's privilege of partaking of Communion within the sanctuary and, on occasion, of preaching there to the assembled faithful[69]—acts which may also have been performed by the Sicilian kings in their capacity as surrogate papal legate.

*Pl. 37*   The second prophet's message is more general: Jonah (2: 2) says: 'I called to the Lord out of my distress and he answered me ...'[70] Certainly, Roger's reign was full of personal as well as political tribulations, including a stormy crossing to Sicily when, it was believed, he was saved through divine intervention. It turns out that the same phrase used in Jonah's message also appears in the psalm from which Roger's royal motto comes (Vulgate Psalm 117: 5).

*Pl. 37*   Looking across to the wall of the southern chapel, the king would have seen directly in front of him six Christological scenes distributed in three tiers: *Joseph's Dream* and the *Flight into Egypt* at the top; *Baptism*, *Transfiguration*, and the *Raising of Lazarus* in the middle; and at the bottom by itself the *Entry into Jerusalem*. Both the *Flight into Egypt* and the *Entry into Jerusalem* have been interpreted as royal advents—subjects which figure allegorically in both the Roman and Frankish reception of kings.[71] Neither *Joseph's Dream* nor the *Transfiguration* seem to have any particularly royal implications, although the latter may have been associated with Roger's legendary landing in Sicily on the Feast of the Transfiguration.[72] The *Raising of Lazarus* was appropriate not only because, like other scenes in this tier, it stressed Christ's superhuman nature, but also because it may have been an allusion to the chapel's function as a burial site.[73] Below, on either side of the *Entry into Jerusalem*, are two patron saints of the Frankish monarchy: *Denis* and *Martin of*

*Pl. 8*   *Tours*. As at Cefalù, Denis has the place of honour next to the apse.

There were several other scenes in the southern chapel which also had special meaning for the monarchy, but if the king was in or near the northern chapel he probably could

*Pls. 39, 42*   not have seen them. On the eastern end wall is the *Nativity*,[74] which appears as an isolated scene between another image of the Saviour with the 'Ego sum lux' text (above) and *St Paul* in the apse conch (below). The *Nativity* is larger in scale than the other scenes, and there is evidence that it and the other subjects and texts in the sanctuary figure in the Roman and Byzantine liturgies for Christmas and were therefore intended to commemorate Roger's coronation day.

*Pl. 44*   The vault mosaic in the southern chapel also had royal significance: *Pentecost* illustrates the evangelical mission conferred upon the Apostles, of whom the Norman king was a latter-day legate. It was also a feast-day often used for coronations and the anointing of bishops with the holy chrism, and was associated with the divine right of kings via descent of the Holy Spirit.[75] It was probably for both of these reasons that Roger chose this day for the foundation of his earliest royal church: the cathedral at Cefalù.[76]

## THE SANCTUARY AREA

*Pl. 16*   Appropriate though the *Pentecost* and *Ascension* were to the monarchy's concept of its sacred mission and its aspiration in the hereafter, the place of these subjects on either side of a vision of the Saviour in the central dome was a common feature in Byzantine schemes.[77] Also conforming to the Byzantine formula is the *Hetoimasia*, the prepared throne,[78] set in the narrow vault between the central square and the apse. In the Byzantine East, scenes from Christ's infancy often occupied lower areas as they do here where the *Annunciation* and *Presentation in the Temple* face each other on the eastern and western arches of the crossing.[79] The Annunciation, being the Incarnation, was associated with transubstantiation; while the *Presentation* located over the sanctuary entrance represents the Lord's entry into his own sanctuary.[80] Because of their eucharistic significance, these subjects were particularly well suited as preambles to the high altar in the apse. But the other Christological scenes were distributed in a most unconventional manner, which cannot be explained by arguing that a conventional Byzantine scheme was here forced into an uncongenial architectural situation, or that King Roger simply had no clear idea of what should be represented in the chapel and that this uncertainty caused subsequent revisions.[81] First of all, the series of scenes does not correspond to the normal cycle of feasts so often used in Byzantine schemes; notably absent are scenes from the Passion, Crucifixion, Anastasis, and Resurrection.[82] It is true that Byzantine models were used for individual scenes (the *Nativity* is a striking example), but these were introduced into completely non-Byzantine programmes created to suit the new monarchy. In the case of the Cappella Palatina, the arrangement in the eastern end accommodated the royal presence somewhere in the northern side of the sanctuary area. But all this was incorporated into a much larger scheme involving the entire chapel.

In order to contradict the prevailing view that these mosaics are merely a provincial pastiche of Byzantine and Roman formulas, there are other unusual features in the scheme which must also be accounted for. Why, for instance, are there three busts of the Pantocrator: in the central dome, in the main apse, and in the eastern end of the southern chapel? Why does the Baptist appear five times in the sanctuary, while Peter, the chapel's titular, appears only three times—and then only amidst other saints: in the main apse and among the Apostles in the *Ascension* and *Pentecost* vaults?

First, let us consider the repetition of the half-length image of the Saviour. Beck has already commented on his appearance in three different contexts.[83] In the central dome, he appears with closed book in a hieratic-dynastic context with ranks of angels, prophets, ancestors of Christ, and evangelists ranged below him. Around the central medallion is the Greek text for 'Heaven is my throne and the earth is my footstool' (Isaiah 66: 1; Acts 7: 49). This text, together with Roger's royal motto, are paraphrased in Peter's sermon at Pentecost (Acts 2: 33–5), thereby further linking the chapel's titular with the king. Then come eight angels (four of whom are in imperial court dress) who, as the agents of illumination, are appropriately set in a radiating pattern with eight windows at their feet. In the spandrels of the drum, eight prophets in half-length display scrolls. Proceeding clockwise from the north-eastern corner are: *Isaiah, Ezekiel, Jeremiah, Jonah, Daniel, Moses, Elijah,* and *Elisha.* At the four central points of the drum are *David* (an eighteenth-century substitute for a window), the *Baptist, Solomon,* and *Zechariah.*[84] The four squinches are occupied by *Matthew, Mark, Luke,* and *John* arranged in a counter-clockwise sequence from the north-eastern corner. The messages on the three surviving scrolls of the evangelists, as

*Pls. 20, 25*

*Pls. 17–18*

*Pl. 26*

*Pl. 39*

*Pls. 25, 18, 39*
*Pl. 16*
*Pls. 20, 31, 44*

*Pl. 25*

*Pl. 16*

*Col. Pl. IV*

well as those held by *Isaiah, Ezekiel, Zechariah,* and *Daniel,* all refer either directly to the Christmas theme or consist of texts used in both the Greek and Latin Christmas liturgies,[85] strengthening our thesis that the mosaics in the sanctuary commemorate Roger II's coronation day. Luke's and Matthew's texts also allude to the Baptist, of whom a relic was preserved in the chapel.[86]

*Pls. 18, 20–1*     In contrast to the image in the dome, the *Pantocrator* in the central apse conch appears with the book opened at the 'Ego sum lux' text. The border framing him has a Latin inscription set upon a ground of silver tesserae. The text, apparently composed for the site, reads:

LANCEA SPONCIA LIGNEA CRUX CLAVIQ[UE] CORONA
DANT EX PARTE METUM COGUN[T] ET FUNDERE FLETUM
PECCATOR PLORA CUM VIDERIS HAEC ET ADORA /
PARTE STAT INDE DEXTRA MICHAEL, GABRIEL QUE SINISTRA
UT MAIESTATI SINT DESERVIRE PARATI

[The lance, the sponge, the wooden cross, the nails and the [thorny] crown in part inspire fear [but also] force [men] to pour forth weeping. Oh sinner, weep when you shall see these things and worship. On the right stands Michael, and Gabriel on the left in order that they may be ready to serve [his] Majesty.[87]]

*Pl. 20*     The two archangels mentioned in the inscription appear directly in front of it, in the presbytery vault on either side of the prepared throne of the Apocalypse (*Hetoimasia*), thereby conferring an eschatological aspect to the Saviour in the apse conch. The area between the altar and presbytery was then understood as the throne of Christ.[88]

But besides alluding to the Second Coming, the instruments of the Passion cited at the beginning of the inscription (and represented with the *Hetoimasia* on the adjacent arch soffit) also refer to the earthly Jerusalem, where their relics were revered in the church of the Holy Sepulchre.[89] The lance mentioned at the beginning of the text was then of considerable topical interest because, according to the Norman chronicler Ordericus Vitalis, the head of the holy lance was discovered during the siege of Antioch, when St Andrew appeared to a poor Provençal clerk and told him where the holy lance was buried in the church of St Peter. Despite controversy concerning its authenticity, the 'discovery' of the lance and the vision itself were of real inspirational force in mustering the Crusaders' morale on their final drive to Jerusalem.[90] This event may have contributed to the choice of Andrew in the northern apse conch of the Palatina, because Antioch (the site of the vision and Peter's first diocese) was, like Jerusalem, a city upon which Roger II had dynastic claims.[91] Furthermore, the lance had imperial associations: Charlemagne fought the infidel with a piece of it embedded in the pommel of his sword; while the relic found at Antioch was taken to Constantinople by Raymond of Toulouse as a gift for the Byzantine emperor.[92] This, or another relic of the lance, was preserved there in one of the royal chapels.[93] Nothing is known of a lance relic in Roger's possession, however.

*Pls. 16, 18,*     Accompanying the *Pantocrator* on the curved apse wall below are four saints standing
*20, 24*     on either side of what was originally a window which was then filled in at the end of the

eighteenth century by a seated Virgin.[94] *Peter*, the chapel's titular, is on the liturgical right (our left). Beside him is *Mary Magdalene*, an 'evangelist' of southern Gaul, and the patron saint of another royal chapel where the queens and princes of Roger II's family were buried.[95] Their companions on the right are *James*, dressed as the patriarch of 　*Pl. 24* Jerusalem, and *John the Baptist*. The pairing of *Peter* and *James* juxtaposes the Churches 　*Pls. 18, 16* of Rome and Jerusalem. James's presence, however, seems not so much a *sotto voce* plea for dispensing with papal primacy[96] as another reminder of the special Sicilian relationship to Jerusalem. But all four saints are appropriate attendants to a vision of the Second Coming. On the adjacent piers framing the apse are two more formidable occupants of 　*Pls. 16, 20* Peter's Roman chair—*Gregory* and *Sylvester*.

The third image of the Pantocrator is on the east wall of the southern chapel, where 　*Pl. 39* the context changes again: here he is the embodiment and source of light and wisdom. This aspect of the Saviour will be taken up later in a general discussion of the light metaphor in the chapel. To sum up, for the present, it can be argued that the three images of the Pantocrator are not repetitions but representations of the Saviour in three different contexts.[97] In the central square the dominant theme is hieratic and dynastic, 　*Pls. 16, 25* in the sense that the prophets and ancestors of Christ are arranged below him; in the 　*Pls. 20, 39* main apse it is eschatological; and in the southern chapel it is anagogical.

As for the fivefold apparition of the Baptist, his manifold presence was justified not 　*Pl. 16* only by the relic in the high altar, but also by the baptismal font once situated near the pulpit at the south-eastern end of the nave at the foot of the raised sanctuary.[98] He accompanies the Saviour in the main apse and the *Hodegetria* in the northern chapel. In 　*Pls. 18, 34* the central square he appears among Christ's ancestors as the last of the prophets and 　*Pl. 37* the first witness of the Incarnation.[99] Two inscriptions appear with him as he stands between *Jeremiah* and *Jonah*. On his scroll is written in Greek (John 1: 29):

ΙΔΕ Ο ΑΜΝΟϹ ΤΟΥ Θ[ΕΟ]Υ Ο ΑΙΡΩΝ ΤΗΝ ΑΜΑΡΤΙΑΝ ΤΟΥ ΚΟϹΜΟΥ.

[Behold the Lamb of God who takes away the sin of the world.] The second inscription is on the gold background (Matthew 3: 10):

ΠΑΝ ΟΥΝ ΔΕΝΔΡΩΝ [*sic*] ΜΗ ΠΟΙΟΥΝ ΚΑΡΠΟΝ ΚΑΛΟΝ ΕΚΚΟΠΤΕΤΑΙ ΚΑΙ ΕΙϹ ΠΥΡ ΒΑΛΛΕΤΑΙ

[Every tree therefore that does not bear good fruit is cut down and thrown into the fire.]

The first text repeats the Baptist's message in the northern chapel and, of course, refers to the infant Jesus in the *Presentation* as well as to the *Pantocrator* overhead. The second inscription, however, is linked to the scenes of *Baptism* and *Pentecost* located directly behind 　*Pl. 37* in the southern chapel. Not only does the *Baptism* represent the fulfilment of the prophecy (even the axe and the tree are included in the scene), but the next line in Matthew (3: 11) refers to the Pentecost as well ('I baptize you with water for repentence, but he who is coming after me is mightier than I . . . he will baptize you with the Holy Spirit and with fire'). The fifth time the Baptist appears in the sanctuary area is in a preaching scene 　*Pl. 28* located in the northern chapel below the blind lunette. This was made during the late eighteenth and early nineteenth centuries, however, and it is impossible to tell if it reflects a lost original.[100]

*Pl. 16*

Finally, we must turn our attention to Peter's minor role in the sanctuary, which is difficult to justify even though his story has the lion's share of the apostolic sequence filling both aisles. However, his image always occupies a place of precedence on the liturgical right appropriate for the chapel's titular: in the apse, in *Pentecost*, and at the western end of the nave. It has been suggested that originally Peter occupied either the main apse conch or that in the northern chapel, where he would have appeared as the pendant to *St Paul* in the *Pentecost* bay. However, no known precedent exists for such an image of Peter in the main apse, which in all three of the royal Norman mosaic schemes was reserved for the Saviour. None of the reasons suggested so far for the replacement of Peter with Andrew seems compelling,[101] and Andrew's presence does not represent a dissonant element within the scheme as a whole.

*Col. Pls. III–IV*

A distinctive feature of the sanctuary mosaics is the use of silver tesserae to achieve a shimmering effect amidst the fields of gold. As at La Martorana, they were used as grounds for most of the important inscriptions and for emphasis of the holiest figures, as well as for supernatural events such as the cross in Christ's various nimbi, for the highlights

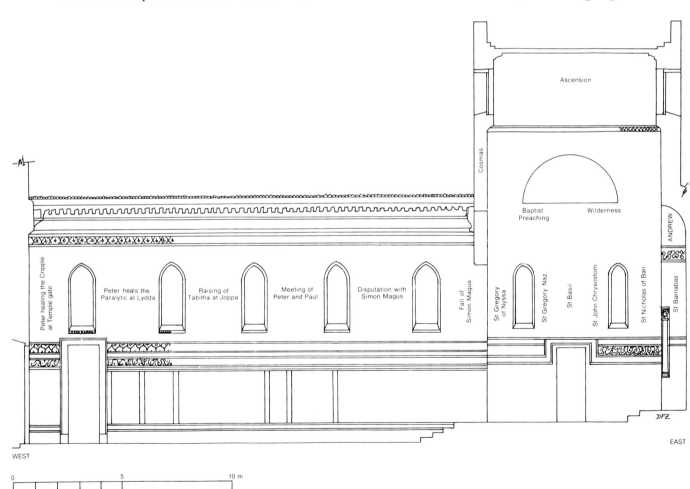

Fɪɢ. 4  Palermo, Cappella Palatina: section of south and north aisles with transept arms

in his garments, for the altar ciborium in the *Presentation*, for the rays of light emanating from the star of Bethlehem, the dove of the Holy Spirit, and the transfigured Christ, and even for paving the road in the *Entry into Jerusalem*. The roundels of most of the saints in the arch soffits of the central square are silver, as distinct from the golden ones in the nave arcades.[102] It is easy to spot those areas of the sanctuary which have been restored, because white was used to replace the original silver tesserae. A similar use of silver can be seen in the fifth- to sixth-century vault of Hagios Giorgios at Thessalonica, as well as in the great *Transfiguration* mosaic in St Catherine's monastery at Mt Sinai.[103]

## THE APOSTOLIC NARRATIVES IN THE AISLES *Pls. 47–56*

Although there were several early Christian precedents for apostolic mural cycles in Rome, the mosaics in the Cappella Palatina have only a superficial relation to them: as far as we know, their similarities lie only in the apostolic theme, and the fact that they proceed in a horizontal band across the walls of a basilica. What the relationship may

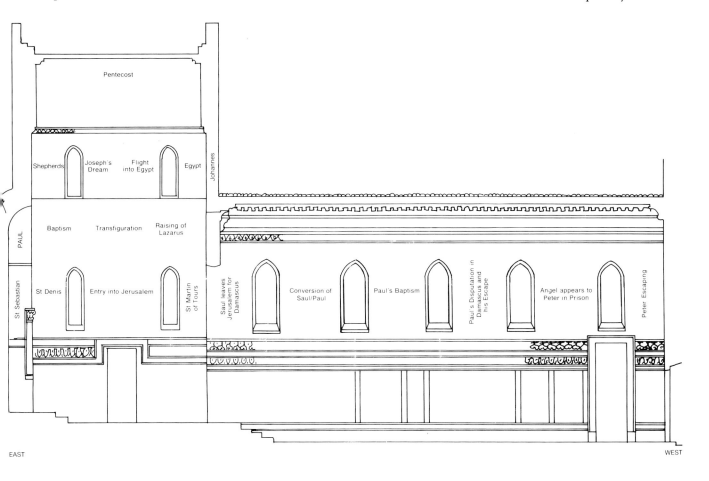

have been to the lost Montecassino cycle is, as yet, impossible to establish.[104] However, many of the individual compositions in the Palatina sequence do resemble contemporary Byzantine manuscript illuminations, which, in turn, may ultimately have been derived from monumental examples which have since been lost.[105] Otherwise, these Sicilian mosaics resist classification; like the rest of this royal scheme, their arrangement is unique.

*Fig. 4*             The apostolic cycle occupies a single band of scenes incorporating five windows in both aisles. Save for the three concluding episodes which are apocryphal, the subjects are taken from the Acts of the Apostles. The biblical sequence of events was rearranged, however, because in the text Peter's missionary activity precedes Paul's—following directly after Pentecost. The Pauline sequence may have been given precedence for two reasons: as a logical development from the southern chapel, where Paul's bust occupies the apse conch,[106] and to allow the Peter story to occupy the liturgical right in the northern aisle.

*Pls. 47, 49–*      The first episode of the Pauline sequence in the southern aisle shows *Paul's Dispatch to*
*50*                 *Damascus*, followed by his *Conversion* along the way (Acts 9: 1–9). Then comes Paul's *Baptism* (Acts 9: 18), followed by the *Disputation in Damascus* and his *Escape* from the city (Acts 9: 19–25). The last two scenes in this aisle, at the western end, are already devoted to St Peter—his *Imprisonment* in Jerusalem (?) and his *Liberation* by an angel (Acts 12: 4–
*Pls. 50–1*           9). Evidently, the designers wanted to link similar events in the lives of the two Apostles. Passing across to the northern aisle, Peter's story is resumed at the western end with *Peter*
*Pls. 52–3*           *and John healing the Lame Man at the Temple Gate* (Acts 3: 2–7), well chosen for its situation at the actual chapel door. This scene, in fact, like its pendant opposite, spans the corner between the aisle and the entrance wall, thereby enhancing the tempo of the action: the angel pulls Peter around the southern corner, while Peter and John look across to the
*Pls. 53–4*           cripple in the temple doorway. This is followed by the *Peter healing the Paralytic at Lydda* (Acts 9: 33–5) and the *Raising of Tabitha at Joppa* (Acts 9: 36, 40–1). The final apocryphal
*Pls. 54–6*           scenes are all set in Rome: the *Meeting of Peter and Paul, Disputation with Simon Magus before Nero*, and the *Fall of Simon Magus*.[107] Directly over the final scene, on the timbers of the roof, are three deacon saints with Peter holding the keys to the heavenly gates.

Just as there is no Crucifixion scene among the Christological sequences, neither are the martyrdoms of Peter and Paul represented in the chapel. In the aisle mosaics,
*Pl. 16*             the emphasis is upon conversion, preaching, and healing—the apostolic mission from Jerusalem to Rome—the example followed by the Norman king who, as surrogate apostolic legate in Sicily, sat at the Apostles' feet at the western end of his palace chapel,[108] or on other occasions sat in the northern chapel, again in the company of the Apostles, as a private witness of Christ's Ascension in the vault.

*Pls. 29, 31*        From the concluding Roman scene at the eastern end of the northern aisle, the topographical sequence, as one mounts the stairs to the northern chapel, is a return to
*Pl. 34*             Jerusalem—to the *Ascension*. Facing the aisle from the apse conch is the bust of *St Andrew*, Peter's elder brother, with the *Hodegetria* and the *Baptist* overhead. The inscription on the *Baptist*'s scroll, 'Behold the Lamb of God', is also the phrase that was used when Andrew brought Simon to Christ who renamed him Peter.[109]

Andrew and Peter were revered as the Apostles to whom the Lord entrusted the East and West, and subsequently they were regarded as the founders of Christian Rome and

Constantinople.[110] The choice of Andrew rather than Peter for the northern apse conch may reflect not only the vision at Antioch, but also the hoped-for reconciliation between Byzantium and Rome in 1161–2.[111] If the latter is true, then this mosaic would date from the reign of Roger's son William I (1154–66).

## GENESIS: PARADISE LOST AND REGAINED

The theme of sacred mission and return to Jerusalem, or Paradise, which is found in the aisles and in the southern and northern chapels is also taken up by the double-tiered Genesis cycle in the nave. Here, too, the arrangement is unconventional. The usual *Pls. 47–50,* scheme formulated in early Christian Rome was to have sequences from the Old and *53–6* New Testaments facing each other on opposite walls of the nave arcade, as at Old St Peter's (known today only through seventeenth-century copies and derivative murals in provincial Romanesque churches).[112] But in the Cappella Palatina both sides of the nave arcade are devoted to the Old Testament. There is only one notable precedent for such an arrangement: the fifth-century Roman mosaics at Santa Maria Maggiore, which, however, are much smaller in scale and surface area.[113] The biblical cycle there does not start out from the very beginning of Genesis: the Creation sequence is absent.[114] Instead, the episodes concern the patriarchs—Abraham, Jacob, Joshua, and Moses. The main idea behind this choice was to portray the Chosen People before the age of grace being fulfilled by the coming of the Messiah, whose infancy is represented upon the triumphal arch amidst symbols of another chosen people—the 'PLEBI [sic] DEI' of Rome.[115] Much of the same theme is embedded in the Cappella Palatina mosaics, but these are also indebted to the mainstream of early Christian representations, which *did* include the Creation scenes. Here the Sicilian scheme certainly profited from the Benedictine revival of early Christian programmes during the late eleventh and early twelfth centuries.[116] Although the outstanding example, Abbot Desiderius's at Montecassino, is lost, another of his churches, Sant' Angelo in Formis, survives.[117] There Old Testament stories were painted on the walls of both aisles—cradling, as it were, the Christological cycle covering the nave arcades.[118] At the Palatina the order is reversed.

Of the thirty-one Genesis scenes on the nave arcades at Palermo, only three are relatively modern substitutions for the original mosaics.[119] The upper tier incorporates five clerestory windows on either side of the nave, while the lower row is fitted into the spandrels of the arches. Either windows or thin vertical strips serve as dividers. Conforming *Pl. 16* to tradition, the cycle starts and finishes on either side of the sanctuary arch. Beginning on the south wall, at the eastern end, are the first seven days of Creation, followed by *Pls. 47–50* *Adam in Paradise* and the *Creation of Eve*; on the north wall, the story continues from the western end with the *Fall*, the *Judgement of Adam and Eve*, *Expulsion from Paradise*, the *Pls. 53–4* *Labours of Adam and Eve*, the *Sacrifice of Cain and Abel*, and the *Curse of Cain*, followed by three scenes made in the eighteenth century by the restorer Cardini: *Lamech informing his *Pls. 54–6* Wives of the Slaying of Cain*, *Enoch's Assumption*, and *Noah with his Family*. The last scene in *Pls. 55–6* this tier is the *Building of the Ark*. Returning to the south wall, the lower tier begins with the *Flood and Noah's Covenant with God*, followed by *Noah's Drunkenness*, the *Tower of Babel*, *Pls. 47–9*

*Pl. 50*

*Pls. 53–4*

*Pls. 55–6*
*Abraham's Welcome of the Angels and their Feast*, and the *Hospitality of Lot*. Across the nave, the story resumes with the *Destruction of Sodom, Abraham's Sacrifice of Isaac, Rebecca watering the Camels and her Journey with Abraham's Servant, Isaac blessing Jacob while Esau hunts, Jacob's Dream and the Anointing of the Altar*, and, finally, *Jacob wrestling with the Angel*.

*Pls. 47, 55*
The subjects are arranged in such a way that there are correspondences between scenes on the same wall as well as across the nave. For instance, the *Creation of Water* is directly above the second *Flood* scene, while *Noah's Descent from the Ark* down a ladder and his *Covenant with God* face *Jacob's Dream* of angels ascending another ladder, accompanied by the anointment of the altar. Thus Noah, as God's first minister, or *rector populi*, who served as priest and law-giver, faces Jacob's priestly act and his own meeting with God in the guise of an angel. Appropriately, both scenes of confrontation with the Deity, involving a covenant and a promise, are placed close to the sanctuary. Similarly, the scenes of the *Deluge* were situated above the area where the baptismal font may once have stood, which coincides with the liturgical association of baptism with the Flood as forms of rebirth and renewal.[120]

Both Noah and Jacob would have had a special significance for the first kings of Sicily as far as their divine right to rule and their sacred mission were concerned. Noah's sacred vicarate was handed down through patriarchs, judges, and kings. This raises the question of why the Palatina Genesis begins not with the patriarchs but with the Creation, and why both sides of the nave were used. In part this reflects the general revival of interest in biblical history and concordance between the Old and New Testaments then under way in France among such theologians as Honorius of Autun, Rupert of Deutz, and the Abbot Suger.[121] At the Cappella Palatina in Palermo, however, the choice of episodes in the Genesis cycle was especially concerned with the arrival of the Chosen People who, through the patriarchs, pursue their providential destiny towards the Promised Land— a theme of topical interest in the era of the crusades and of more than allegorical significance for the Norman conquerors of Sicily, who, although having reached one of their promised lands, still felt compelled to justify their mission through biblical parallels. This 'infusion' of monarchical propaganda into an Old Testament pictorial cycle is not unique. Much the same thing was done for the Byzantine Emperor Basil I in a ninth-century manuscript concerning the Joseph story.[122] The Old Testament, with its many holy rulers, was the perfect source of justification for new monarchies such as those of Sicily and England which also sought a degree of independence from Rome,[123] and it also fitted in very well with the old Frankish idea of the restoration of a Davidic monarchy.

However, there is a special reason why the Old Testament fills both sides of the nave, beginning with the *Creation* and concluding with *Jacob*. Of course, Jacob was an ante-type of Christ[124] and, like so much of the imagery in the sanctuary, these subjects appear in the Greek Christmas liturgy, which begins with the first thirteen lines of Genesis followed immediately by Balaam's prophecy ('a star shall come forth out of Jacob, and

*Pls. 55–6*
a sceptre shall rise out of Israel': Numbers 24: 17). 'ISRAHEL', the new name given to Jacob by the angel, appears in the mosaic on the golden ground adjacent to the sanctuary arch. The choice of Jacob and the link with Balaam's prophecy is another allusion to Roger's coronation on Christmas Day. The positioning of both Jacob scenes at the

threshold of the sanctuary is beautifully calculated; on waking from his dream Jacob says: 'This is none other than the house of God, and this is the gate of Heaven' (Genesis 28: 17). Whereupon, just as the mosaic shows, he takes his stone pillow and anoints it as an altar.[125] It was believed during the twelfth century that Jacob's pillow was preserved near the choir of the Christianized Temple in Jerusalem.[126]

Taken as a whole, this mosaic sequence of *Creation* to *Jacob* is essentially concerned with mankind's return to Paradise—whether in the guise of the geographical Holy Land or the visionary Promised Land of Israel. Inside the sanctuary, the *Annunciation* (or Incarnation) *Pls. 16, 18* makes Israel synonomous with the 'house of Jacob' mentioned in Luke's account of this *Col. Pl. III* event (Luke 1: 33). Similarly, 'the gate of heaven' perceived at the end of Jacob's dream was a phrase that was also used for the annunciate Virgin,[127] which accounts for the frequent representation of the Annunciation across an arch. Just as the Jacob episodes herald the return to Paradise via the Promised Land, so also Byzantine liturgical literature interpreted the Annunciation.[128] If one stands within or below the central square of the *Pl. 18* Cappella Palatina, the *Annunciation* is viewed together with the Latin verses framing the *Pantocrator* in the apse. Even the holy lance with which this inscription begins was also regarded as opening Paradise to mortals.[129] The same idea recurs in the adjacent *Ascension* *Pls. 16, 31* vault where Christ returns to Paradise. The Ascension also figures in the context of genesis and rebirth; a contemporary Benedictine wrote that it was the Ascension that began the rule of Mary who 'gave birth to Him who restored all things to the beauty of the first creation'.[130] There is a thematic symmetry between the northern and southern chapels, therefore: birth and rebirth; physical ascent and spiritual descent via the *Nativity, Ascension,* *Pl. 16* and *Pentecost*. The arrangement of the mosaic imagery is full of such interconnections.

The fact that *Jacob/Israel* is set close to the *Ascension* and to the area reserved for the king at the north-eastern corner of the Cappella Palatina is a magnificent device as far as the entire pictorial programme is concerned; in the account of the Ascension in Acts (1: 6–11), the assembled Apostles ask Jesus: ' "Lord, will you at this time restore the kingdom of Israel?" To which the Saviour replies: ". . . you shall receive power when the Holy Spirit has come upon you; and you shall be my witness in Jerusalem".' What more eloquent prophecy could there be for the Apostles of Pentecost, for apostolic legates, or—for that matter—for the anointed Sicilian king with his dynastic claim upon Jerusalem?

## LIGHT AND THE CHRISTMAS THEME

The idea of achieving birth and rebirth through the Creator and the Holy Spirit is expressed in the Palatina mosaics quite literally as en*light*enment—through light as the agent of divine wisdom. This is communicated not only through the choice and arrangement of subjects, but by their accompanying inscriptions and by the very use of the mosaic medium with its light reflecting golden ground. The chief image in the central apse sums up the entire concept with its accompanying text: 'I am the Light of the World; he who *Pls. 18, 21–2* follows me will not walk in darkness' (John 8: 12).[131] The ubiquitous presence in the sanctuary of Christ's precursor, the Baptist, is also justified by the theme of light,[132] for

Jesus compared him to 'a burning and shining lamp' (John 5: 35), and described him as a 'witness to the light . . . The true light that enlightens every man . . .' (John 1: 6–9).

The light theme initiates the narrative sequences in the nave and aisles and permeates

*Pls. 47–8*

the central square and southern chapel. The first Creation scene illustrates this beautifully; in fact, Creation here is rendered as illumination.[133] To achieve this, the mosaic inscriptions taken from Genesis 1: 1–3 were deliberately placed so that the creation of light appears uppermost between the Creator's hand and the actual clerestory window, while the creation of heaven and earth are set below on the left with the creation of water on the lower right. In the aisle below, among the first scenes of the apostolic cycle, is *Paul's Conversion*, brought about by a shaft of light.

Returning to the central square, the Latin inscriptions are arranged so that the passages concerning light correspond exactly with the adjacent pictorial imagery. For instance,

*Pls. 18, 20*

along the arch between Gabriel and Mary in the *Annunciation*, are the words:

LVMEN . VITA . VIA . EN . REPLE[N?]T . TE . VIRGO .

MARIA . FELIX . QVAE . VERBIS . CREDIS . NEC .

CORDE . SVP[ER]BIS

[The Light, the Life, the Way; Behold, fill you, O Virgin Mary, happy you who trust the words [of the angel] and do not become proud in your heart.[134]]

The entire wall surface upon which the *Annunciation* is rendered curves out and upwards, making the upper area shimmer. Immediately above the *Annunciation*, there was originally a window admitting light (like the one that can still be seen at La Martorana); which in the mosaic coincided with the celestial sphere from which the hand of God and the dove of the Holy Spirit emerge.[135] Directly opposite the *Annunciation*, a band of silver tesserae

*Pls. 16–17, 26*

displays another message involving illumination above the *Presentation in the Temple*. These words are part of a longer inscription encircling the central square. The entire text is given here, with slashes to indicate the corners of the wall and with the phrase accompanying the *Presentation* italicized:

ALES HOMO VITVLVS LEO PRECONES SIMVL ISTI +/

PRETENDVNT FORMAM DOCVERVNT QVAM FORE CRISTI +/

*QVAM TENEBRIS MUNDI LUCEM VITAMQVE DEDISTI*/

SICVT AB ETERNO . DEITAS . PIA . DISPOSVISTI/ .

[The bird, the man, the calf, the lion: all these heralds revealed and [still] proclaim who Christ [really] is *and what light and life you gave to the darkness of the world* as from eternity you, pious deity, had arranged.[136]]

*Col. Pl. III*
*Pls. 16–18*

These inscriptions accompanying the *Annunciation* and *Presentation* are beautiful reciprocals for the 'Ego sum lux' message in the apse, which is aligned with these related words and images in the central square.

*Pls. 39, 44*

The theme of light, with the Holy Spirit as its agent, dominates the southern sanctuary chapel. As we have already seen, this necessitated the repetition of the Saviour's bust with the 'Ego sum lux' inscription—this time rendered only in Greek. This *Pantocrator* occupies the uppermost area of the narrow east wall. His text appears directly above the *Nativity*,    *Pls. 39, 42* with the Star of Bethlehem shown as an emanation of the words in the open book.[137] The Christmas feast, first introduced by John Chrysostom at Antioch *circa* 375, coincided with the pagan feast of *sol invictus*.[138] Chrysostom composed parts of the Greek Christmas liturgies which are still in use. The Christmas and Ephiphany rites are full of phrases which equate the Saviour with light in various guises ('sun', 'the true Light', 'Light of lights', 'star', 'sun of righteousness', 'to give light to those who sit in darkness', 'King of the sun', 'word all-shining', 'the light no man can approach', 'Light from light')—images which are reflected in the Palatina sanctuary mosaics created by Greek artisans.

The Latin inscription between the Star and the Saviour's words associates the Star of    *Pls. 39, 42* Bethlehem with the birth of the sun:

STELLA PARIT SOLEM ROSA FLOREM FORMA DECOREM

[The Star brings forth the sun; rose the flower; comeliness, splendour ...[139]]

As the birth of the 'Light of lights', the Nativity was understood as a second Genesis and is so expressed in both the Greek and Latin Christmas liturgies.[140] Furthermore, this mosaic seems to embody Balaam's prophecy, 'a star shall come forth out of Jacob and a sceptre shall rise out of Israel' (Numbers 24: 17)—a familiar passage used in Christmas commentaries and sermons as well as in the Greek Christmas liturgy.[141] Here again is another link between the first and last episodes of the Genesis cycle in the nave and also the *Annunciation* in the central square. In fact, the Greek Christmas liturgy contains the following relevant passages: 'Today the Virgin gives birth to the maker of the universe. The cave brings forth Eden, and the star makes known Christ, sun to those in darkness ... rejoice Jerusalem ... today the age-old bond of Adam's condemnation has been untied. ... Paradise has been opened to us ...'[142] If, as Kitzinger has suggested, the mosaicists here were Greek, they would have been familiar with this interpretation of the subject— and some of the clerics at Roger's court clearly were.[143]

The inscription above the *Nativity* which circumscribes the chapel at the base of the vault is written in Leonine verse and unites the *Nativity* with the *Pentecost* represented on    *Pls. 16, 39,* the long narrow ceiling. The entire text (with slashes to indicate the corners of the ceiling)    *44* reads as follows:

+STELLA PARIT SOLEM ROSA FLOREM FORMA DECOREM/

FIT SONVS E COELIS ET JVXTA SCRIPTA JOHELIS

IMBVIT AFFATVS SANCTI VEHEME/NTIA FLATVS

PECTORA M/VNDORVM SVCCENDENS DISCIPVLORVM

VT VITAE VERBVM PER EOS TERAT OMNE

SVPERBVM/[144]

[The star brings forth the sun; rose the flower; comeliness splendour. There comes a sound out of heaven, and in accordance with the writings of Joel, [the] force of holy breath [i.e. the Holy Spirit] fills the breasts of the purified disciples enflaming [them] so that through their efforts the word of life can crush every arrogance.[145]]

*Pls. 16, 41*
Joel's prophecy, mentioned here, is represented on the arch spandrel below where the prophet is shown pointing to the vault with a scroll partly inscribed with the text from Peter's sermon at Pentecost (Acts 2: 17), which is based upon Joel 2: 28:

ΤΑΔΕ ΛΕΓΕΙ Κ[ΥΡΙΟ]C ΕCΤΑΙ ΕΝ ΤΑΙC

ΕCΧΑΤΕC ΙΜΕΡΑΙC ΕΚΧΕΩ ΑΠΟ ΤΟΥ

ΠΝ[ΕΥΜΑΤΟ]C ΜΟΥ.

[And in the last days it shall be, the Lord declares, that I will pour out my Spirit.[146]]

*Pl. 42*
*Isaiah*, on the opposite spandrel, is pointing towards the adjacent *Nativity*, with a foot and the ends of his fluttering mantle entering the scene. The text on his scroll was used for the Greek liturgy for both Christmas Eve and Christmas Day (Matthew 1: 23, based upon Isaiah 7: 14):[147]

ΙΔΟΥ Η ΠΑΡΘΕΝΟC ΕΝ ΓΑCΤΡΙ ΕΞΕΙ

ΚΑΙ ΤΕΞΕ [*sic*] ΥΙΟΝ.

[Behold, the virgin will have in her belly and will bear [a] son.]

*Pls. 37–8*
In fact, all of the imagery on the walls of the chapel has to do either with light or with the Holy Spirit. Angels, as personifications of light (or illumination), appear in *Joseph's Dream* and the *Flight into Egypt*. In the *Baptism*, the dove of the Holy Spirit seems to be a materialization of the light descending upon Christ from an actual window. Here again there is a recurrence of the theme of rebirth as illumination; baptism was understood to represent rebirth, enlightenment, a return to Paradise, and therefore among the Greeks (and in the Gallican liturgy as well) the feasts of Christ's birth and baptism were celebrated together on Epiphany—6 January, the day of the Adoration of the Kings.[148] The *Transfiguration* is another subject involving illumination, placed here between two other kinds of transformation and rebirth: the *Baptism* and the *Raising of Lazarus*.[149] Both the *Flight into Egypt* and the *Entry into Jerusalem* are likewise associated with the theme of royal advent, which is also intrinsic to Epiphany and the Nativity. Furthermore, the *Entry into*
*Pl. 44*
*Jerusalem* was included in the Latin Christmas liturgy.[150] As for the *Pentecost* overhead, the dove of the Holy Spirit rests upon the closed book of the central medallion, while each seated Apostle is inspired by his own personal dove. Just as Christ was compared to a sun or a star, so Chrysostom compared the Apostles of Pentecost to 'lights' and 'stars'.[151]

Pentecost also figures in both the Greek and Latin Christmas liturgies, but how closely twelfth-century Sicilian sacramentaries may have resembled the Roman missal is now difficult to establish.[152] However, a comparison of the Palatina mosaics with Roman liturgical texts for Christmas shows that they have a lot in common. During the Middle Ages, three Christmas Masses were said in three different churches in Rome at midnight, dawn, and midday. The churches were Santa Maria Maggiore, Sant' Anastasia, and St Peter's.[153] Many of the psalms and gospel texts used for these services allude to the Nativity not only as the materialization of the Word, or Logos, but also as the light of the world and dispeller of darkness.[154] The Baptism, Transfiguration, Entry into Jerusalem, and Pentecost are also mentioned.[155] Jacob's name is invoked, the Davidic monarchy, and even the Almighty's footstool (mentioned in the Palatina's dome inscription) recurs as the Messiah's throne.[156] Psalm 109/110, in which the new king is invited to ascend the throne and is described as bearing the dignity of priesthood while the defeat of his enemies is assured, is used several times.[157] Both the Latin dawn Christmas Mass and the Greek rite for Epiphany use lines from Psalm 117/118.[158] This is the psalm from which Roger II's royal motto was taken: 'Dextera Domini fecit virtutem, dextera Domini exaltavit me.' Roger II was crowned at the break of Christmas Day.[159]

The one subject absent from both the Latin and Greek Christmas and Epiphany liturgies is the *Raising of Lazarus*. Although not all of the psalms, prophetic texts, and scriptural passages were shared by both rites, the Messianic imagery is much the same—the advent of light and the righteous son sitting at the Lord's right hand, for example.[160] In the crossing, apart from *Solomon* and possibly *Elijah*, all of the inscriptions accompanying *Pl. 16* the prophets and evangelists are texts which are used in either the Greek or Latin liturgies for Christmas and Epiphany. The fact that so many of the subjects and inscriptions in the sanctuary area were included in these Christmas rites inevitably suggests that the programme was largely intended to commemorate Roger's coronation and the installation of the new monarchy.[161]

In both the mosaics and their accompanying inscriptions, light and the Holy Spirit appear as the agents of divine wisdom and illumination; angels are also used metaphorically for the same idea.[162] There are, in fact, an unusual number of them, and in the *Pentecost* four angels appear quite gratuitously—for nothing in the Scriptures accounts *Pl. 44* for their presence here.[163] Elsewhere, they are expected participants—as in the central *Pl. 25* dome, where they stand above eight light-giving windows. Two more angels, the so-called guardians of the bema, are on the presbytery vault, while another pair are on the arch *Pls. 16, 20,* separating the nave from the central square. Apart from Gabriel in the *Annunciation* and *18* the angels guiding Peter, five more appear in the *Nativity* (Luke 2: 13–14), and several of *Pls. 39, 42,* them accompany Jacob in the concluding episodes of the Jacob sequence. This pro- *55–6* liferation of angels is due to the contemporary interest in texts then attributed to St Denis, frequently identified with Dionysius the pseudo-Areopagite.[164] In these tracts, angels were perceived as the transmitters of divine illumination to mankind and therefore of crucial importance for salvation. Among the examples of their activity were cited Zaccharias and the Angel, the Annunciation, Joseph's Dream, the Nativity, the Annunciation to the Shepherds, and the Flight into Egypt.[165] With the exception of the Zaccharias episode, all of these subjects are represented in the sanctuary area of Roger's royal chapel.

Altogether, the mosaics of the Cappella Palatina display an intense involvement with the theology of light—or illumination in its material and metaphysical senses. Just as Roger II's first mosaics were being set at Cefalù and Palermo, new editions and commentaries of works attributed to St Denis were completed by Honorius of Autun and Hugh of St Victor. In 1137 Hugh dedicated his commentary on the *Celestial Hierarchy* to King Louis VII of France, who twelve years later was rescued by a Sicilian ship and brought to Calabria, where he met Roger.[166] Louis wrote about the meeting to Abbot Suger of Saint Denis, with whom Roger was also in touch.[167] The wide appeal of the pseudo-Dionysius's texts (*Celestial Hierarchy* and *Divine Names*) was due to their formulation of anagogy: the ascent from the material world towards the immaterial source of harmony, radiance, and light which creates, animates, and unifies.[168] This invisible sun, this 'Father of lights', was identified as God the Father, while Christ was described as the 'first radiance' revealing the Father to the world. Roger II's correspondent, Abbot Suger, was steeped in these ideas which inspired the adornment of the royal abbey church of St Denis, which was finished just as Roger began the mosaic programmes at Cefalù and Palermo.[169] It was at St Denis that Suger introduced stained-glass windows on a grand scale for the first time. Roger used mosaics in much the same way as Suger had used stained glass: both are materials which rely on light—either passing through the windows or reflecting from the golden tesserae. Each reveals sacred imagery in its own way— literally making visible divine things which otherwise could not be seen.[170] Evidently Roger, like Suger, believed that material brilliance 'should brighten the minds so that they may travel, through the true lights, to the True Light where Christ is the true door'.[171] The presence of St Denis, the reputed author of this anagogical system, in a place of honour at both Cefalù and the royal chapel in Palermo is as much a tribute to his theological ideas as to the Frankish monarchy.[172]

In the Cappella Palatina, the golden tesserae pour down the vaults to the arches, and along the nave and aisles. The pavement and the high dado are made of white marble richly inlaid with green, red, and golden patterns, which a contemporary compared to an eternal springtime meadow.[173] What Roger had begun at Cefalù was fulfilled in his palace chapel. If Cefalù's apse and presbytery represent a royal gate to heaven, the Cappella Palatina corresponds materially to the heavenly Jerusalem come down to earth described in Revelation (21: 10, 18–21). This passage was paraphrased by Bruno of Segni (c.1048–1123), an older contemporary of Roger II's. Although he probably wrote with the mosaics of Montecassino in mind, his text applies just as well to Roger's royal chapel: '... truly this city is pure gold, which is like clear glass ... everywhere gold shines, everywhere all things shine with the light of wisdom ... this gold is said to be like clear glass, for gold may shine, but what is within is not seen ...'[174]

In 1142, Peter of Cluny referred to Roger as a new Solomon.[175] He was probably thinking only of the King's wisdom and justice, because Cefalù and the Cappella Palatina were still far from completion,[176] but he may already have recognized Roger's aspirations for Jerusalem in both its terrestrial and celestial aspects. The mosaics in the Cappella Palatina exalt the biblical subject-matter and glorify the monarchy allegorically. For a ruler who even before his coronation was known by such biblical epithets as 'sun of justice' and 'light of wisdom',[177] with a claim upon the earthly Jerusalem and with a royal motto expressing the conviction that he sat at the Lord's right hand, it was entirely consistent that his chapel should have been conceived of as a physical replica of the heavenly kingdom[178]—as a return to Paradise and the celestial city of 'pure gold'.

## THE PROCESSION OF SAINTS AND VIRTUES

Between the capitals of the nave arcade and the lower tier of the Genesis cycle there is a series of holy figures. Four male saints face each other on either side of the nave. Starting at the south-eastern end, they are: *Julian*, *Cataldus*, *Leo the Great*, and *Athanasius* on

*Pls. 16, 47, 49–50, 53–5*

the southern arcade, with *Blaise, Augustine, Ambrose,* and *Sabinus* on the northern side.[179] Roger II possessed a relic of St Cataldus, who was a patron saint of Palermo.[180] Cataldus, who made a pilgrimage to the Holy Land, also occupies a similar site in the church of the Nativity in Bethlehem.[181] There are two more saints at the western ends of either aisle: *Felix of Nola* and *Jerome.*[182] On the other side of the arcade walls, looking into the aisles, are twelve large foliated medallions of holy women. Moving once more from south to north they are: *Scholastica, Thecla, Radegonda,* and *Margaret; Christine, Euphemia, Perpetua,* and *Candida.* In addition to these, the spandrels of the southern aisle contain further medallions with the Pauline virtues of *Charity, Hope,* and *Faith,* which in commentaries on the Apocalypse were sometimes regarded as corner-stones of the heavenly Jerusalem.[183] In the northern aisle, there are medallions of SS *Petronilla, Prassede, Euphrosina,* and *Colomba.*

*Pls. 51–2*

*Pl. 16*

According to the Roman martyrology, the three virtues included here were sisters who were martyred under Hadrian, and their feast-day coincides with that of *St Peter in Chains,* which is represented opposite them on the southern aisle wall.[184] While allegories of the virtues in the form of monumental female figures were seen in western churches from the twelfth century onwards, there are no known examples in Byzantium.[185] Roundels of the virtues were also included in the later Norman mosaics at Monreale, but the most complete set of all is in St Mark's in Venice, where in the late twelfth century they were given a much more conspicuous site in the outer ring of the central dome.[186] The Palatina virtues, therefore, are the earliest known examples among medieval wall mosaics.

*Pl. 50*

## THE DATING OF THE MOSAICS

The mosaics in the Cappella Palatina belong to a well-co-ordinated plan with several related messages: the commemoration of Roger's coronation, the apostolic mission, the aspirations for Jerusalem in this world and the next. All of these are articulated into an all-encompassing theme—the justification of the new monarchy. The arrangement is so eloquently contrived that it must be assumed that the scheme was foreseen from the start. The style of the mosaics, however, lacks this consistency. Those in the crossing and side chapels—restorations and replacements notwithstanding—are of finer quality and are more intrinsically Greek. In fact, this area of the chapel has many Greek inscriptions, while the mosaics in the nave and aisles have none. The glass and stone tesserae on the sanctuary walls are used with greater skill, elegance, and ingenuity. Connections have been established between some of the saints here and those at Cefalù.[187] Further similarities have been discerned in the mosaics commissioned by Roger II's Admiral George of Antioch for his church of La Martorana.[188] Brenk noticed that even the workmanship of the porphyry columns in the Palatina's apse is identical with that at La Martorana.[189] It seems more than likely, therefore, that teams of the same craftsmen were used in both churches at Palermo, which were begun and decorated at about the same time.[190]

*Col. Pl. V*

*Pls. 9, 13*

The mosaics in the nave and aisles are much more Latin—i.e. more Roman—in style. This may partly be due to the nature of the subject-matter—discursive narratives with a

*Col. Pl. VI*

long tradition in the West. Except for the earlier Pauline scenes and many of the medallions lining the soffits of the nave arcade, these mosaics are clumsier than the ones in the sanctuary; the colours have less sparkle, less life in the contrasts, less subtlety in the transitions of light and shade.[191] The Genesis cycle, which in style seems to be half-way between the sanctuary and aisle mosaics, has been variously dated between *c.*1150 and 1171.[192]

*Pl. 25*

*Pl. 35*

The difference in style between the sanctuary mosaics and most of those in the rest of the chapel implies a lapse of time and various campaigns of work. The original team of mosaicists left before completing the job; either local craftsmen were trained to succeed them or others were imported from Byzantium or the Italian mainland. No comparable works remain to sustain the latter possibility, however. Not a single document has survived to tell us how the work was begun and completed. The only date in the building is 1143 in the base of the cupola—three years after Roger II's charter of endowment. The rest is speculation. For instance, does *St Theodore*'s presence in the northern chapel justify a date of soon after 1147, when the Normans came into possession of his relic?[193] As late as 1155, the pope was still addressing the ruler of Sicily as 'Signore', or Lord—not as king— but between the Treaty of Benevento in 1156 and the accession of Pope Alexander III in 1159, Rome finally recognized the Sicilian monarchy with all its privileges, the surrogate apostolic legateship was renewed, and William I finally made common cause with the papacy.[194] All these events would have encouraged the strong pro-Roman cast of the apostolic cycle in the aisles, as well as of the Apostles accompanying *Christ in Majesty* above the king's throne on the entrance wall.[195] During his reign, William succeeded in driving out the last of the Byzantines from Southern Italy, and this might account for the total absence of Greek inscriptions in the nave and aisles, which have nothing of the cosmopolitan flavour of the sanctuary mosaics which are a faithful reflection of Roger II's taste. A contemporary chronicler, Romuald of Salerno (writing *c.*1178), attributed all the chapel's decorations to William I's reign (1154–66).[196] In view of the inscription of 1143 in the cupola, however, this can only be understood in the sense that the son finished his father's project.[197] Some of the mosaics have even been dated to William II's reign.[198]

*Pl. 19*

Since Roger's Christmas coronation is alluded to repeatedly in the mosaics, one might expect to find similar references to his son William I's coronations. This is difficult to detect, however. William was crowned twice: once in Roger's lifetime to ensure the succession, and again after Roger's death.[199] Both coronations were at Easter—another favourite day for such rites.[200] As the fulfilment of Christmas, Easter uses some of the same liturgical texts,[201] one of which, the Paschal Psalm (92/93: 1–2), includes these appropriate dynastic phrases: 'The Lord reigns; he is robed in majesty ... The throne is established of old; thou art from everlasting.' Psalm 109/110: 1–2 alludes to the defeat of enemies by the just ruler, and also includes paraphrases of the royal motto as well as the cupola inscription: 'The Lord said to my lord: "Sit at my right hand, till I make your enemies your footstool." The Lord sends forth from Zion your mighty sceptre. Rule in the midst of your foes ...' But these texts are as appropriate to Roger as they are to William, and to either Christmas or Easter. Only the choice of St Andrew instead of Peter for the

I. Cefalù cathedral: detail of orant *Virgin* in the apse.

II. Cefalù cathedral: detail of angel from presbytery vault.

III. Palermo, Capella Palatina: view of apse and sanctuary from nave looking east.

IV. Palermo, Capella Palatina: *St Luke*, crossing squinch.

northern apse conch might conceivably reflect the attempted *rapprochement* between Rome, Sicily and Byzantium in 1158–62.[202]

When William died in 1166, his death was kept secret for some time because of the troubled political situation in Sicily.[203] How near the mosaics were to completion is unknown. Some think they were not finished until 1170 or even later; it has even been suggested that the apse *Pantocrator* and the royal dais on the west wall are late twelfth-century afterthoughts.[204] In any case, William was buried in the crypt of the Cappella Palatina, but twenty years later his remains were transferred to the new royal abbey mausoleum at Monreale.[205]

*Fig. 2*

# APPENDIX

## Table of Inscriptions and Subjects Appearing in the Sanctuary Mosaics which are included in the Liturgies for Christmas and Epiphany*

### INSCRIPTIONS
(for the texts see n. 84)

| | |
|---|---|
| Ezekiel (Baruch 3: 35/36) | Greek Christmas Eve, Greek Christmas Day |
| Jeremiah (Ezekiel 44: 2) | Greek Christmas Day |
| Jonah (2: 2/3 = Psalm 117/118: 5) | Greek Christmas Day (Mattins, Canticle 6, 2nd Canon) |
| Daniel (2: 45) | Greek Christmas Day |
| Moses (Exodus 3: 2–4) | Greek Christmas Day, Greek Epiphany |
| Elisha (2 Kings 2: 21) | Greek Epiphany |
| Zechariah (9: 9) | Latin Christmas (Dawn Mass) |
| Matthew (1: 1–2) | Greek Christmas Day |
| (2: 1) | Greek Christmas Eve, Greek Christmas Day, Latin Epiphany |
| John (1: 1) | Greek Christmas Day, Latin Christmas (Dawn and Daylight Masses) |
| Luke (1: 5 = Matthew 2: 1) | Greek Christmas Eve, Greek Christmas Day, Latin Epiphany |
| Isaiah (7: 14 = Matthew 1: 23) | Greek Christmas Eve, Greek Christmas Day |

* For the texts used in the Greek and Latin rites, see *The Festal Menaion*, trans. Mother Mary and K. Ware (London and Boston, 1984), 199–289, 295–387; the *Roman Missal*; I. Schuster, *The Sacramentary*, i (London, 1924), 356–77, 399–404.

## SUBJECTS

*Nativity*
(Psalm 92/93: 1–5)  Greek Christmas Day, Greek Eve of Epiphany, Greek Epiphany, Latin Christmas (Dawn Mass)
(Isaiah 9: 6)  Greek Christmas Eve, Greek Christmas Day, Latin Christmas (Dawn Mass)

*Adoration of Shepherds*
(Luke 2: 15–20)  Greek Christmas Eve, Greek Christmas Day, Latin Christmas (Dawn Mass)

*Adoration of Magi*
(Matthew 2: 1–12)  Greek Christmas Eve, Greek Christmas Day

*Light Theme*
(Genesis 1: 1–13)  Greek Christmas Day, Greek Epiphany
(Hebrews 1: 3)  Greek Christmas Eve, Greek Christmas Day, Greek Epiphany, Latin Christmas (Daylight Mass)
(Isaiah 9: 2)  Greek Christmas Day, Greek Forefeast of Epiphany, Latin Christmas (Dawn Mass)
(Isaiah 9: 6)  Greek Christmas Eve, Greek Christmas Day, Latin Christmas (Daylight Mass)
(John 1: 1–14)  Greek Forefeast of Christmas, Greek Christmas Day, Latin Christmas (Daylight Mass)
(Malachi 4: 2)  Greek Christmas Day, Greek Epiphany
(Baruch 3: 35/36)  Greek Christmas Eve, Greek Christmas Day
(Baruch 4: 4)  Greek Christmas Day

*Balaam's Prophecy*
(Numbers 24: 17)  Greek Forefeast of Christmas, Greek Christmas Day

*Baptism*
(Titus 3: 4–7)  Greek Eve of Epiphany, Greek Epiphany, Latin Christmas (Dawn Mass)
(Psalm 92/93: 1–5)  Greek Epiphany
(Luke 3: 1–18)  Greek Eve of Epiphany, Greek Epiphany

*Joseph's Dream*
(Matthew 1: 18–21)  Greek Christmas Eve, Greek Christmas Day, Latin Christmas Eve

*Flight into Egypt*
(Matthew 2: 12–23)  Greek Christmas Eve, Latin Vigil of Epiphany

*Transfiguration*
(Psalm 88/89: 11–14)  Latin Christmas (Daylight Mass)

*Entry into Jerusalem*
(Psalm 96/97: 1–4)  Latin Christmas (Dawn and Daylight Masses)
(Zechariah 9: 9)  Latin Christmas (Dawn Mass)

*Pentecost*
(Isaiah 11: 2)  Greek Christmas Day, Greek Epiphany

| (Titus 3: 4–7) | Greek Eve of Epiphany, Greek Epiphany, Latin Christmas Day (Dawn Mass) |
| (Acts 19: 1–8) | Greek Eve of Epiphany |
| (Luke 3: 16) | Greek Eve of Epiphany, Greek Epiphany |

[1] E. Kitzinger, 'The Mosaics of the Cappella Palatina in Palermo: An Essay on the Choice and Arrangement of the Subjects', *Art Bulletin*, 31 (1949), 270.

[2] G. Di Stefano, *Monumenti della Sicilia normanna*, ed. W. Krönig (2nd edn., Palermo, 1979), 38; L. Boglino, *Storia della Real Cappella di S. Pietro della reggia di Palermo* (Palermo, 1894), 8, 41 n. 3; U. Falcando, *Storia*, ed. G. del Re (Naples, 1845), 394 n. 16; O. Demus, *The Mosaics of Norman Sicily* (London, 1950), 25, 58 nn. 2–4.

[3] Demus, *The Mosaics of Norman Sicily*, 58 nn. 2, 4.

[4] It is conceivable that Roger knew about Justinian's church dedicated to SS Peter and Paul built near the royal palace in Constantinople as a token of his desire for peace between Rome and Byzantium: F. Dvornik, *Early Christian and Byzantine Political Philosophy: Origins and Background*, 2 vols. (Washington, DC, 1966), ii. 830 f.

[5] Demus, *The Mosaics of Norman Sicily*, 25; Kitzinger, 'The Mosaics of the Cappella Palatina', 269 n. 2.

[6] M. Bloch, *The Royal Touch: Sacred Monarchy and Scrofula in England and France*, trans. J. E. Anderson (London, 1973), 116.

[7] Demus, *The Mosaics of Norman Sicily*, 59 n. 11. V. F. Hopper (*Medieval Number Symbolism* (New York, 1938), 77 f.) explains that, according to Irenaeus and Lactantius, the limit of the world was supposed to be 6,000 years, but that some other theologians maintained that, thanks to Christ's dispensation, another 1,000 years had been granted.

[8] Demus (*The Mosaics of Norman Sicily*, 59 f. nn. 11–12) gives the much restored Greek text; cf. I. Beck, 'The First Mosaics of the Cappella Palatina in Palermo', *Byzantion*, 40 (1970), 125 f. Our variation of Demus's translation is due to J. McManamon.

[9] F. Chalandon, *Histoire de la domination normande en Italie et en Sicile*, 2 vols. (Paris, 1907), ii. 93 f.; Demus, *The Mosaics of Norman Sicily*, 59 n. 7; Kitzinger, 'The Mosaics of the Cappella Palatina', 269 n. 2; C. Brühl, *Diplomi e cancelleria di Ruggero II* (Palermo, 1983), 76: 'Nos autem pro salute animarum predecessorum nostrorum Roberti Guiscardi et Rogerii comitis, patris nostri, et matris nostre Adelasie et Elvire regine, uxoris nostre . . .'

[10] Demus, *The Mosaics of Norman Sicily*, 25 f.; Beck, 'The First Mosaics', 121 ff.; B. Patera, *L'arte della Sicilia normanna nelle fonti medievali* (Palermo, 1980), 17 ff., 83 f. On the basis of a marginal note in a Rogerian martyrology (Biblioteca Comunale, Palermo, MS 2 Qq-E2), Monsignor Rocco claims that the chapel's dedication coincided with the endowment charter of 28 Apr., which followed a Byzantine custom of dedicating churches on Sundays soon after Easter: B. Rocco, 'La Cappella Palatina di Palermo: Lettura teologica', *Beni culturali ambientali: Sicilia*, 4 (1983), 21. N. Nersessian, on the other hand, gives the consecration date as Palm Sunday 1140 ('The Cappella Palatina of Roger II: The Relationship of its Imagery to its Political Functions', Ph.D. diss. (University of California at Los Angeles, 1981), 1; no source given), which in that year fell on 31 March.

[11] E. Kitzinger, 'The Date of Philagathos' Homily for the Feast of Sts. Peter and Paul', in *Byzantino-Sicula*, ii: *Miscellanea di scritti in memoria di Giuseppe Rossi Taibbi* (Palermo, 1975), 301–6; Patera, *L'arte della Sicilia*, 17, 19, 61 nn. 17 and 17 *bis*. M. Gigante, 'La civiltà letteraria', in *I bizantini in Italia* (Milan, 1982), 626 f.

[12] Kitzinger, 'The Mosaics of the Cappella Palatina', 273 n. 21; Demus, *The Mosaics of Norman Sicily*, 322; D. Hiley, 'The Norman Chant Traditions: Normandy, Britain, Sicily', *Proceedings of the Royal Musical Association*, 107 (1980–1), 17.

[13] Observations of Lucio Trizzino, the architect, who supervised the maintenance of the chapel and has written an unpublished history of the chapel's structure and modifications. Typescript entitled 'Cappella Palatina: Dissesti e restauri' (n.d.), Palermo (Archives of the Soprintendenza beni culturali e ambientali, Palermo; Palermo 1979). See addendum, p. 101 below

[14] M. and C. Valenziano, 'La Supplique des chanoines de la cathédrale de Cefalù pour la sépulture du roi Roger', *Cahiers de civilisation médiévale*, 21 (1978), 150; J. Deér, *The Dynastic Porphyry Tombs of the Norman Period in Sicily* (Cambridge, Mass., 1959), 4 ff., 10; id., 'Das Grab Friedrichs II.', in J. Fleckenstein (ed.), *Probleme um Friedrich II.* (Sigmaringen, 1974), 365; Demus, *The Mosaics of Norman Sicily*, 25.

[15] Kitzinger, 'The Mosaics of the Cappella Palatina', 270; Demus, *The Mosaics of Norman Sicily*, 27 f.

[16] This was pointed out to me by B. Brenk. See Di Stefano, *Monumenti della Sicilia*, 16, 22, 39, pls. XXIII, XXIX.

[17] Observations of L. Trizzino, whose measurements of the nave show that the south wall splays outwards 22 cm. from a vertical plumb line, while the north wall is 18 cm. out of plumb. For discussion of the roof's style, structure, and iconography, see Nersessian, *The Cappella Palatina of Roger II*, 152–76; for Romuald of Salerno's dating of the ceiling, see Demus, *The Mosaics of Norman Sicily*, 28. For the imagery on the wooden ceiling, see also D. Gramit, 'I dipinti musicali della Cappella Palatina di Palermo', *Schede medievali*, 10 (1986), 5–55.

[18] Demus, *The Mosaics of Norman Sicily*, 59 f. nn. 11, 12; Beck, 'The First Mosaics', 125. Whether SS Sergius and Bacchus was also a palace chapel is controversial: C. Mango, 'The Church of Saints Sergius and Bacchus at Constantinople and the Alleged Tradition of Octagonal Palatine Churches', *Jahrbuch der österreichischen Byzantinistik*, 21 (1972), 189; and R. Krautheimer, 'Again Saints Sergius and Bacchus at Constantinople', *Jahrbuch der österreichischen Byzantinistik*, 23 (1974), 251 ff. According to A. van Millingen (*Byzantine Churches in Constantinople: Their History and Architecture* (London, 1912), 64), this church was built by Justinian as a 'special thank offering for his crown'.

[19] Patera, *L'arte della Sicilia*, 19.

[20] W. Krönig, *Il duomo di Monreale e l'architettura normanna in Sicilia* (Palermo, 1965), 178 ff. For the classical spoils used in a similar fashion at Monreale, see L. Trizzino, 'Die Kathedrale von Monreale: Was für eine Collage!', *Daidalos*, 16 (15 June 1985), 67 f.; for more general information on the use of spoils, see C. Klapisch-Zuber, *Les Maîtres du marbre: Carrare, 1300–1600* (Paris, 1969), 25 ff.; A. Esch, 'Spolien: Zur Wiederverwendung antiker Baustücke und Skulpturen im mittelalterlichen Italien', *Archiv für Kulturgeschichte*, 51 (1969), 1–64.

[21] Chalandon, *Histoire de la domination normande*, ii. 584; Demus, *The Mosaics of Norman Sicily*, 60 n. 24.

[22] All of the royal dead, except for the king and his heirs, were to be buried near this monastery in the adjacent cemetery of S. Giorgio Nuovo: Brühl, *Diplomi e cancelleria*, 176; cf. L. White, *Latin*

*Monasticism in Norman Sicily* (Cambridge, Mass., 1938), 128, 130; Deér, *Dynastic Porphyry Tombs*, 2 f.

[23] Chalandon, *Histoire de la domination normande*, ii. 632, 638; K. Kehr, *Die Urkunden der Normannisch-Sicilischen Könige* (Innsbruck, 1902), 70–7; Deér, *Dynastic Porphyry Tombs*, 2; H. Enzensberger, *Beiträge zum Kanzlei- und Urkundwesen der normannischen Herrscher Unteritaliens und Siziliens* (Kallmünz Opf., 1971), 50 ff.; Nersessian, *The Cappella Palatina of Roger II*, 185 f.

[24] Chalandon, *Histoire de la domination normande*, ii. 584.

[25] Boglino, *Storia della Real Cappella*, 72 n. 11; Kitzinger, 'The Mosaics of the Cappella Palatina', 274 n. 29; Rocco, 'La Cappella Palatina di Palermo', 23.

[26] U. Falcando, *Storia*, ed. del Re, 287: 'Aliorum quoque Regum ac gentium consuetudines diligentissime fecit inquiri, ut quod in eis pulcherrimum aut utile videbatur . . .'.

[27] Boglino (*Storia della Real Cappella*, 33) believed that the original altar was set just in front of the apse conch in the bema, but that it was moved back into the apse proper in 1708 when it was also remodelled. Trizzino's list of restorations ('Cappella Palatina', 7) mentions that the present altar dates from another reworking in 1788. For a late 12th-century view of the chapel and its altar, see Pietro da Eboli, *Liber ad honorem Augusti*, ed. G. B. Siragusa (Rome, 1906), plate III from Bern, Burger Bibliothek MS 120, c. 4 (97). This sketch shows the altar in front of the apse, roughly corresponding to the crossing. Trizzino maintains that the building's structure could not have supported a heavy altar in this position.

[28] Philagathos, Migne, *Patrologia Graeca*, 132, homily 55, col. 954: 'Locus ille, in quo arcanum peragitur sacrificium marmoreo thorace septum, et circumscriptum est sacerdotibus, ubi et requiescere, et tuto consistere, et aspectum, spectaculo licet oblectare. Idque claustrum etiam ab accessu prohibet, si quia temerarius ac profanus adyta penetrare contendat.' Panels from the dismantled enclosure were sent to Spain in 1680, and in 1719 others were used for the remodelling of the throne dais at the west end of the Chapel: Boglino, *Storia della Real Cappella*, 30; B. Rocco, 'I mosaici delle chiese normanne in Sicilia: Sguardo teologico, biblico, liturgico. II. La Cappella Palatina', *Ho Theologos*, 11–12 (1976), 131 f.; id., 'La Cappella Palatina di Palermo: Lettura teologica', *Beni culturali ambientali: Sicilia*, 4 (1983, pub. 1985), 27; Patera, *L'arte della Sicilia*, 83 ff.; Nersessian, *The Cappella Palatina of Roger II*, 269 f. nn. 3–4; Trizzino, 'Cappella Palatina', 6.

[29] Trizzino, 'Cappella Palatina', 5. The loge was dismantled between 1838 and 1841; Boglino, *Storia della Real Cappella*, 37 f. For the arguments in favour of an original Norman loge, see Demus, *The Mosaics of Norman Sicily*, 52; E. Kitzinger, review of Demus, *The Mosaics of Norman Sicily*, in *Speculum*, 28/1 (1953), 146; Beck, 'The First Mosaics', 126–9, 152, 158 ff.

[30] Trizzino, 'Cappella Palatina', 5. The two windows are still clearly visible on the exterior wall. Cf. Beck, 'The First Mosaics', 127 f.

[31] Van Millingen, *Byzantine Churches*, 69 f., cites an imperial viewing-gallery in a chapel in Constantinople dedicated to the Theotokos (Mother of God). There were other Byzantine loges in the Saviour's chapel attached to the Chalke and at SS Sergius and Bacchus, as well as several 12th-century Russian examples: C. Mango, *The Brazen House: A Study of the Vestibule of the Imperial Palace of Constantinople* (Arkæologisk-Kunsthistoriske Meddelelser, Det Kongelige Danske Videnskabernes Selskab, 4/4; Copenhagen, 1959), 18, 28, 87. For Oviedo, see E. Dyggve, 'Le Type architectural de la Cámara Santa d'Oviedo et l'architecture asturienne', *Cahiers archéologiques*, 6 (1952), 125–33. For the Byzantine emperor's route of entrance to Hagia Sophia from the royal palace, see Mango, *The Brazen House*, 26 n. 20, 88; id., *Materials for the Study of the Mosaics at St. Sophia at Istanbul* (Washington, DC, 1962), 37 f. For clarification of the hitherto confused ideas of imperial

loges in Constantinople see C. Strube, *Die westliche Eingangsseite der Kirchen von Konstantinopel in justinianischer Zeit* (Wiesbaden, 1973), *passim*; and C. Delvoye, 'Empore', *Reallexikon zur byzantinischen Kunst*, ii (Stuttgart, 1967), cols. 129–44.

[32] For the arguments against the existence of a permanent loge based on the lack of structural evidence, see Trizzino, 'Cappella Palatina'.

[33] K. M. Swoboda, 'The Problem of the Iconography of Late Antique and Early Medieval Palaces', *Journal of the Society of Architectural Historians*, 20/2 (1961), 88 f.; I. Lavin, 'The House of the Lord: Aspects of the Role of Palace Triclinia in the Architecture of Late Antiquity and the Early Middle Ages', *Art Bulletin*, 44 (1962), 1–27; cf. J. Christern, 'Zum Verhältnis von Palasttriklinium und Kirche', *Istanbuler Mitteilungen*, 13–14 (1963–4), 108–12. See also Slobodan Ćurčić, 'Some Palatine Aspects of the Cappella Palatina in Palermo', *Dumbarton Oaks Papers*, 41 (1987), 125–44, which appeared while the present volume was already in the press. Ćurčić (ibid. 140–2) describes three rooms in the imperial palace in Constantinople which contained elements (e.g. a wooden ceiling of Islamic workmanship) also to be found in Palermo's Cappella Palatina.

[34] H. Fichtenau, 'Byzanz und die Pfalz zu Aachen', *Mitteilungen des Instituts für österreichische Geschichtsforschung*, 59 (1951), 1–25, 41, 48 ff.; W. E. Kleinbauer, 'Charlemagne's Palace Chapel at Aachen and its Copies', *Gesta*, 4 (1965), 2–11; I. Forsyth, *The Throne of Wisdom: Wood Sculptures of the Madonna in Romanesque France* (Princeton, 1972), 88.

[35] Also noted by Nersessian, *The Cappella Palatina of Roger II*, 110 ff. For discussion of the heavenly and earthly thrones juxtaposed, see Fichtenau, 'Byzanz und die Pfalz', 41, 48 ff.; E. Kitzinger, 'The Cult of Images in the Age before Iconoclasm', *Dumbarton Oaks Papers*, 8 (1954), 126; O. Demus, *The Mosaics of San Marco in Venice*, 4 vols. (Chicago and London, 1984), i. 266, 377 n. 227.

[36] S. Der Nersessian, 'Two Images of the Virgin in the Dumbarton Oaks Collection', *Dumbarton Oaks Papers*, 14 (1960), repr. in *Études byzantines et arméniennes*, i (Louvain, 1973), 62; Lavin, 'The House of the Lord', 17, 22 f.; A. Cameron, 'Images of Authority: Elites and Icons in late Sixth-century Byzantium', *Past and Present*, 84 (1979), 17 f.; Demus, *The Mosaics of San Marco*, i. 377 n. 227.

[37] A. Terzi, S. Cavallari, *et al.*, *La cappella di S. Pietro nella reggia di Palermo* (Palermo, 1873–85), 22; Demus, *The Mosaics of Norman Sicily*, 34, 37; Trizzino, 'Cappella Palatina', 7—the window was filled in between 1797 and 1800; cf. Nersessian, *The Cappella Palatina of Roger II*, 34, who doubts the Norman date for the window.

[38] B. Brenk kindly pointed out to me that Charlemagne's palace chapel at Aachen was also furnished with two bronze doors and that it too was sometimes used as an audience hall. Such double-portalled royal edifices may also have been a deliberate recollection of Jerusalem: see N. Kenaan-Kedar, 'Symbolic Meaning in Crusader Architecture: The Twelfth-century Dome of the Holy Sepulchre Church in Jerusalem', *Cahiers archéologiques*, 34 (1986), 115, on the double portals of the church of the Holy Sepulchre as well as those at the Golden Gate, both in Jerusalem. Kenaan-Kedar sees the rebuilding of the Holy Sepulchre by the Crusaders as symbolic of the new Latin kingdom with an allusion to Christ's entry into Jerusalem.

[39] For the various restorations of the throne dais, see Boglino, *Storia della Real Cappella*, 30 f.; Trizzino 'Cappella Palatina', 6, citing the reconstruction of 1719; Nersessian, *The Cappella Palatina of Roger II*, 269 f. nn. 3–4; and n. 28 above.

[40] See Appendix, pp. 82, 84.

[41] Kitzinger, 'The Mosaics of the Cappella Palatina', 284; id., 'The Date of Philagathos' Homily', 305; Demus, *The Mosaics of*

*Norman Sicily*, 52, 57–78; Deér, *Dynastic Porphyry Tombs*, 37 ff.; H. Buchtal, 'Early Fourteenth-century Illuminations from Palermo', *Dumbarton Oaks Papers*, 20 (1966), 105; Rocco, 'I mosaici delle chiese normanne', 17 (1978), 53 n. 5, believes the mosaic was planned from the beginning, although it was executed in the late 12th century. For different reasons from mine, Beck ('The First Mosaics', 132 f., 162) also believes that this mosaic and the royal dais below it belong to the original Rogerian programme.

⁴² Eusebius associated the phrase with the Ascension: J. Daniélou, *Bibbia e liturgia: La teologia biblica dei sacramenti e delle feste secondo i padri della chiesa* (Milan, 1965), 416 ff.; Migne, *Patrologia Graeca*, 23. 1342C. The phrase also occurs in the Greek liturgy for the vespers of the feast of the Annunciation; *The Festal Menaion*, trans. Mother Mary and Kallistos Ware (London and Boston, 1985), 440.

⁴³ For the mosaic in Charlemagne's palace chapel at Aachen, see W. Schöne, 'Die künstlerische und liturgische Gestalt der Pfalzkirche Karls der Grossen in Aachen', *Zeitschrift für Kunstwissenschaft*, 15 (1961), 127 f., 140 ff., figs. 4, 7; H. Schnitzler, 'Das Kuppelmosaik der Aachener Pfalzkapelle', *Aachener Kunstblätter*, 29 (1964), 37–9.

⁴⁴ J. Kollwitz, review of A. Stange, 'Das frühchristliche Kirchengebäude als Bild des Himmels', in *Byzantinische Zeitschrift*, 47 (1954), 169.

⁴⁵ R. J. H. Jenkins and C. A. Mango, 'The Date and Significance of the Tenth Homily of Photius', *Dumbarton Oaks Papers*, 9–10 (1956), 133–4, 137 ff.; Demus, *The Mosaics of San Marco*, i. 238.

⁴⁶ C. A. Mango, *The Homilies of Photius, Patriarch of Constantinople* (Cambridge, Mass., 1958), 177, 187 f.

⁴⁷ P. Testini, 'Osservazioni sull'iconografia del Cristo in trono fra gli apostoli', *Rivista dell'Istituto nazionale d'archeologia e storia dell'arte*, NS 11–12 (1963), 263. Cf. Beck ('The First Mosaics', 132 f., 162), who interprets the mosaic as a *Traditio legis* and dates it before 1150 on the basis of a relief on the west front of Sessa Aurunca cathedral. I do not agree with her, since neither of the Apostles receives anything from Christ (see C. Weyer-Davis, 'Das Traditio-Legis-Bild und seine Nachfolge', *Münchner Jahrbuch der bildenden Kunst*, 3rd ser., 12 (1961), 7–45). For the later dating of the Sessa Aurunca relief, see V. Pace in M. D'Onofrio and V. Pace, *Italia romanica: La Campania* (Milan, 1981), 81 f.

⁴⁸ See ch. 2 nn. 12, 13 above; Nersessian, *The Cappella Palatina of Roger II*, 212–16. Alexander of Telese's chronicle was written at the behest of King Roger's sister Matilda.

⁴⁹ This was Queen Sibylla, the widow of Tancred and the mother and regent of William III: Pietro da Eboli, *Liber ad honorem Augusti*, pl. XLI, Bern, Burger Bibliothek, MS 120, c. 42 (135).

⁵⁰ Also recognized by Demus, *The Mosaics of Norman Sicily*, 53; Beck, 'The First Mosaics', 132 f., 156; Nersessian, *The Cappella Palatina of Roger II*, 94.

⁵¹ Peter of Cluny (also known as Peter the Venerable) compared Roger to Solomon in 1142: *Letters*, bk. iv, no. 37, in Migne, *Patrologia Latina*, 189, col. 369, cited by E. Curtis, *Roger of Sicily and the Normans in Lower Italy 1016–1154* (New York and London, 1912), 210, and D. C. Douglas, *The Norman Fate 1100–1154* (Berkeley and Los Angeles, 1976), 123 (with erroneous Migne reference). His letters to Roger were written between 1139 and 1142: see C. Valenziano, 'La basilica cattedrale di Cefalù nel periodo normanno', *Ho Theologos*, 19 (1978), 105 ff. He and Roger shared an interest in Arabic literature; Peter had the Koran translated into Latin for the first time: Curtis, *Roger*, 147 f.

⁵² Observed by Piero Bertolucci and also noted by Ćurčić, 'Some Palatine Aspects', 143. For the history of the spiral column in this context, see H. Rosenau, *Vision of the Temple: The Image of the Temple of Jerusalem in Judaism and Christianity* (London, 1979),

67. Monsignor Rocco sees *Solomon* as a portrait of Roger II's son, (1983/5), Roger the duke of Apulia: 'La Cappella Palatina', 31. In the crossing mosaics, *Solomon* appears between *Mark* and *Luke*—a familiar combination by the late 11th century in consecration rites for new churches in which the new church was compared to Solomon's Temple: Kenaan-Kedar, 'Symbolic Meaning in Crusader Architecture', 113.

⁵³ Kindly pointed out to me by Eileen Roberts. See F. Pottino, *La Cappella Palatina di Palermo* (Palermo, 1976), 36; Trizzino, 'Cappella Palatina', 7—dated between 1797 and 1800; cf. Demus, *The Mosaics of Norman Sicily*, 63 n. 91; C. Pasca (*Descrizione della imperiale e regal Cappella Palatina di Palermo* (Palermo, 1841), 99) wrote that *David* was entirely remade by restorers, and Monsignor Rocco also believes that *David* and not a window originally occupied the site: 'La Cappella Palatina', 73 n. 37; see also E. Kitzinger, 'Two Mosaic Ateliers in Palermo in the 1140's', in *Artistes, artisans et production artistique au Moyen Âge (Colloque international, Université de Rennes, 2–6 mai 1983)*, i (Paris, 1986), 279 f.

⁵⁴ V. Lazarev, *Storia della pittura bizantina* (Turin, 1967), 236; cf. Kitzinger ('The Mosaics of the Cappella Palatina', 272 f. n. 20), who believes that the *Pantocrator* replaced an earlier image, possibly of Peter; while Demus (*The Mosaics of Norman Sicily*, 53 f.) suggests that the Saviour replaced an image of the Virgin.

⁵⁵ The *Ascension* was completely restored in 1950: Beck, 'The First Mosaics', 136. There are many blue nimbi like those of the angels in the vault at Cefalù. For another *Ascension* situated in a barrel vault, see the fresco at Santa Sophia, Lake Ohrid, Yugoslavia, dated by Demus (*The Mosaics of San Marco*, i. 174) c.1050.

⁵⁶ Demus, *The Mosaics of Norman Sicily*, 51 ff., 309; Kitzinger, 'The Mosaics of the Cappella Palatina', 285.

⁵⁷ Demus, *The Mosaics of Norman Sicily*, 51 ff.; Kitzinger, review of Demus, 146; Rocco, 'La Cappella Palatina', (1983/5), 65. The condition of the tesserae shows traces of interventions, and the unsymmetrical disposition of both the *Baptist* and the *Hodegetria* has been explained in various ways: to accommodate a royal view looking at these walls from an oblique angle, or (in the case of the *Hodegetria*) to be seen by those entering the south-western door of the building.

⁵⁸ John 1: 35–42. Demus (*The Mosaics of Norman Sicily*, 51 f.) sees the *Baptist* as an afterthought. It has been argued that *Andrew* commemorated another royal chapel; ibid. 25, 55. Kitzinger ('The Mosaics of the Cappella Palatina', 273 n. 20) is inclined to believe that the saint was intended for the apse conch from the outset, while Rocco ('I mosaici delle chiese normanne', 17 (1978), 55), Beck ('The First Mosaics', 131), and Nersessian (*The Cappella Palatina of Roger II*, 114) believe that he was a later substitute for *St Peter*. For an earlier example of Andrew on the left side of a church dedicated to Peter, see Old St Peter's in Rome: H. Grisar, *Das Missale im Lichte römischer Stadtgeschichte* (Freiburg, 1925), 96 f.

⁵⁹ Cf. Kitzinger, 'The Mosaics of the Cappella Palatina', 273 f.; J. A. Jungmann, *Missarum sollemnia*, 4th edn. ii (Vienna, 1958), 7 f. nn. 13, 15.

⁶⁰ Demus, *The Mosaics of Norman Sicily*, 34, 42.

⁶¹ Ibid. 322; Rocco, 'I mosaici delle chiese normanne', 17, (1978), 56 n. 75.

⁶² Rocco, 'La Cappella Palatina' (1983/5), 70, notes the same trio is also represented at the eastern end of Monreale. At Monreale, these saints are on the wall just behind the king's throne. For S. Parasceve, also known variously as *Venera*, *Veneria*, and *Veneranda*, see R. Janin, 'Parasceve Vergine', in *Bibliotheca sanctorum*, x (Rome, 1968), col. 330; N. Ferrante, *Santi italo-greci in Calabria* (Reggio Calabria, 1981), 94, 158, 240 f. n. 4; Beck ('The First Mosaics', 142 ff.) suggested that originally this trio included a portrait of the king: cf. Kitzinger, 'The Mosaics of the Cappella Palatina', 285; Demus, *The Mosaics of Norman Sicily*, 42 f.

[63] S. Der Nersessian, 'The Illustrations of the Homilies of Gregory of Nazianzus, Paris Gr. 510', *Dumbarton Oaks Papers* 16 (1962), 202 repr. in *Études byzantines et arméniennes* (Louvain, 1973), i. 82.

[64] Demus, *The Mosaics of Norman Sicily*, 43; Kitzinger, 'The Mosaics of the Cappella Palatina', 274; Beck, 'The First Mosaics', 131.

[65] See above, p. 10. On St Nicholas see also Kitzinger, 'The Mosaics of the Cappella Palatina', 284 f.

[66] H. Holloway, *A Study of the Byzantine Liturgy* (London, n.d.), 14, 39. Der Nersessian, 'Two Images of the Virgin' (1973), 66 f. Also mentioned in the rite are SS Cosmas, Damian, Theodore, Demetrius, and Stephen, all of whom are present in the mosaics of this chapel. See also Ćurčić, 'Some Palatine Aspects', 139, who sees the central group of SS Gregory, Basil, and Chrysostom as representative of the recently introduced cult of the Three Hierarchs.

[67] For the Greek text used in the mosaic see n. 84 below.

[68] A northern gate or door also corresponds to the arrangement of the Byzantine iconostasis where such a door was used by deacons. Some of the same images in this part of the iconostasis are also to be found in the northern chapel of the Palatina (Mary and St Nicholas of Myra): C. Kucharek, *The Byzantine–Slav Liturgy of St. John Chrysostom: Its Origin and Evolution* (Allendale, NJ, 1971), 209, 211 n. 5.

[69] O. Treitinger, *Die oströmische Kaiser und Reichsidee: nach ihrer Gestaltung im höfischen Zeremoniell* (Jena, 1938), 136 f., 139; D. J. Geanakoplos, *Byzantine East and Latin West: Two Worlds of Christendom in Middle Ages and Renaissance* (New York, 1966), 70 f.; T. F. Mathews, *The Early Churches of Constantinople: Architecture and Liturgy* (University Park and London, 1971), 172 f.; S. Der Nersessian, 'Program and Iconography of the Frescoes of the Parecclesion', in *The Kariye Djami*, iv (Princeton, 1975), 346; Kitzinger, 'The Mosaics of the Cappella Palatina', 277, relates the text to the Annunciation; Dvornik, *Early Christian and Byzantine Political Philosophy*, ii. 644 f.

[70] For the Greek inscription used in the mosaic see n. 84.

[71] Kitzinger, 'The Mosaics of the Cappella Palatina', 279–83; E. Kantorowicz, 'The King's Advent and the Enigmatic Panels in the Doors of Santa Sabina', *Art Bulletin*, 26 (1944), 210 f., 218 f.; id. *Laudes regiae: A Study in Liturgical Acclamations and Medieval Ruler Worship*, 2nd edn. (Berkeley and Los Angeles, 1958), 71 ff.

[72] See ch. 2 n. 3 above.

[73] Deér, *Dynastic Porphyry Tombs*, 4 ff., 10; id., 'Das Grab Friedrichs II.', 365; Der Nersessian, 'The Illustrations of the Homilies of Gregory of Nazianzus', i. 85.

[74] Demus believes that the *Nativity* was reduced after Roger II's death to make room for the triple tier of scenes on the south wall: *The Mosaics of Norman Sicily*, 49, 218; Beck, 'The First Mosaics', 134. The difference in scale between the *Nativity* and the other scenes on the south wall may reflect the greater importance of the subject rather than a separate campaign of work.

[75] See ch. 2 nn. 3 and 5 above.

[76] 7 June 1131; White, *Latin Monasticism*, 189.

[77] Kitzinger, 'The Mosaics of the Cappella Palatina', 277; Demus, *The Mosaics of Norman Sicily*, 199, 203, 218.

[78] Beck, 'The First Mosaics', 148; Demus, *The Mosaics of Norman Sicily*, 203, 215.

[79] Ibid. 200.

[80] A further meaning may be that the *Presentation* as a royal advent is linked with the Genesis cycle in the nave in the sense that it marks the coming of the new law and the end of the old: Kitzinger, 'The Mosaics of the Cappella Palatina', 281 ff.

[81] Demus, *The Mosaics of Norman Sicily*, 196. Beck, like the present writer, sees no anomalies in the scheme, but rather an original Norman formulation: 'The First Mosaics', 119, 132 ff.

[82] Kitzinger, 'The Mosaics of the Cappella Palatina', 275 f.; Demus, *The Mosaics of Norman Sicily*, 218.

[83] Beck, 'The First Mosaics', 132 f., 149.

[84] These and the following Greek texts in the sanctuary were checked with great care by J. McManamon, G. Fioravanti, and M. Bettini, who have indicated the errors of the mosaicists as well as departures from the Septuagint text. Expansions of abbreviations are in square brackets. In the mosaics, omega usually appears in lower case.

*Isaiah* (Matthew 1: 23 based upon Isaiah 7: 14):
YION.
(Behold, the virgin will have in her belly and will bear [a] son.) Repeated by *Isaiah* in the arch spandrel of the southern chapel.

*Ezekiel* (Baruch 3: 35):
ΟΥΤΟC Ο Θ[ΕΟ]C ΗΜΩΝ ΟΥ ΛΟΓΗCΘΗCΕΤΑΙ ΕΤΕΡΟC ΠΡΟC ΑΥΤΟΝ.
(This is our God, no other can be compared to him.)

*Jeremiah* (Ezekiel 44: 2):
ΤΑΔΕ ΛΕΓΕΙ Κ[ΥΡΙΟ]C Η ΠΥΛΗ ΑΥΤΗ ΚΕΚΛΕΙCΜΕΝΗ ΕCΤΑΙ ΟΥΔΕΙC ΟΥ ΜΗ ΔΙΕΛΘΗ ΔΙ ΑΥΤΗC.
(But the Lord said these things, This gate shall remain shut . . . no one shall enter by it.)

*Jonah* (Jonah 2: 2):
ΕΒΟΗCΑ ΕΝ ΘΛΙΨΗ ΜΟΥ ΠΡ[Ο]C Κ[ΥΡΙΟ]Ν ΤΟΝ Θ[ΕΟ]Ν ΜΟΥ ΚΑΙ ΕΙCΗΚΟΥCΕ ΜΟΥ.
(I called in my distress to my Lord the God and he heard me.)

*Daniel* (Daniel 2: 45):
ΕΘΕΩΡΟΥΝ ΕΩC ΟΥ ΕΤΜΗΘΗ ΛΙΘΟC ΑΠΟ ΟΡΟΥC ΑΝΕΥ ΧΕΙΡΩΝ.
(I was looking until a stone was cut from the mountain without hands.) This is a contamination of Daniel 2: 34 and Daniel 2: 45.

*Moses* (Exodus 3: 2):
ΚΑΙ ΕΙΔΟΝ ΚΑΙ ΕΚΑΙΕΤΟ Η ΒΑΤΟC ΚΑΙ ΟΥ ΚΑΤΕΦΛΕΓΕΤΟ.
(This varies slightly from the Septuagint, which used 'He' instead of 'I': 'And I looked and the bush was burning and it was not consumed'.) This is a case where the Greek is a translation of the Vulgate and differs from the Septuagint: the procedure probably explains many of the departures from the Septuagint in the inscriptions. This passage and other variants were already associated with the Virgin by Bernard of Clairvaux (d. 1153) and Richard of St Victor (d. 1173): Bernardo di Chiaravalle, *Lodi della Vergine Maria*, ed. D. Turco (Rome, 1984), Sermon II. 5, pp. 5, 63 f.; B. Nolan, *The Gothic Visionary Perspective* (Princeton, 1977), 36 f. In the crossing, *Moses* is in the spandrel to the right of *Solomon* and opposite the *Annunciation*.

*Elijah*:
ΖΗ Κ[ΥΡΙΟ]C ΕΙ ΕCΤΑΙ ΥΔΩΡ ΕΠΙ ΤΗC ΓΗC.
(The Lord lives, if there will be water on the earth.)
The text is a puzzling contraction and interpolation partly based upon 1 Kings 17: 1, 12, 14.

*Elisha* (2 Kings 2: 21 (Septuagint) ):
ΤΑΔΕ ΛΕΓΕΙ Κ[ΥΡΙΟ]C ΙΑΜΑΙ ΤΑ ΥΔΑΤΑ ΤΑΥΤΑ ΚΑΙ ΟΥΚ ΕCΤΑΙ ΑΤΕΚΝΩΝ [*sic*] ΕΞ ΑΥΤΩΝ.
(These things says [the] Lord: I have made this water wholesome . . . miscarriage shall not come from it.)

*Solomon* (Psalm 41: 9 (Septuagint) ):
Ο ΕCΘΙΩΝ ΑΡΤΟΥC ΜΟΥ ΕΜΕΓΑΛΙΝΕΝ [*sic*] ΕΠ ΕΜΕ ΠΤΕΡΝΙCΜΟΝ.
(The one who ate of my bread has lifted his heel against me.)

*Zechariah* (Zechariah 9: 9):

ΧΑΙΡΕ CΦΟΔΡΑ ΘΥΓΑΤΕΡ CΙΩΝ.
(Rejoice greatly, O daughter of Zion.)
A text used in the Latin Christmas liturgy.
*Matthew* (Matthew 1: 1–2):
LIBER [GENE]RAT[IONIS] JESV XPI FILII DAVID
FILII ABRAHAM / ABRAHAM GE[N]VIT ISAAC.
(Jesus' royal descent from David through Jacob.)
*John* (John 1: 1):
IN PRINCIPIO ERAT VERBV[M] ET VERBV[M] ERAT
APVD DEV[M] ET DEVS ERAT VERBV[M].
(In the beginning was the Word, and the Word was with
God, and the Word was God.)
*Luke* (Luke 1: 5):
FVIT IN DIEBVS HERODIS REGIS.
(In the days of Herod the King.)
     This is the phrase used for the birth of the Baptist; also
used by Matthew (2: 1) for Christ's birth. Mark's message
is the work of a restorer, but, like the others, probably came
from the first verses, which in this case again relate the
coming of the Baptist as Christ's precursor.
[85] For the messages of *Isaiah, Ezekiel, Zechariah,* and *Daniel,* see
n. 84 above and appendix to this chapter.
[86] For the relic, see Kitzinger, 'The Mosaics of the Cappella
Palatina', 272 n. 18.
[87] The inscription has lacunae and evident signs of restoration:
Demus, *The Mosaics of Norman Sicily,* 37. The English translation
is by J. Monfasani and M. Hammond.
[88] C. Walter, *Art and Ritual of the Byzantine Church* (London,
1982), 201.
[89] During the 5th and 6th centuries they were preserved in
the church on Mount Zion: B. Kötting, *Peregrinatio religiosa:
Wallfahrten in der Antike und das Pilgerwesen in der alten Kirche*
(Regensburg and Münster, 1950), 98. These, or other relics of
the same objects, together with the sponge and the cross were
also in the church of the Holy Sepulchre: A. Heisenberg, *Grabeskirche und Apostelkirche: Zwei Basiliken Konstantins. Untersuchungen
zur Kunst und Literatur des ausgehenden Altertums,* 2 vols. (Leipzig,
1908), i. 192, 194.
[90] Orderic Vitalis, *The Ecclesiastical History,* ed. M. Chibnall, 6
vols. (Oxford, 1969–80), v. bk. IX, 101 ff., 109; J. Prawer, *Colonialismo medievale: Il regno latino di Gerusalemme,* trans. F. Cardini
(Rome, 1982), 34; H. E. Mayer, 'Das Pontifikale von Tyrus und
die Krönung der lateinischen Könige von Jerusalem', *Dumbarton
Oaks Papers,* 21 (1967), 181; C. W. Jones, *San Nicola: Biografia di
una leggenda* (Bari, 1983), 246 f.; S. Runciman, 'The Holy Lance
found at Antioch', *Analecta bollandiana,* 68 (1950), 197–209; id.,
*A History of the Crusades: The Kingdom of Jerusalem and the Frankish
East 1100–1187,* 2 vols. (Cambridge, 1952), i. 241–6.
[91] Chalandon, *Histoire de la domination normande,* ii. 124, 133.
[92] L. H. Loomis, 'The Oriflamme of France and the War-cry
"Monjoie" in the Twelfth Century', in *Studies in Art and Literature
for Belle da Costa Greene* (Princeton, 1954), 76; id., 'The Holy Relics
of Charlemagne and King Athelstan: The Lances of Longinus
and St Mauricius', *Speculum* 25 (1950), 441 f.; Runciman, 'The
Holy Lance', 202.
[93] Jenkins and Mango, 'The Date and Significance of the
Tenth Homily of Photius', 136.
[94] Pasca (*Descrizione della imperiale e regal Cappella Palatina,* 26)
records that the cartoon for the Virgin was supplied by the painter
Gaspare Serenario; see also Boglino, *Storia della Real Cappella,* 32;
Demus, *The Mosaics of Norman Sicily,* 37, 71 n. 237; Kitzinger,
'The Mosaics of the Cappella Palatina', 272 n. 18.
[95] E. Kantorowicz, *Laudes regiae: A Study in Liturgical Acclamations and Medieval Ruler Worship,* 2nd edn. (Berkeley and Los
Angeles, 1958), 160 f.; Demus, *The Mosaics of Norman Sicily,* 191
n. 19. A royal burial chapel dedicated to the Magdalen was in

Palermo cathedral (see ch. 4 n. 39). Roger II contributed to
several religious foundations dedicated to the Magdalen: White,
*Latin Monasticism,* 158, 211 f.; Rocco ('I mosaici delle chiese normanne', 17 (1978), 56 n. 75) refers to the church of the Magdalen
suffragan to the Palatina located nearby within the precincts of
the *carabinieri* headquarters just to the north of the royal palace.
[96] Demus, *The Mosaics of Norman Sicily,* 54, 72 nn. 243–4, and
Rocco, 'I mosaici delle chiese normanne', 17 (1978), 56 n. 75,
refer to a relic of St James in the high altar.
[97] Also noticed by Beck (see n. 83 above).
[98] Krönig, *Il duomo di Monreale,* 56; Rocco, 'I mosaici delle
chiese normanne', 17 (1978), 47 ff.
[99] Der Nersessian, 'Two Images of the Virgin', 65 f.
[100] Demus, *The Mosaics of Norman Sicily,* 43; Beck, 'The First
Mosaics', 131, 144 who sees the imagery here as a continuous royal
procession directed towards the Hodegetria; Trizzino, 'Cappella
Palatina', 8, 31 f. Demus (ibid. 268) suggested that scenes from
Christ's Passion may have been planned for this area; see also
n. 161 below.
[101] Kitzinger, 'The Mosaics of the Cappella Palatina', 272 f. n.
20; Demus, *The Mosaics of Norman Sicily,* 55; Lazarev, *Storia della
pittura bizantina,* 236; Nersessian, *The Cappella Palatina of Roger II,*
114; n. 58 above.
[102] A blue nimbus appears at the top of the arch soffit between
the central square and the northern chapel.
[103] W. E. Kleinbauer, 'The Orants in the Mosaic Decoration
of the Rotunda at Thessaloniki: Martyr Saints or Donors?', *Cahiers
archéologiques,* 30 (1982), 40 f. n. 2; G. H. Forsyth and K. Weitzmann, *The Monastery of St. Catherine at Mt. Sinai: The Church and
Fortress of Justinian* (Ann Arbor, 1973), ii. 12. See also Hagia
Sophia in Constantinople; R. Krautheimer, *Architettura paleocristiana e bizantina* (Turin, 1986), 246.
[104] Demus, *The Mosaics of Norman Sicily,* 296 f.; S. Waetzoldt,
*Die Kopien des 17 Jahrhunderts nach Mosaiken und Wandmalereien in
Rom* (Vienna and Munich, 1964), 55 ff., 66 f. The Montecassino
biblical cycle in the atrium consisted of murals (not mosaics); H.
Bloch, *Monte Cassino in the Middle Ages,* 3 vols. (Rome, 1986), i,
53 f., 122 ff. It is unknown if apostolic scenes were included here
or among the narthex mosaics.
[105] Demus, *The Mosaics of Norman Sicily,* 297, 299; L. Eleen,
'Acts Illustrations in Italy and Byzantium', *Dumbarton Oaks Papers,*
31 (1977), *passim* and 265.
[106] Between the apse conch and the altar stand full-length
figures of SS *Sebastian* and *Philip,* relics of whom were embedded
in the altar of this chapel: Rocco, 'I mosaici delle chiese normanne', 17 (1978), 56 n. 75. *St Anna with Mary* replaced a window in
the 18th century: Demus, *The Mosaics of Norman Sicily,* 34. During
the Middle Ages, Sebastian, Peter, and Paul were regarded as the
patron saints of Rome. Philip is associated with the prophecy
of Paul's martyrdom (Acts 21: 8–11).
[107] For the apocryphal scenes of St Peter in Rome, see *Bibliotheca sanctorum,* x (Rome, 1968), cols. 595–639 citing, among
others, Irenaeus, Clement of Alexandria, and Tertullian.
[108] Cf. Demus, *The Mosaics of Norman Sicily,* 296–9.
[109] John 1: 29, 36, 40–2.
[110] F. Dvornik, *The Idea of Apostolicity in Byzantium and the Legend
of the Apostle Andrew* (Cambridge, Mass., 1958), 3, 231 f.
[111] Ibid. 285, for the negotiations between Pope Alexander III
and Manuel I Comnenos.
[112] Kitzinger, 'The Mosaics of the Cappella Palatina', 271;
Waetzoldt, *Die Kopien des 17. Jahrhunderts, passim;* Demus, *The
Mosaics of Norman Sicily,* 205 ff., 224 f.; W. Tronzo, 'The Prestige
of St. Peter's: Observations on the Function of Monumental
Narrative Cycles in Italy', in *Pictorial Narrative in Antiquity and the
Middle Ages* (Studies in the History of Art, 16; National Gallery
of Art, Washington, DC, 1985), 93–112.

[113] Kitzinger, 'The Mosaics of the Cappella Palatina', 271.

[114] For interpretations of the Old Testament scenes at S. Maria Maggiore, see: H. Karpp, *Die frühchristlichen und mittelalterlichen Mosaiken in Santa Maria Maggiore zu Rom* (Baden-Baden, 1966); B. Brenk, *Die frühchristlichen Mosaiken in S. Maria Maggiore zu Rom* (Wiesbaden, 1975); S. Spain, 'The Promised Blessing: The Iconography of the Mosaics of S. Maria Maggiore', *Art Bulletin*, 61 (1979), 518–40; M. L. Heuser, review of Brenk, *Die frühchristliche Mosaiken*, in *Art Bulletin*, 61 (1979), 473–7.

[115] Brenk, *Die frühchristlichen Mosaiken*, 35 ff., 42, 112, 125.

[116] Demus, *The Mosaics of Norman Sicily*, 245, 252–7, notices that some of the scenes at Montecassino relied on Byzantine models. On the other hand, he notes that, starting in the late 11th century, Old Testament cycles in France and England figured importantly and quite independently of the Italian revival: id., *The Mosaics of San Marco*, ii. 94.

[117] At Montecassino, the biblical cycle adorned the corridors of the atrium. It is not known what subjects were illustrated in the nave and aisles of the church: H. Bloch, 'Monte Cassino, Byzantium and the West in the Early Middle Ages', *Dumbarton Oaks Papers*, 3 (1946), 195, 198 ff.; id., *Monte Cassino in the Middle Ages* (Rome, 1986), i. 88 f., 122 ff.

[118] O. Demus, *Romanische Wandmalerei* (Munich, 1968), 114–17.

[119] Id., *The Mosaics of Norman Sicily*, 34 f., 44, 67 nn. 169–71.

[120] G. Schiller, *Ikonographie der christlichen Kunst*, i (Gütersloh, 1966), 139; Rocco, 'I mosaici delle chiese normanne', 17 (1978), 48 f.

[121] E. Mâle, *L'Art religieux du XII$^e$ siècle en France*, 2nd edn. (Paris, 1924), 158 f.; A. Esmeijer, Divina quaternitas: *A Preliminary Study in the Method and Application of Visual Exegesis* (Amsterdam, 1978), 19–25, 30 (kindly brought to my attention by Mrs Karen Wright); E. Panofsky, *Abbot Suger on the Abbey Church of St. Denis and its Treasures*, 2nd edn. (Princeton, 1979), 180 f.

[122] M. Riddle, 'Illustration of the "Triumph" of Joseph the Patriarch', *Byzantine Papers: Proceedings of the First Australian Byzantine Studies Conference, Canberra, 17–19 May 1978* (Canberra, 1981), 75 f., 80 n. 46, also cites another example at Sopoćani.

[123] H. Böhmer, *Kirche und Staat in England und in der Normandie in XI. und XII. Jahrhundert* (Wiesbaden, 1968), 227 f., 236 f., 252. Charlemagne's intimates were already allowed to call him David: P. E. Schramm, 'Sacerdotium und Regnum im Austausch ihre Vorrechte: "Imitatio imperii" und "imitatio sacerdotii"', in *Beiträge zur allgemeinen Geschichte*, 4/1 (Stuttgart, 1970), 76. Schramm also noted that the Old Testament kings were first acclaimed by the people: 'Das Alte und das Neue Testament in der Staatslehre und Staatssymbolik des Mittelalters' (same volume), 139. To an extent this was also true of Roger II, who was acclaimed king by the barons and clergy gathered at Salerno, and this was subsequently confirmed by Anacletus II's bull issued at Benevento on 17 Sept. 1130: E. Caspar, *Roger II (1101–1154) und die Gründung der Normannisch-Sicilischen Monarchie* (Innsbruck, 1904), 92 ff.

[124] Der Nersessian, 'The Illustrations of the Homilies', 83, citing Justin and Origen.

[125] C. M. Kauffmann, 'Jakob', in *Lexikon der christlichen Ikonographie*, ii (Rome, Freiburg, Basle and Vienna, 1970), 373 ff., citing several early commentators who described the dream as a gate of heaven. Cf. Esmeijer, Divina quaternitas, 93.

[126] H. Vincent and F. M. Abel, *Jérusalem: Recherches de topographie, d'archéologie et d'histoire*, ii (Paris, 1922), 972 f. Cf. J. Phocas, 'A Brief Description … of the Holy Places in Palestine', in *Palestine Pilgrims' Text Society*, 5 (London, 1896), 20. This account, written in 1185, describes a church on the eastern side of Jerusalem known as the 'Holy of Holies' which was built on the foundations of Solomon's Temple. On the left side of this church, in a vaulted chamber, was a mosaic of Jacob's dream with the stone of Bethel exhibited beneath it.

[127] For the Virgin as *Porta coeli*, see A. Salzer, *Die Sinnbilder und Beiwörter Mariens in der deutschen Literatur und lateinischen Hymnenpoesie des Mittelalters* (Darmstadt, 1967), 525 f, 541 ff.

[128] For Jacob and the conquest of the Promised Land, see K. Schefold, 'Altchristliche Bilderzyklen: Bassussarkophag und S. Maria Maggiore', *Rivista di archeologia cristiana*, 16 (1939), 306; A. Grabar, *Christian Iconography: A Study of its Origins* (London and Henley, 1980), 96; *Festal Menaion*, 439 f., notes that Jacob's ladder is invoked in the Great Vespers of the Annunciation feast thus: '… hail, thou bridge that leads to heaven, and ladder raised on high that Jacob saw … hail thou restoration of Adam, the Lord is with thee.'

[129] Loomis, 'The Oriflamme of France', 76.

[130] Eadmer of Canterbury, cited by H. Graef, *Mary: A History of Doctrine and Devotion*, i (New York, 1963), 217, citing from Eadmer's *Tractatus* (published erroneously as Anselm in Migne, *Patrologia Latina*, 59, col. 548A–B); cf. ed. H. Thurston and T. Slater (Freiburg im Breisgau, 1904), 11.

[131] I have been unable to consult what must be a relevant essay, G. P. Wetter, '"Ich bin das Licht der Welt": Eine Studie zur Formelsprache des Johannes Evangeliums', *Beiträge Religionswissenschaft*, 1/187 (1913–14), cited in B. Brenk, 'Los primeros mosaicos dorados del arte cristiano', *Paleta*, 38 (n.d.), 16.

[132] Cf. Rocco, 'I mosaici delle chiese normanne', 17 (1978), 47 ff.

[133] Cf. O. von Simson, *The Gothic Cathedral* (London, 1956), 52.

[134] The translation is by J. Monfasani, M. Hammond, and R. Stefanini.

[135] See n. 53 above.

[136] The English rendering is by J. Monfasani, M. Hammond, and R. Stefanini. For a recent discussion of the words 'lux', 'lumen', etc., see J. Gage, 'Gothic Glass: Two Aspects of a Dionysian Aesthetic', *Art History*, 5/1 (1982), 38 ff.

[137] W. Krönig, 'Considerazioni sulla Cappella Palatina di Palermo', in *Atti del Convegno internazionale di studi ruggeriani, 21–25 aprile 1954* (Palermo, 1955), i. 257; Rocco, 'I mosaici delle chiese normanne' (1976), 149 ff. For a different interpretation of the *Pantocrator* in this area, see Kitzinger, 'The Mosaics of the Cappella Palatina', 278 ff., who suggests a link to Pentecost and an eschatological theme—as do W. Krönig, 'Zur Transfiguration der Cappella Palatina in Palermo', *Zeitschrift für Kunstgeschichte*, 19 (1956), 168 and Beck, 'The First Mosaics', 149 f.

[138] I. Schuster, *The Sacramentary*, i (London, 1924), 361; G. A. Wellen, *Theotokos: Eine ikonographische Abhandlung über das Gottesmutterbild in frühchristlicher Zeit* (Utrecht, 1960), 14. For the Oriental cult of *Sol invictus* and its existence in Rome, see H. P. l'Orange, *Studies on the Iconography of Cosmic Kingship in the Ancient World* (New Rochelle, 1982), 42, 107 ff.

[139] The English rendering is by J. Monfasani, M. Hammond, and R. Stefanini.

[140] Ladner, *The Idea of Reform*, 291; M. E. Frazer, 'Church Doors and the Gates of Paradise: Byzantine Bronze Doors in Italy', *Dumbarton Oaks Papers*, 27 (1973), 161, citing Gregory Nazianzenus. The Greek Christmas liturgies include Genesis 1: 1–13, and Hebrews 1: 1–12: E. Mercenier and F. Paris, *La Prière des églises de rite byzantin*, ii (Amary s/Meuse, 1939), 114, 116, 311, 340. The Latin liturgy uses the same text from Hebrews.

[141] Balaam's prophecy (Numbers 24: 17) is included in the Greek Christmas rite: Mercenier and Paris, *La Prière des églises*, 126. For the texts of Athanasius and Leo the Great, see E. Kirschbaum, 'Der Prophet Balaam und die Anbetung der Weisen', *Römische Quartalschrift für christliche Altertumskunde und Kirchengeschichte*, 49 (1954), 131 f., 135. St Ambrose: '… Christus est stella; orietur enim stella ex Jacob et exsurgit homo ex Israhel':

Wellen, *Theotokos*, 15. Bernard of Clairvaux referred to the Virgin as 'the noble star of Jacob': Bernardo di Chiaravalle, *Lodi*, ed. Turco, Sermon II, 17, p. 7. A Christmas homily of Gregory Nazianzenus shares much the same imagery as the *Nativity* mosaic, as well as including other subjects represented near it—e.g. the Baptism, the Transfiguration, and the Conversion of St Paul: Der Nersessian, 'The Illumination of the Homilies of Gregory of Nazianzus', 80 f.

[142] Ladner, *The Idea of Reform*, 291; *Festal Menaion*, 265 (see ch. 1 n. 33 above); F. J. Dölger (*Antike und Christentum: Kultur und religionsgeschichtliche Studien*, v (Münster, 1936), 9), discusses Jesus as the Sun of Justice and the Apostles as its rays; id., vi (Münster, 1950), 21 ff., for the 'Christian Helios'; Dvornik, *Early Christian and Byzantine Political Philosophy*, ii. 620 ff., 681; E. Kantorowicz, '*Puer exoriens*: On the Hypapante in the Mosaics of S. Maria Maggiore', in *Selected Studies* (Locust Valley, 1965), 36. For a discussion of rulers who have either been compared to a star or revealed by light, see S. G. MacCormack, 'Christ and Empire, Time and Ceremonial in Sixth Century Byzantium and Beyond', *Byzantion*, 52 (1982), 300 f.; ead., *Art and Ceremony in Late Antiquity* (Berkeley, 1981), 45. An Arabic poem, written in honour of Roger II's son and namesake, also uses the same simile: Curtis, *Roger of Sicily*, 311.

[143] Kitzinger, 'Two Mosaic Ateliers', 277. Philagathos from Rossano, who preached in the chapel during its first year, was a Basilian cleric who encouraged Greek culture in Sicily and Calabria see n. 11 above and Patera, *L'arte della Sicilia*, 11.

[144] In the context of the phrase and the mosaic imagery, the words 'Rosa florem' recall Bernard of Clairvaux's interpretation of Nazareth (Mary's home at the time of the Annunciation) as 'flower': Bernardo di Chiaravalle, *Lodi*, ed. Turco, Sermon I, 3, p. 43.

[145] The English rendering is by J. Monfasani, M. Hammond, and R. Stefanini.

[146] The English translation is by M. Hammond. The variations from the Septuagint were pointed out to me by J. McManamon.

[147] Mercenier and Paris, *La Prière des églises*, ii. 107, 327. The mosaic text differs slightly from the Septuagint.

[148] H. Grisar, *Analecta romana* (Rome, 1899), i. 593; J. Quasten, 'Oriental influence in the Gallican Liturgy', *Traditio*, 1 (1943), 74 n. 116; Ladner, *The Idea of Reform*, 291, for the Nativity as a second Genesis and return to Eden; Frazer, 'Church Doors and the Gates of Paradise', 161; *Dionigi l'Areopagita: Tutte le opere*, ed. P. Scazzoso (Milan, 1981), 141; G. Constable, 'Renewal and Reform in Religious Life: Concepts and Realities', in R. L. Benson, G. Constable and C. D. Lanham (eds.), *Renaissance and Renewal in the Twelfth Century* (Cambridge, Mass., 1982), 46 f.

[149] Krönig, 'Zur Transfiguration der Cappella Palatina', 162 f., 168 ff. Krönig cites a similar site for the Transfiguration in another mid-12th-century chapel with an altar dedicated to *SS Peter and Paul* at Schwarzrheindorf near Bonn.

[150] Psalm 96–97; Zechariah 9: 9. Cf. Rocco ('La Cappella Palatina' (1983/5), 49) interprets the *Entry into Jerusalem* in terms of light in Isaiah 60: 1.

[151] Dölger, *Antike und Christentum*, vi. 33 ff.; M. Maccarone, 'Il pellegrinaggio a San Pietro e il giubileo del 1300', *Rivista di storia della chiesa in Italia*, 34/2 (July–Dec. 1980), 392, citing Chrysostom's commentary on Romans. For Peter and Paul as the Dioscuri or as stars related to Christ-Sol, see Weyer-Davis, 'Das Traditio-Legis Bild', 32 ff.

[152] Schuster, *The Sacramentary*, 5–11; cf. Kantorowicz (Laudes regiae, 158 ff.), who refers to a 15th-century Gallican missal in Palermo, which was probably a copy of a 12th-century original.

[153] Schuster, *The Sacramentary*, 361–75.

[154] Isaiah 9: 2, 6; John 1: 1–12.

[155] Psalm 88/89: 12, 15; Paul to Titus 3: 4–7; Zechariah 9: 9.

[156] Schuster, *The Sacramentary*, 366, 370, 372; Psalms 92/93, 109/110: 1–2, 131/132: 1–3, 5, 7, 11–12; Isaiah 66: 1.

[157] This psalm was probably composed for a coronation: H. G. May and B. M. Metzger, *The New Oxford Annotated Bible* (New York and Oxford, 1971), 744.

[158] However, the Roman rite uses other lines from this psalm—i.e. 5, 23, 26–7. The Greek rite for Epiphany uses 117/18: 1–4, 26, 27.

[159] According to Falcone Beneventano, Roger, like Charlemagne, was crowned on Christmas night: A. Marongiu, 'Concezione della sovranità di Ruggero II', in *Atti del Convegno internazionale di studi ruggeriani, 21–25 aprile, 1954* (Palermo, 1955), i, 218.

[160] See appendix at end of ch. 3 below.

[161] For a table of the subjects and inscriptions appearing in the sanctuary mosaics which are included in the liturgies for Christmas and Epiphany, see the appendix at the end of this chapter. For the Roman rite, see the *Missale romanum* and Schuster, *The Sacramentary*, 361–77. There were from 12 to 18 subjects in the classical cycle of feasts represented in Middle Byzantine churches, and some of them have a similar sequence to the Palatina. But in Roger II's palace chapel, the Crucifixion, Harrowing of Hell, and Death of the Virgin are absent. Nevertheless, the triple tier of scenes in the southern chapel resembles the arrangement on a panel from the iconostasis beam of the church of St Catherine at Mt Sinai: K. Weitzmann, *Studies in Classical and Byzantine Manuscript Illumination* (Chicago and London, 1971), 308, fig. 305.

[162] M. T. d'Alverny, 'Les Anges et les jours', *Cahiers archéologiques*, 9 (1957), 273 f., 277, 282, kindly brought to my attention by V. Pacc.

[163] Cf. Demus, *The Mosaics of Norman Sicily*, 313 ff., who, although noting their unique number, concludes that they were merely ornamental. Yet there is nothing in the Palatina mosaics which is haphazard. In the *Pentecost*, for instance, Peter and Paul are given places closest to Christ at the eastern end. Among the Apostles, the evangelists are distinguished from the rest by the bound volumes they hold instead of scrolls.

[164] Panofsky, *Abbot Suger*, 18 ff.; von Simson, *The Gothic Cathedral*, 104 ff.; E. Bellini in *Dionigi*, ed. Scazzoso, 110 f., ch. 9: 2–3 of the *Celestial Hierarchy*. For translations of Dionysius's works from the late 9th century onwards, see A. M. Friend, 'Carolingian Art in the Abbey of St. Denis', *Art Studies*, 1 (1923), 67–75.

[165] *Dionigi*, ed. Scazzoso, *Celestial Hierarchy*, ch. 4.4, pp. 95 f. For the immense popularity of these texts during the 12th century, see Hopper, *Medieval Number Symbolism*, 108; Nolan, *The Gothic Visionary Perspective*, 35 n. 1. During the 11th and 12th centuries there was a similar revival in Byzantium: Walter, *Art and Ritual*, 215.

[166] See ch. 2 n. 61 above; Caspar, *Roger II.*, 403 ff.; Panofsky, *Abbot Suger*, 2, 18 ff., 23 ff.; Esmeijer, *Divina quaternitas*, 130 n. 22; H. Wieruszowski 'The Norman Kingdom of Sicily and the Crusades', in K. M. Setton *et al.* (eds.), *A History of the Crusades*, ii (Madison, Milwaukee, and London, 1969), 14 f. n. 20; von Simson, *The Gothic Cathedral*, 105; n. 164 above.

[167] Caspar, *Roger II*, 404 ff.; Kitzinger, 'The Mosaics of the Cappella Palatina', 290 n. 127.

[168] I am paraphrasing Panofsky here, *Abbot Suger*, 20; Nolan, *The Gothic Visionary Perspective*, 36. For an excellent survey of angel hierarchies during the Middle Ages, see J. Barclay Lloyd, 'The Trinity amid the Hierarchies of Angels: A Lost Fresco from S. Clemente in Rome and an Iconographic Tradition of the Angelic Choirs', *Arte cristiana*, 708 (1985), 167–80.

[169] For Suger's friendship and correspondence with the king, see A. Lecoy de la Marche, *Œuvres complètes de Suger* (Paris, 1867), 208, 245 f., 292, 384; Kitzinger, 'The Mosaics of the Cappella

Palatina', 290 n. 128, citing Migne, *Patrologia Latina*, clxxxvi, cols. 1415, 1417. For a reassessment of Suger's use of the ideas of the pseudo-Dionysius, see P. Kidson, 'Panofsky, Suger and St. Denis', *Journal of the Warburg and Courtauld Institutes*, 50 (1987), 4–11, 17. For the gift of mountain crystal from Roger which eventually reached Suger, see n. 5 in the Introduction above; Panofsky, *Abbot Suger*, 79, 221 f.; Caspar, *Roger II.*, 406 n. 2, 571 f.; C. Valenziano, 'La basilica cattedrale di Cefalù', 102–4.

[170] The resemblance has also been noted by Gage ('Gothic Glass', 42 f.) who, however, discusses them in the context of conspicuous display rather than in their metaphysical function. For related theological texts, see von Simson, *The Gothic Cathedral*, 50–5.

[171] Translation of Suger's inscription at Saint Denis: Panofsky, *Abbot Suger*, 23, 47, 49. For a Basilian interpretation of the Light theme in the Palatina, see Nersessian, *The Cappella Palatina of Roger II*, 76 ff., 85, 90 ff. Kitzinger ('The Mosaics of the Cappella Palatina', 277 f.) notes that light symbolism 'plays a conspicuous role in both Eastern and Western liturgical and homiletic texts pertaining to Pentecost', and sees the *Pantocrator* repeated here as stressing the eschatological aspect of the Pentecost.

[172] It was then commonly believed that St Denis (the first bishop of Paris), Denis the Areopagite, and the pseudo-Dionysius were all the same person; J. M. Wallace-Hadrill, *The Frankish Church* (Oxford, 1983), 127, 246, 300. See also Kitzinger, 'The Mosaics of the Cappella Palatina', 289 ff.; Lazarev, *Storia della pittura bizantina*, 237 f. During William I's reign, Peter of Blois, probably familiar with the pseudo-Dionysius's texts, served as tutor to the future William II. For a short time he became chancellor of the realm, but he left Sicily in the summer of 1168: von Simson, *The Gothic Cathedral*, 190 n. 17, 192 n. 24; Chalandon, *Histoire de la domination normande*, ii. 321, 346.

[173] Cf. Demus, *The Mosaics of Norman Sicily*, 26; Philagathos of Cerami in a homily delivered in the chapel; Patera, *L'arte della Sicilia*, 84.

[174] Cited by Nolan, *The Gothic Visionary Perspective*, 13 f.; cf. von Simson, *The Gothic Cathedral*, 11 n. 27. Bruno was abbot of Montecassino from 1105 to 1111. His words are a striking reflection of the contemporary fascination with the anagogical ideas of the pseudo-Dionysius.

[175] See n. 51 above.

[176] Cf. Beck, 'The First Mosaics', 134 f., 137 ff., 146 f., 153 f., 163, who argues that all the mosaics in the eastern end of the church were carried out before 1148– possibly as early as 1143. See also n. 187 below.

[177] See pp. 3, 5 n. 33, 49 n. 142 above.

[178] Cf. E. Catafygiotu Topping, 'Romanos, on the Entry into Jerusalem: A Basilikos Logos', *Byzantion*, 47 (1977), 66, and *passim*.

[179] Each saint is accompanied by an identifying label. For a layout of the scheme, see Rocco, 'I mosaici delle chiese normanne', 17 (1978), pl. v, and our plate 16.

[180] For the recently discovered relic (the ivory head of St. Cataldus' pastoral staff), see B. Rocco, 'La Cappella Palatina di Palermo. Lettura teologica (Parte seconda)', *Beni culturali ambientali: Sicilia*, 5 (3–4, 1984, pub. 1987), 64 f., Plate xxii, 98 n. 34. The 7th-century saint was buried in Taranto: G. Carata, 'Cataldo', *Bibliotheca sanctorum*, iii (Rome, 1963), cols. 950 ff.

[181] R. W. Hamilton, *The Church of the Nativity, Bethlehem: A Guide* (Jerusalem, 1968), 72; Rocco, 'I mosaici delle chiese normanne', 17 (1978), 34 n. 34.

[182] Rocco, 'I mosaici delle chiese normanne', 17 (1978), 35 f.; this saint was included in the chapel's martyrology.

[183] Ibid. 36–9, pl. V. See also A. Katzenellenbogen, *Allegories of the Virtues and Vices in Medieval Art from Early Christian Times to the Thirteenth Century* (London, 1939), 22, 53 n.; M.-T. Gousset, 'Un aspect du symbolisme des encensoirs romans: La Jérusalem céleste', *Cahiers archéologiques*, 30 (1982), 97. These virtues inside

their curling foliate frames seem to be branches from the 'Tree of Virtues': see e.g. the mid-12th-century illustration in *De fructibus carnis et spiritus*, Salzburg, Studienbibliothek, MS Sign. V.I. H. 162, illustrated in Katzenellenbogen, *Allegories of the Virtues and Vices*, fig. 67.

[184] In some 12th-century liturgical books these virtues appear in the company of many of the same saints represented on the aisle side of the southern nave arcade: Rocco, 'I mosaici delle chiese normanne', 17 (1978), 36; Katzenellenbogen, *Allegories of the Virtues and Vices*, 53 n., where these virtues are located in the 'south transept' [*sic*].

[185] Demus, *The Mosaics of San Marco*, i. 186 f., 253 f., colour plates 5, 59–62, black-and-white plates 273–304.

[186] Ibid. 186.

[187] Demus, *The Mosaics of Norman Sicily*, 47 ff.; Beck, 'The First Mosaics', 120 f., 138 ff., 148 ff., believes that the *Pentecost* vault and the upper tier of scenes below it were completed by 1143; while Lazarev, *Storia della pittura bizantina*, 238, dates all the transept mosaics between 1143 and 1150; Kitzinger, 'The Date of Philagathos' Homily', 305, dates the south transept to between 1145 and 1150; Nersessian, *The Cappella Palatina of Roger II*, 217 f., believes that all the sanctuary mosaics belong to Roger II's lifetime.

[188] Kitzinger, 'The Mosaics of the Cappella Palatina', 286–8; Lazarev, *Storia della pittura bizantina*, 238; Beck, 'The First Mosaics', 137, 139–41, 147.

[189] Brenk's observations made on site in March 1985.

[190] Demus, *The Mosaics of Norman Sicily*, 82 ff., dates the Martorana mosaics between 1143 and 1151. Cf. Kitzinger ('Two Mosaic Ateliers', 277 f.), who believes that the teams of Byzantine mosaicist's at work in the two churches were not the same.

[191] Demus, *The Mosaics of Norman Sicily*, 56 f.

[192] Kitzinger ('The Mosaics of the Cappella Palatina', 282, 287 f.), Demus (*The Mosaics of Norman Sicily*, 58), and Beck ('The First Mosaics', 129) date the Genesis and the apostolic cycle after 1160. Lazarev, *Storia della pittura bizantina*, 238 dates them entirely to William I's reign (1154–66). In 1953 Kitzinger (review of Demus, 147), stated that he believed the apostolic cycle was planned from the outset, and that it was partly executed in William I's reign.

[193] See ch. 2 n. 42.

[194] Chalandon, *Histoire de la domination normande*, ii. 176, 232 ff., 291 f., 302; G. B. Siragusa, *Il regno di Guglielmo I in Sicilia* (Palermo, 1929), 59 f.; Wieruszowski, 'The Norman Kingdom of Sicily', 30.

[195] Demus, *The Mosaics of Norman Sicily*, 58, 225; Lazarev, *Storia della pittura bizantina*, 236.

[196] Patera, *L'arte della Sicilia*, 36.

[197] Demus, *The Mosaics of Norman Sicily*, 47.

[198] Kitzinger, 'The Mosaics of the Cappella Palatina', 284 n. 88; Demus, *The Mosaics of Norman Sicily*, 58; Beck, 'The First Mosaics', 123 n. 2.

[199] Chalandon, *Histoire de la domination normande*, ii. 121, 152, 169.

[200] See ch. 1 n. 16. Baldwin II of Jerusalem, for instance, was crowned on Easter Day (14 Apr. 1118) and again on Christmas Day 1119.

[201] Schuster, *The Sacramentary*, 371, 373.

[202] Dvornik, *The Idea of Apostolicity*, 285; cf. Demus, *The Mosaics of Norman Sicily*, 55.

[203] Deér, 'Das Grab Friedrichs II.', p. 364; M. and C. Valenziano, 'La Supplique des chanoines', 150.

[204] Kitzinger, 'The Mosaics of the Cappella Palatina', 288; Demus *The Mosaics of Norman Sicily*, 52, 58.

[205] For a late 12th-century illustration of the funeral, see Pietro da Eboli, *Liber ad honorem Augusti*, pl. 111; Bern, Bürger Bibliothek, MS, 120, c. 4 (97). For William's burial and transfer to Monreale, see Deér, *Dynastic Porphyry Tombs*, 4 ff., 10, 15; id., 'Das Grab Friedrichs II.', 365, 367, 375.

# 4

# MONREALE: THE LEGACY PROCLAIMED
## (Plates 57–118)

WILLIAM I's two sons (William and Henry, prince of Capua) were left in the care of their mother Margaret of Navarre, who acted as queen-regent.[1] Some weeks after his father's death, the elder son was acclaimed king by an assembly of barons and high clergy. On the same day, 9 May 1166, William II was crowned in Palermo cathedral by Romuald, archbishop of Salerno, who was also a royal chronicler.[2] Unlike the coronations of his father and grandfather, no great feast-day was chosen for the event; it happened to coincide with the Feast of St Gregory Nazianzenus. The occasion was no longer marked by strained relations with the papacy. Pope Alexander III, who had recently returned from France, took up residence in William's domain at Benevento in 1167.[3]

Although the queen dowager did not have to contend with papal hostility, she was faced with feudal rivalry. Possibly with the idea of remaining aloof from these local quarrels, she surrounded herself with French advisers—chief among whom were Stephen de la Perche and the learned Peter of Blois.[4] But the protest against these foreigners was so great that they were forced to leave barely two years later.[5] Matthew of Ajello became the young king's chief adviser and he remained in this capacity throughout the reign. And replacing Peter of Blois as William's tutor was Walter 'Ophamil', deacon of Agrigento and a member of the royal council.[6] In 1169, in spite of the queen mother's protests, he became archbishop of Palermo and was subsequently a thorn in the side of the monarchy.[7] Able and ambitious, Walter remained in office for the next twenty years, and from the start he and Matthew of Ajello were antagonists.[8] Somehow the king managed them both; Ajello defended the interests of the Crown against the arrogance of feudal barons and prelates, and he vigorously promoted the foundation of the royal abbey of Monreale.[9]

Monreale was as much the product of royal piety as an attempt to check the ambitious archbishop of Palermo. By 1171, William had come of age and, as acting apostolic legate, he had the right to initiate new monastic establishments as well as new dioceses.[10] The foundation of Monreale was an exercise of this power.[11] Its site—on a hill overlooking Palermo—was part of a royal park which included a small church or chapel called Hagia Kiriaka ('Sunday church') by the former Greek Metropolitan. It was claimed that its ancient foundation was the basis for the See of Palermo, whereas Walter 'Ophamil''s cathedral on the plain below merely replaced a mosque called the 'Friday church'.[12] This may not have been a case of special pleading by the king's men; at Agrigento there was a similar example of a cathedral *extra muros* for the Christian community during Muslim domination of the island.[13]

The earliest known reference to William II's new ecclesiastical establishment is

*Pl. 118*

1 March 1174.[14] To finance the royal abbey, the bishop of Messina ceded Santa Maria de Maniace, which had recently been enriched by the king's mother.[15] This was the first of a series of endowments designed to provide funds and at the same time to curtail the independence of the great ecclesiastical estates by subordinating them to the new royal foundation.[16] Construction was already under way when the pope officially approved of the project, late in 1174.[17] The papal bull of 30 December stated (as was the custom with Benedictine establishments) that the monastery was to be subject only to the Holy See; the king retained the right to approve the choice of the abbot.[18] All this was to anticipate possible objections from the archbishop of Palermo.[19] The bull further specified that the monastery was to follow the Benedictine rule and that the abbot was to be invested with full episcopal insignia.[20] The intention to give the place archiepiscopal status must have been an open secret for another nine years. In 1183, the monastery figured as an archbishopric in the bull of 4 February and the name of Monreale appeared for the first time.[21] Walter 'Ophamil' started rebuilding Palermo cathedral at just about the same time as the Monreale project began.[22]

Monreale was the last of four royal abbeys founded by the d'Hautevilles.[23] Instead of turning to the seat of the Benedictine order at Montecassino, the king called upon the Cluniac Benedictines of Cava dei Tirreni near Salerno to inhabit the monastery. Montecassino had accepted the monarchy with poor grace and was therefore never allowed to have establishments in Sicily.[24] The monks from Cava, on the other hand, had always been welcome to the Norman kings. By 1131, the Cluniacs already had three priories on the island when Roger II gave them the church of Sant'Angelo at Petralia.[25] And in 1151, Roger's second wife Queen Sibilla was buried at Cava in an ancient marble sarcophagus, and the king's motto is to be found in a cloister there.[26]

On 14 January 1176, after Pope Alexander III's renewal of the bull founding Monreale, King William sent an embassy to the abbey of the Trinity at Cava inviting these Benedictines to the newest royal abbey.[27] Six weeks later a hundred monks reached Monreale, enough of which must have been built to accommodate them.[28] A royal charter was granted and a great endowment made on Assumption Day, 15 August 1176.[29] Until then, documents simply refer to this royal abbey as *Sancte Marie Nove*, or 'New St Mary's'.[30] Perhaps this was to distinguish it from three older churches of the same name: S. Maria di Gerusalemme (the former palace chapel in Palermo), S. Maria de Maniace (Queen Margaret's foundation), and Palermo cathedral.[31] The king made further donations on Assumption Day 1178, followed by many more throughout his reign.[32] Eventually, the abbey's large new cathedral was dedicated to Mary's Assumption—the same title as that of Palermo's new cathedral begun at about the same time.[33] Many years later, after Monreale's importance had waned, its name was changed to that of the Virgin's Nativity.[34]

Echoes of the Holy Land already present in the very first royal foundation at Cefalù resound again at Monreale, the final, and by far the largest, ecclesiastical project of the Norman Crown. This is evident not only in the choice of Monreale's title, but also in its intended function as a royal mausoleum. Although Assumption Day was the feast used to initiate the First Crusade, the idea of Mary's corporeal assumption into heaven was not a universally accepted belief.[35] However, it was a theme especially revered by the

Cluniac Benedictines of Cava, whom the first Latin ruler of Jerusalem (Godfrey of Bouillon) had invited to come to the Holy Land as custodians of the Virgin's putative tomb at Gethsemane.[36] This Palestinian church was still in ruins in 1106–7, but it was subsequently rebuilt by (among others) Queen Melisende of Jerusalem (wife of King Fulk, d. 1161) who was buried there.[37] This church, dedicated to the Assumption, was known to the Crusaders as Our Lady of Jehosaphat. There is a connection between this royal gift in the Holy Land and Monreale—another royal foundation which bears the same title, was cared for by the same monks, and was also the burial site of the dowager queen of Sicily, who was interred there in 1183.[38] A few years later, William II brought up the royal dead from Palermo.[39] Not very much is known about the appearance of Monreale's namesake in the Holy Land; twelfth-century accounts described it as encased in marble with 'a dome-like structure of gold and silver' over the Virgin's tomb.[40]

## PLAN OF THE BUILDING

*Pl. 57*

Monreale cathedral is 102 metres long and 40 metres wide, with approximately 7,600 square metres of mosaics lining its upper walls.[41] The structure was executed with astonishing speed; hardly ten years after it was begun the pope praised the king for having built the church so quickly, and added that its like had not been seen since antiquity.[42] This was in 1183. How rapidly the mosaics were completed is less certain. Demus attributes them to a team of first-class Byzantine mosaicists, who may have been imported for the task after the Norman capture of Salonika in 1185.[43] The mosaics may not be that Greek, however. Nothing comparable is known in contemporary Byzantium, and the mosaicists might have been Greek-trained, whether in Sicily or on the South Italian mainland. What about the legacy left by the Greeks who worked at Montecassino a century earlier? Biblical cycles in fresco filled the atrium of the abbey there in a way comparable to those in the nave and aisles of Monreale, which may also have been used by the monks for processions and meditations.[44] The provenance of the mosaicists and the date of their activity remains one of the vexed questions of medieval art history. Equally mysterious is the function of the enormous nave and aisles—covered with biblical cycles—in a Cluniac monastery church where all the services were conducted within the sanctuary.

Not a single document or inscription has survived to tell us when any of the work was done except for the bronze doors at the western end of the nave, which were signed and *Pls. 58–9* dated by Bonanno of Pisa in 1186.[45] During the next year the coffins of William II's brothers, father, and grandfather were brought to the new cathedral, which was intended to be the dynastic burial site of the d'Hauteville kings, for whom the monks were to pray continuously. As the royal mausoleum, Monreale finally replaced Cefalù and Palermo cathedral, which had previously quarrelled over this privilege.[46]

In several respects, Monreale's structure expanded ideas which had been expressed in the earlier churches of the Norman kings. Cefalù's intended function as a royal mausoleum was finally realized, and at the same time mosaic features of both Cefalù and the Palatina were incorporated into the new cathedral.[47] Monreale's ground-plan (see Fig. 5) resembles *Pl. 57* Catania and Cefalù cathedrals in so far as there are three apses, a deep presbytery, strong *Pl. 1*

*Pls. 3, 61*

*Pls. 57, 68–*
*9, 74–8*
*Pls. 61, 82–*
*90*

*Fig. 5*

crossing-piers, and a slightly projecting transept.[48] There are also engaged columns in the apses as well as on the crossing-piers.[49] As in other Cluniac abbey churches, the transept is subdivided: the eastern third of the span is a corridor of vestibules framed by tall, pointed arches set in front of the three apses; the remaining two-thirds is made up of a large, almost square crossing, flanked by narrow rectangular chambers. The nave, which is forty-three metres high, is framed by arcades consisting of nine wide ogival arches on either side. The great monolithic granite columns are all classical spoils, as are the composite capitals, skilfully assembled by the Normans and carefully transported from unknown classical sites.[50] This grandiose use of ancient and exotic materials is reminiscent of Desiderius's use of them at Montecassino and what Suger contemplated for St Denis.[51]

Until the mid-seventeenth century, a barrier separated the nave and aisles from the sanctuary area which includes the crossing and transept. It has been estimated that this wall was about half as high as a nave column.[52] According to a late sixteenth-century report, there were originally only nine altars—all of them in the sanctuary: in the three

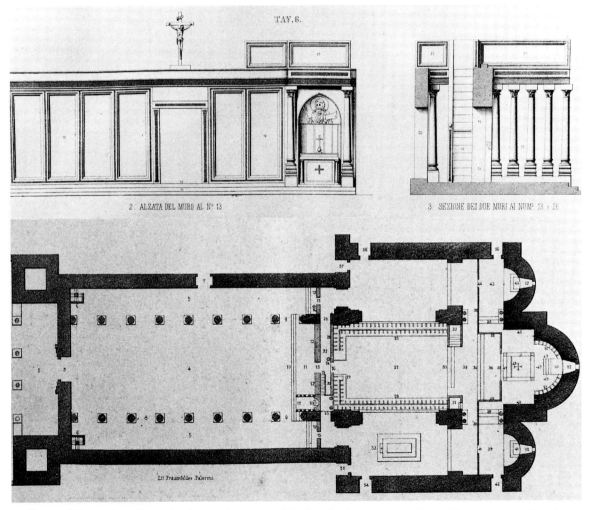

FIG. 5 Monreale cathedral: plan and section with Gravina's reconstruction of the sanctuary barrier

apses, outside the four corners of the crossing, in the Baptist's chapel situated underneath the raised ambo just outside the southern end of the sanctuary barrier, and another near William I's tomb in the southern arm of the transept.[53] This corresponds more or less to Cluniac arrangements, which, however, sometimes accommodated three altars in the central apse, with the high altar placed in front of them.[54] None of the original altars are visible; that in the main apse is buried within a baroque structure.[55] The original throne of the abbot-archbishop has vanished, too, and its location in the sanctuary is unknown. The present episcopal throne in the south-east corner of the crossing is a late concoction; on its site earlier was a narrow ambo.[56] But the royal throne opposite it is a repaired original.[57] A porphyry baptismal font, previously set in the second bay of the south aisle, was remodelled in the sixteenth and nineteenth centuries.[58] Today its base is in a niche in the southern aisle wall, which also accommodates a mosaic bust of the Baptist in its conch—a refugee from the dismantled chapel once located at the southern end of the sanctuary barrier.[59]

*Pl. 69*
*Pls. 103*
*Col. Pl. VIII*

There was probably always an unimpeded view down the length of the nave to the apse. The transept is raised above the nave and aisles by a shallow flight of three stairs. The climax of the main view is the most imposing of all the Sicilian Pantocrators located in the main apse conch, which at its base measures twelve metres wide—a quarter of the nave's height. This enormous icon is framed by a succession of four arches: at either end of the crossing, at the presbytery, and at the apse.

*Pl. 61*

*Pl. 64*

The brightest light is in the crossing—which was the royal enclosure and possibly served as the monks' choir as well. Its rectangular shape meant that the builders could not raise a cupola, as had been done earlier at both the Cappella Palatina and La Martorana.[60] Instead, a high lantern with many windows was used, which now admits a strong light augmented by the reflection of the gold mosaics covering the walls. Originally, there were more windows, but these were soon filled in by the mosaicists to accommodate the many scenes represented there. The presence of these windows was disclosed by recent repair work, which uncovered cakes of coloured glass together with fragments of Arabic stucco screens used to filter the light.[61] Such windows were probably used throughout the church and would have enhanced the sparkle of the mosaics, but by the sixteenth century these screens had been replaced by perforated lead panels, which must have made the interior much darker.[62]

*Pls. 95, 100–2*

As for the roofing, small cross-vaults were built in front of the chapels flanking the apse, but the rest consist of open-timbered trusses—replaced several times through the centuries.[63] Little or nothing remains of any Norman flooring. The oldest bits are the angular Saracenic interlaces at the eastern end.[64] The fifteenth-century pavement in the northern arm of the transept may have used material from an earlier floor for its Cosmatesque patterns and its spritely animals of inlaid white marble. The *opus sectile* work in the crossing was completely redone in 1915.[65] Until the late sixteenth century, the nave floor seems to have been merely packed earth or clay, while the high marble dado in the aisles was added less than a century ago.[66]

*Pl. 75*
*Col. Pl. VII*

The walls of the interior are smooth and unarticulated—clearly with an all-over mosaic mantle in mind—the most ambitious scheme ever carried out in this medium.

Architecturally, Monreale's interior has been described as simply a vessel for a pictorial theme.[67] The entire spectacle approaches Paul the Silentiary's sixth-century account of Hagia Sophia, where the mosaics were compared to heaven and the inlaid marble revetments to the Garden of Eden.[68]

## THE DISTRIBUTION OF THEMES

*Pls. 58–9*      Bonanno's bronze doors at the western entrance to the nave herald the major theme of the biblical sequences within: namely, the fulfilment of sacred history in Christ's Ascension and Mary's Assumption—their triumph over mortality and entry into the celestial Jerusalem. Mary, as the titular of the church, is situated on the liturgical right. The 'Ego sum lux' inscription at the top of Christ's half of the door is echoed down the length of

*Pls. 61–2, 67*      the church by the display of the same text in the Pantocrator's open book in the main apse conch.

Although Mary is Monreale's titular, her role is subordinated to the coming of the Saviour. As in the Cappella Palatina, a Genesis cycle unfolds around the nave arcade and is directed towards the crossing, where Christ's story begins and circulates in con-centric fashion from the transept around the aisles. The apostolic sequences of Peter and Paul fill the easternmost corners of the transept on either side of the presbytery. Again as in the Palatina, a series of half-length holy women enclosed by foliate medallions are set in the spandrels of the nave arcade looking into the darker aisles.[69] The great piers of the transept are covered on all sides with tiers of saints beloved of Sicily and the Cluniac Benedictines of Cava.

*Pl. 86*      There are also a few isolated scenes which appear as interjections—historical episodes from a less remote past. At the western end of the nave, clustered around the portal, are three miracles of South Italian bishop martyrs: *SS Castus*, *Cassius*, and *Castrensis*. The latter (on the left of the door as one enters) had some relevance for the monarchy, because his relics were brought as a wedding present by Alfano, bishop of Capua, when William II married Joan princess of England, on 13 February 1177 in the Cappella Palatina.[70] Two

*Pls. 104–5*      scenes, both honouring the monarchy, appear on either side of the crossing: *Christ crowning King William II* and *William II presenting Monreale to the Enthroned Virgin*. The royal thread of the Norman monarchy glitters here and there down the length of the church, in inscriptions as well as imagery, coming to a bold climax above the actual throne where the biblical basis for d'Hauteville rule is openly declared at last, while its aspirations are absorbed into the fulfilment of its sacred destiny.

## THE MARIAN IMAGERY

*Pl. 57*      The Marian imagery is also aligned along the central axis of the church—from the entrance to the apse. Included among Mary's many allegorical associations and attributes were that she was the gate of life and the door to Salvation.[71] At Monreale, therefore, she

*Pls. 60, 64,*    was represented in a series of doorways and entrances: outside, in the former entrance
*98–9*      portico; inside, in the tympanum over the main portal, and on the presbytery arch.

Before their destruction in the eighteenth century, the exclusively Marian subjects in the northern half of the entrance portico illustrated the *Birth of the Virgin* and the *Presentation in the Temple* on the narrow end wall, followed by the *Dormition* and *Assumption* on the wider wall left of the portal.[72] In the other half of the portico, Mary's story joins Christ's infancy. To the right of the door were two royal advents: the *Nativity* and the *Adoration of the Magi*. Two temple scenes occupied the narrower end wall: the *Presentation of Jesus in the Temple* (facing Mary's *Presentation* at the opposite end) and *Christ among the Doctors*. There were angels and prophets on the arcade wall of the porch opposite the façade, each set across from an appropriate scene. *Michael*, the angel of the Last Judgement, looked at the *Dormition* and *Assumption*; while *Gabriel*, the angel of the Incarnation, faced the *Nativity* and *Adoration of the Magi*. Above the central columns of the porch were two prophets: *Isaiah*, on Mary's side, held the inscription: 'Egredietur Virgo de radice Jesse' (Isaiah 11: 1).[73] The pendant figure opposite Christ's *Nativity* was *Balaam*, the prophet of the Messiah's birth. His inscription, 'Orietur stella ex Jacob' (Numbers 24: 17),[74] linked Jacob's mission with Christ's birth. By 1596 these mosaics were already in a ruinous state and in 1770 they were destroyed.[75]

Inside the entrance portal, in the recessed tympanum, there is an abbreviated version *Pl. 60* of the *Hodegetria*, the protectress of kings. No longer hidden in the depths of the sanctuary *Pl. 34* as she was in the Cappella Palatina, she intitiates here the central axis of the interior. Represented in half-length, Mary holds a much-restored infant Jesus with a now empty scroll. On the gold ground, a Greek inscription identifies her as the Mother of God (Theotokos).[76] Over her head is a starred sphere representing heaven, and on the recessed surfaces on either side the archangels Michael and Gabriel bow in homage. In the mosaic lintel below is written:

SPONSA SVE PROLIS O STELLA PVERPERA SOLIS
PRO CVNCTIS ORA SED PLVS PRO REGE LABORA

[The bride of her offspring. Star, bringer forth of the sun, pray for all, but [even] more work for the king.]

As in the southern sanctuary chapel of the Palatina,[77] this text again takes up Balaam's prophecy and the theme of light. It alludes to Mary as the apocalyptic *mulier amicta sole* as well as to her intercessory role at the Last Judgement. And it introduces the Sicilian monarchy by invoking the Virgin's sponsorship of the new cathedral's donor.

The donation panel on the south-eastern pier of the crossing is a sequel to the portal *Pl. 105* lunette. The enthroned queen with open hands accepts the church which is being offered in her name by the bowing king identified as 'REX GVILIELMVS S[E]C[VN]D[V]S'. His good work is blessed by the hand of God, while two angelic witnesses hover overhead.

On the triumphal arch framing the presbytery apse, the *Annunciation* occupies its *Pls. 62, 64* traditional place. At the very centre of the apse, below the *Pantocrator* and above a large ogival window, Mary appears enthroned again. But this time she is rendered in hieratic *Pls. 62–3* frontality as queen of the celestial court with the blessing Christ-child seated upon her knees. A Greek inscription identifies her as the Panachrantos, the Immaculate One,[78] thereby making explicit the notion of Mary's corporeal assumption because doctrinally this was only possible if she herself was immortal—born free of original sin. The final acts of Mary's Assumption were her coronation and enthronement with Christ. In the Latin West these events were usually represented as scenes of action, such as the Virgin ascending amidst angels or Christ crowning Mary.[79] Among the Greeks, however, the static icon of the enthroned (but uncrowned) queen was preferred, and it is to this tradition that Monreale's *Panachrantos* belongs. In fact, she has been attributed to late Comnenian artists,[80] who rendered her as the throne of the divine Child—the incarnation of divine wisdom. This type of seated Virgin and Child, therefore, was known as the 'Throne of Wisdom'.[81] In this respect, the Monreale designers surely based their mosaic queen upon the imperial model in the apse conch of Hagia Sophia in Constantinople,[82] where the son she holds embodies the name of the church—that of the Holy Wisdom. Another *Pls. 64–5* personification of this idea appears at Monreale in the medallion on top of the gabled arch separating the nave from the sanctuary, where a crowned and orant female is accompanied by the words, 'SAPIENTIA DEI'.[83]

*Pl. 57*       From the portico to the apse there is a calculated progression in the Marian imagery which originally ran from a cycle of narrative scenes to the iconic *Hodegetria* tympanum, down the length of the church to scenes of ceremonial isolation such as the *Donation* panel and the *Incarnation/Annunciation*, and terminating finally in the hieratic *Panachrantos*, who rules over the double tier of holy figures in the apse as Queen of the saints in heaven as well as of earthly kingdoms.[84]

## THE APSE AND PRESBYTERY

*Pls. 62, 68–* The dominating *Pantocrator* is the fulfilment of all the prophecies represented by the texts *9, 71* and images on the arch framing the apse and on the two arches spanning the corridor between the presbytery and the crossing. These figures and their messages can only be seen together in the bema—just in front of the presbytery. On the wall above the two transept arches, there are six prophets on either side distributed in a double tier: two between the windows above and four at their feet below. Apart from general messages of *Pls. 69, 71* obeisance and prophecies of the Messiah's coming, those on the southern arch (*Isaiah, Habbakuk, Jeremiah, 'Amos, Obadiah,* and *Joel*) allude to the Incarnation and Last Judgement—themes incorporated by the adjacent *Annunciation* and *Pantocrator*.[85] All the specific- *Pl. 68* ally royal messages are on the northern arch, which is on the liturgical right. Here stand *Jacob, Zechariah, Malachi, Jonah, Ezekiel,* and *Moses*.[86] Three out of the six scrolls concern kings; not only the King of kings in the apse conch, but also the Sicilian king who sat on his throne just below on the same side of the transept. Malachi's text is the antiphon used in the Roman pontifical for the reception of emperors,[87] and Zechariah's words are a reciprocal of the Pantocrator's 'Ego sum lux' inscription displayed in the apse.

*Pls. 66, 3, 20* The great presbytery niche immediately in front of the apse combines details which had been used earlier at Cefalù and in the Palatina. At the summit of the vault is the *Hetoimasia* (or prepared throne of the Second Coming)[88] and ranked below on either side are pairs of seraphim and angels. At first, only a single gigantic angel was contemplated

for either side—as in the Palatina.[89] On the outer face of the apse proper are nine *Pl. 62*
medallions of the ancestors of Christ culminating with *Emmanuel* (God with us, in Greek,
Matthew's name for the son to be born of the Virgin (1 : 23) ). All of the others have Latin
labels and messages. Starting from the lower left these are: *Nathan, Daniel, Elijah, David,*
*(Emmanuel), Solomon, Samuel, Gideon,* and *Elisha.*[90] On the supporting piers are *John* and
*Matthew*, each of whom carries a scroll with the opening words in Greek of their respective
gospels.[91] Like the other figures in this horizontal row which spans the presbytery and *Pls. 62, 68–*
apse, these saints are represented in attitudes of movement: both turn inwards towards *70, 72–3*
the apse. This tier consists of Apostles and evangelists arranged on either side of the
Virgin, each with attendant angels according to his relative importance. Proceeding from
left to right they are: *Philip, Bartholomew, Luke, John, James, Peter, Archangel Michael, the*
*Panachrantos, Archangel Gabriel, Paul, Andrew, Matthew, Mark, Thomas, Simon Zelotes.*

By contrast, all the saints in the tier below are represented in rigid frontality with
identifying inscriptions in Latin—presumably because most of them belong to the Greg- *Pls. 72–3*
orian list of the canon of the Mass.[92] From left to right they are: *Agatha, Anthony Abbot,*
*Blaise, Martin, Stephen, Peter of Alexandria, Clement I* (window), *Sylvester, Thomas of Canterbury,*
*Lawrence, Nicholas of Bari, Hilary, Benedict, Mary Magdalene.* Nine out of fourteen of these
were titulars of ecclesiastical properties which had been ceded to Monreale.[93] But they
are present here for other reasons too. For instance, the patron saints of the French and
Sicilian monarchies, *SS Martin* and *Nicholas*, are given pride of place immediately below *Pl. 62*
*John* and *Matthew* who frame the apse. Then there are early popes (*Clement* and *Sylvester*),
advocates of Mary's virginity (*Peter of Alexandria* and *Hilary*),[94] deacons (*Stephen* and
*Lawrence*), the founders of Eastern and Western monasticism (*Anthony* and *Benedict*), and
*Thomas of Canterbury*, canonized by Alexander III in 1173.[95]

Finally, on the crossing-arch, facing the *Incarnation*, are a pair of angels, each of whom
occupies a spandrel with *Veronica's Veil* situated high up between them. This can only be
seen from the rear of the apse and underwent some heavy restoration from the fifteenth
century onwards.[96] The two Greek stylites (*SS Daniel* and *Simeon*) beneath Gabriel and *Pl. 62*
Mary in the *Annunciation* replaced actual columns which were part of the original
structure.[97]

## THE LATERAL APSES AND THEIR VESTIBULES:
## SS PETER AND PAUL

As guardians of the Cluniac Benedictines, as well as co-founders of the Roman Church, *Pl. 57*
Peter and Paul have chapels on either side of the main apse with its Marian altar and
colossal *Pantocrator*.[98] The importance of these Apostles coincided here with the king's
status as an apostolic legate. As with all Cluniac monasteries, Monreale's abbot was subject only to the pope and so bypassed Sicily's primate in Palermo.[99] During William II's
reign, the apostolic aspect of the royal mission was no longer a source of discord and
relations with the papacy were friendly. Monreale was built with papal support and
Sicilian troops protected the pope on the Italian mainland.[100] Alexander III negotiated

William's marriage with the English princess and shortly afterwards Sicilian ships took him to Venice for the peace treaty with the Holy Roman Emperor.[101]

Besides Cluniac custom, there were several other precedents for placing the chapels of Peter and Paul on either side of the transept. In Old St Peter's in Rome, there was a Petrian cycle in the right transept, just as there was at Monreale.[102] In the Cappella Palatina, Paul's altar occupies this position, while the apostolic cycle of scenes goes around the aisles. At Monreale, these scenes are distributed around the wall of the transept vestibules where each Apostle has his altar.[103] Peter's location on the right was probably justified by his association with St Peter's chair in Rome, to which the Cluniacs were directly subject. The door from the monastery at Monreale leads directly to his chapel (Pl. 57), and from his throne in the apse conch Peter blesses all who enter.

*Pl. 16*

*Pl. 75*

*Pls. 74–5, 78*        The isolated enthronement of Peter and Paul in their respective chapels is very unusual, even though as bishops they were entitled to a throne. Although there are earlier as well as twelfth-century murals of the Apostles enthroned as a group—as in the lost mosaic in Hagia Sophia, in the Palatina *Pentecost* in Palermo, and the Russian fresco of the *Last Judgement* at Vladimir[104]—the only other example known to me of an Apostle enthroned alone in a comparable site is the later mosaic of *St Matthew* in Salerno cathedral, made before 1260.[105] Otherwise images of the enthroned Peter are to be found on civic and monastic seals, over a doorway at Sessa Aurunca Cathedral,[106] and in the Lateran *Coronation* mosaic.

*Pl. 44*

The inscription accompanying *Peter* in his apse conch proclaims him prince of the Apostles and keeper of the keys to the heavenly kingdom:

SANCTVS PETRVS P[RI]NCEPS AP[OSTO]LOR[VM]
CVI TRADITE SVNT CLAVES REGNI CELORVM.

*Pl. 75*        Framing the apse are four standing bishop saints: *Sixtus*, *Savinus*, *Boniface*, and *Germanus*. Paul's inscription at the opposite end of the transept praises him as a preacher of the truth and doctor to the Gentiles:

SANCTVS PAVLVS AP[OSTO]L[V]S PREDICATOR
VERITATIS DOCTOR GENTIVM.

*Pl. 81*        The quartet of saints framing this apse are all fathers of the Eastern and Western Churches: *John Chrysostom*, *Gregory*, *Ambrose*, and *Augustine*. In the context of the transept mosaics, Peter and Paul appear as guardians of the future kingdom of the just. The eschatological vision in the main apse and presbytery exalts this kingdom, which is witnessed and guaranteed by the founders of the Roman Church.[107] This is an expansion of the same idea already found in the fifth-century mosaics on the triumphal arch of Santa Maria Maggiore in Rome, where Peter and Paul adore the prepared throne which is accompanied by an inscription naming the Chosen People ('Plebi Dei')—in this case, of Rome.[108]

Although restricted to the confines of two transept chapels, the series of apostolic scenes at Monreale includes more episodes than the aisles of the Cappella Palatina. In Peter's chapel the scenes are not arranged chronologically throughout. Both lunettes—over the

apse conch and on the south wall—are devoted to *Peter's Liberation from Prison by an Angel* *Pls. 74, 76*
(Acts 12: 6–8). On the southern end wall of the transept, two tiers of scenes continue the
story beneath the lunette: the *Raising of Tabitha* (Acts 9: 40 f.) is followed by three
apocryphal Roman episodes (the *Meeting of Peter and Paul*, the *Disputation* and the *Fall of
Simon Magus*). The setting for the last scene continues on the pilaster on the right, giving
a certain three-dimensional character to an abbreviated view labelled 'Roma'. Then, in
the lunette of the western arch, the story resumes with the subject which—as in the
Palatina—was appropriately chosen for its site near a doorway, i.e. *Peter and John healing
the Lame Man at the Temple Gate* (Acts 3: 3). The lunette on the northern arch follows with
*Peter healing the Paralytic at Lydda* (Acts 9: 32–3). The final scene, *Peter's Crucifixion in Rome*, *Pl. 74*
is represented by itself on the reverse side of the western arch—as a kind of frontispiece
to Peter's chapel for those approaching from the west.[109] The identification of the scene's
locale, 'Roma', is written in large letters in the gold ground and is repeated in the scene
of *Paul's Martyrdom* situated on the corresponding wall in the northern arm of the transept. *Pls. 78–9*

Whereas miracles dominate the Peter sequence, it is conversion and preaching which
are illustrated by the scenes in the Pauline cycle. Here they follow a chronological order
which begins immediately above the apse conch. As in the Cappella Palatina, the first *Pl. 78*
episode is *Paul's Departure from Jerusalem to persecute the Christians at Damascus* (Acts 9: 1–3).
This is followed in the southern lunette by *Paul's Conversion* (Acts 9: 3 4), where the
miracle is dramatized by the actual light which falls on the scene from windows on the
adjacent walls. On the western wall, opposite the apse, *Blind Paul is led to Damascus* (Acts
9: 8–9) where, in the next lunette (on the northern wall), his sight is restored and he *Pl. 80*
meets *Ananias* (Acts 9: 10–12). In the double tier of scenes below; Paul is *Baptized*, *Disputes
with the Jews*, *Flees Damascus*, and *Consigns a Letter to the Disciples at Antioch* (Acts 9: 18,
21–2, 25; 15: 30). In the vault overhead is a medallion of the *Pantocrator* with a closed *Col. Pl. VII*
book, while in Peter's chapel this space is occupied by *Emmanuel*. *Pl. 77*

Although it has been argued that it was the same Byzantine manuscript illustrations
that ultimately inspired the apostolic cycles at both the Cappella Palatina and Monreale,
the styles of these mosaics are quite different.[110] At the Palatina, the compositions are *Pls. 47, 49–*
more self-contained; the windows there serve as dividers, whereas at Monreale they are *56*
often absorbed into the scenery, as in the *Angel's Apparition to St Peter in Prison* or in the
*Baptism of St Paul*. Frequently, the mosaicists unified consecutive episodes within the
confines of a single scene, which, together with the dramatic postures and gestures, give
an unprecedented sense of urgency and movement to all the narrative sequences at
Monreale.[111]

## THE GENESIS CYCLE IN THE NAVE *Pls. 82–91*

The Old Testament occupies the largest continuous wall surface in the church. Its stories
occupy both sides of the nave arcade, starting and finishing on either side of the sanctuary
arch and continuing, without a break, across the western end of the nave. It is a larger
version of the scheme in the Cappella Palatina adjusted to a Marian church. Here, too,
the story is told in a double tier of scenes. Nine windows separate the upper row on either

side of the nave, while below, narrow vertical strips perform the same function. The surfaces are handled with great inventiveness and sensitivity to the effects of light. The entire storiated area is literally lifted up from the rest of the wall surface by the fact that it sprouts from ornamental vases placed above each column capital. The degree of relief varies from five to ten centimetres and the edges are marked by a continuous red band.

*Pls. 86, 62–4*
*Pl. 57*

The Monreale Genesis consists of forty-two scenes as opposed to the thirty-two at the Palatina.[112] Yet the cycle begins and ends with the same episodes. Despite its greater length, no new themes were introduced; the same stories were simply expanded. Compared to the earlier series, however, the Monreale rendering is much closer to the biblical text. The story of the *Creation of Eve* and the *Fall* was amplified more than any other in the series in order to stress the link between the old dispensation and the new. A deliberate parallel was drawn between Eve and Mary, Monreale's titular:[113] Eve's *Creation* and *Introduction to Paradise* fill the western end of the nave directly opposite the *Annunciation* and the *Panachrantos* far down in the celestial paradise of the apse. The source of original sin is contrasted with the Virgin as the means of salvation—the 'Immaculate One'—just as the tree of the forbidden fruit on the west wall faces repeated representations of the tree of life at the corners of the sanctuary and presbytery arches.[114] Notwithstanding arguments for a Byzantine prototype for the Monreale Genesis, the parallel between Eve and Mary was a Western theme. At Monreale this was expressed pictorially by the disposition of the subject-matter, whereas at St Mark's in Venice, for instance, this was rendered by inscriptions.[115]

*Pl. 82*

The Genesis cycle begins with a narrow sliver of a scene fitted into the area available between the sanctuary arch and a window: an *en face* Creator, a miniature *Pantocrator*, wills the sky and water into being. Much more space is left for the *Creation of Light*, which has a scene all to itself. The upper tier concludes on the opposite wall with another narrow scene, *Noah's Covenant with God*. At the Palatina this event was combined with the *Building of the Ark*. At Monreale, the *Building of the Ark* is one of the two largest scenes in the cycle and initiates the lower tier on the south wall. The Flood and its coming marked a new era in the history of salvation, and it was set among the first Genesis scenes, with the waters of creation located directly overhead. An intentional parallel may have been drawn here with the nearby Baptist's chapel, for baptism was also understood as initiating a new life.[115a] Five more Noah scenes follow, but the final scene on this wall is *Abraham's Hospitality to the Angels*. The adjacent west wall continues with the *Angels visiting Lot* and the *Destruction of Sodom*. The Abraham story resumes on the western end of the north wall with *Abraham's Covenant with God*, and concludes with *Jacob wrestling with the Angel*, which is directly below *Noah's Covenant with God*.

*Pls. 91, 56, 82*

*Pls. 82–4*
*Pls. 85–6*

*Pls. 87, 90*

*Pl. 91*

Appropriately, these confrontations with the Deity are located next to the sanctuary entrance. The promises of deliverance made to these patriarchs and, as in Jacob's case, the promise of land,[116] are fulfilled inside the transept beyond. Both Jacob and Noah are used as vehicles for symbol and allegory here. Noah's large ark, for instance, was a well-known simile for Mary as a tabernacle of the new covenant.[117] There is a further allegorical link between *Jacob wrestling with the Angel* and Mary and Gabriel in the *Annunciation*—scenes which in the Greek East were sometimes both included in Marian cycles.[118] The

*Pl. 82*

scriptural texts simply lent themselves to their association in an architectural context, and they are also found together in medieval consecration rites as well as in Marian exegetical literature.[119] The 'gate of heaven' which Jacob recognizes on waking from his dream is the Annunciate Mary, and in Luke's account of the Annunciation, therefore, Jesus 'will reign over the house of Jacob forever' (Luke 1: 32–4). At Monreale, there are *Pls. 91, 64–5* two gates which are related to Jacob: the adjacent one guarded by 'Sapientia Dei' and the pair of angels at the nave entrance to the sanctuary, and the *Annunciation* on the *Pl. 61* presbytery arch—the gate disclosing the glowing vision of the celestial court.

Both Noah and Jacob were charged with a sacred mission which is resumed by the Saviour, his Apostles, and the Sicilian king enthroned in the sanctuary. It is not accidental that *Noah* and *Jacob* reappear in the arch soffit above the king's throne. At Monreale, *Pls. 57, 68–9* Jacob's role is particularly large. As well as his conspicuous position at the conclusion of the Genesis cycle at the sanctuary gate, his relation to Monreale's titular was referred to by Balaam in the lost portico mosaic and yet again in the central presbytery vestibule, where he appears between the *Annunciation* and the king of Sicily's throne with a message appropriate to them both.[120] However, just as in the palace chapel in Palermo, the underlying theme behind the distribution of scenes in the Monreale Genesis is Paradise created, Paradise lost, and the promise of Paradise regained.[121]

## THE ANGELIC HOST

At Monreale, even more than at the Cappella Palatina, angels help to blend the Old Testament with the New through their role as agents of wisdom and enlightenment. They are omnipresent here—they serve as guardians at every gate and portico, and dozens more appear in the frieze of intertwined medallions along the top of both sides of the *Pls. 82–91,* nave (there are forty-two altogether here) and in the gables of the transept.[122] The idea *106, 110* that they personified enlightenment goes back to Augustine as well as to the pseudo-Dionysius.[123] This notion is illustrated quite literally in the second Genesis scene, where *Pl. 82* angels personify the *Creation of Light*—a rare formulation of the subject. The same imagery was used a century earlier for the *Creation of the Firmament* in one of the Salerno ivories.[124]

## THE CROSSING

The crossing, or sanctuary, is a broad rectangular enclosure raised above the surrounding *Pl. 57* floor level of both the nave and transept. Besides the barriers between the nave at one end and the presbytery at the other, the original situation with respect to the transept is unknown. Today all access to the arms of the transept is completely blocked off by a high marble dado, on top of which organs have been installed. Both the dado and the organs are modern, as are the choir-stalls on the north and south sides inside the crossing. There was probably a monks' choir here, but whether it was a free-standing enclosure or set between the lateral arches is uncertain. The only original piece of furnishing left here is the elevated dais for the royal throne at the north-east corner. Just outside the south-west *Fig. 5* corner of the crossing barrier was a chapel dedicated to the Baptist.[125]

*The Arch Soffits*

*Pl. 57*     The mosaics on the four great arch soffits consist of twenty-six medallions with busts
of prophets and ancestors of Christ—a theme also used at Cefalù in the presbytery
lunettes. At Monreale, this was greatly expanded and beautifully arranged so as to
acknowledge in appropriate places the Messiah, the Sicilian king, and even the Bene-
*Pls. 64, 92–*   dictine order. The five largest roundels are on the western arch dividing the sanctuary
*3, 82*      from the nave. It is a royal gate, because all the personages are either kings or closely
related to kings. From left to right (or north to south) they are: *Solomon Rex, Jesse,
Obadiah, David Rex*, and *Rehoboam*. Solomon's position on the liturgical right is particularly
*Pl. 92*     appropriate, because this is also the side of the royal throne. Furthermore, the words on
his scroll ('AVDI FILI PRECEPTA') are those with which the text of the Benedictine rule
begins.[126] As David's father, Jesse was also the ancestor of Mary—Jesse's 'sprout'. Obadiah
belongs in this company because he was a descendant of David and for several other
reasons too: as a gatekeeper, as a prophet of lands repossessed (Obadiah 19–21), and as
an exile who returned to Jerusalem—particularly appropriate for the Sicilian king with
claims on Jerusalem.

*Pls. 97–8*      All the medallions on the northern arch represent the crowned kings of Judea, David's
ancestors. This is the side of William's throne. From west to east they are: *Joathom, Joram,
Asa, Abias, Jehosaphat, Ozias*, and *Achaz*. On the arch soffit between the sanctuary and the
*Pls. 57, 68–*   presbytery several of the nave patriarchs reappear close to the king's throne: *Judas
9, 103*      *Maccabeus, Isaac, Noah, Melchizedek, Enoch, Abraham*, and *Jacob*. As the priest-king of Salem,
*Melchizedek* occupies the loftiest place and looked down upon the precinct of the high
altar as well as upon the enthroned apostolic legate below. The other six figures were also
associated with allegorical virtues: *Enoch* and *Noah* with prudence, and *Abraham, Isaac*,
*Pls. 57, 96,*   and *Jacob* with temperance.[127] On the southern arch, from west to east, we have: *Boaz,
99*          *Nason, Aram, Phares, Esrom, Aminabad*, and *Salmon*. Although the subjects of many of the
medallions are included in Matthew's list, there does not seem to be any basis for supposing
that there were originally forty-two in order to coincide with the generations in the Gospel
text.[128] *Melchizedek, Enoch*, and *Noah*, for instance, do not belong to this series.


*Further Prophets*

There are two further Old Testament figures in the crossing which not only link the
Genesis cycle in the nave with the Christological sequences in the transept, but also exalt
*Pls. 96–7,*    the status of the king, who could easily read their messages from his throne. These are
*101*        *Malachi* and *Isaiah*, who occupy the spandrels of the arch framing the nave. Malachi's
*Pls. 68, 103*   scroll repeats the same text held by the less conspicuous figure near the presbytery
(Malachi 3: 1):

ECCE EGO MITTA[M] ANG[E]L[V]M MEV[M] ET
PR[A]E[PARABIT]

[Behold, I send my angel and he shall prepare [the way before my face. And the Lord whom you
demand and the angel of the Covenant whom you desire, shall suddenly come to his temple].]

The pictorial precedent at Monreale for an angel leading the Chosen People of Israel is the story of *Jacob and the Angel* represented on the nave wall just outside this arch. As the last of the Old Testament prophets, Malachi was the perfect choice for its site, because his message anticipates Gabriel's Annunciation to Mary (as well as the *Nativity* and *Presentation in the Temple* represented overhead). Malachi's message also refers to the Baptist's chapel originally situated beneath him just outside the sanctuary entrance.[129] The message also reverberates in the angelic imagery inside the presbytery arch.[130] But these words were also associated with earthly rulers. The early Franks used them before marching into battle, and the phrase was picked up later in ceremonials used for acclamation, reception, and coronation of kings.[131] The *Malachi* mosaic, therefore, refers not only to Christ's entry into the sanctuary but also constitutes the greeting to earthly monarchs—including the Norman king who sat on his throne below.[132]

*Pls. 57, 91, 96–7*

*Pl. 101*

*Fig. 5*

Isaiah's message in the opposite spandrel is just as explicit in its relevance for the Sicilian monarchy (Isaiah 61: 1):

*Pls. 97, 101*

SP[IRITV]S D[OMI]NI SVP[ER] ME
P[RO]PT[ER] QVOD

[The spirit of the Lord God is upon me because [the Lord has anointed me to bring good tidings to the afflicted].]

The line comes from a passage concerning the mission to Zion. In the context of the imagery in the crossing it is especially appropriate for the *Baptism* mosaic, as well as for the anointed Norman king enthroned below.

*Pl. 103*

### The Holy Warriors and Other Saints

Opposite *Isaiah* and *Malachi* over the eastern crossing arch, are six warrior saints who face the western approach to the sanctuary. This was a common feature of centralized schemes of the Greek East, where they were also situated close to the presbytery.[133] At Monreale, Latin inscriptions identify them as: *John Miles, Mercurius, George, Theodore, Demetrius*, and *Paul Miles*. With the exception of the first and last in the series, the others had been used earlier at either Cefalù or the Cappella Palatina. Besides commemorating visions beheld by the Normans, some of these saints were also invoked in Frankish royal ceremonial.[134]

*Pls. 57, 64, 95*

*Pls. 9, 35–6*

Many other saints beloved of the Benedictines and Norman Sicily keep watch from all the piers and spandrels of the sanctuary and transept arches. At the nave entrance to the sanctuary, *Marcianus* and *Gerlandus* face one another. According to Sicilian tradition, Marcianus was consecrated as bishop of Syracuse by St Peter himself[135] while Gerlandus, an early bishop of Agrigento, was said to be related to Count Roger I, one of the conquerors of Sicily. On the piers at either side of the northern arch are *Lambertus* and *Gennarus*—both Benedictine bishops. *Gennarus* stands on the western face of the throne pier. King William I transferred his bones from Benevento to Cava.[136] The corresponding pier-faces on either side of the eastern arch are occupied by the thrones of the king and

*Pls. 92, 82, 94*

*Pl. 97*

*Pl. 57*

*Pl. 96*

archbishop. On either side of the southern arch are Bishops *Ursinus* and *Cataldus*. Ursinus was a reputed witness of the Last Supper, Crucifixion, and Pentecost, who later went to Gaul as a missionary. Cataldus, who is in the Cappella Palatina also, is present here as a patron saint of Palermo, and is set appropriately on the pier-face next to *Gerlandus*, the bishop of Agrigento.

Several of the saints facing *into* the crossing from the piers and spandrels belong in groups or pairs, and sometimes they appear in parallel positions on either side of the same arch or in a vertical sequence. This is the case with *Vitus* and *Modestus*, who occupy the uppermost places in either spandrel of the southern arch. *Marcellinus* and *Marcus*, another pair, appear just below them.

*Pls. 103, 105*

Without enumerating all of the saints, a few more groups and pairs do need to be mentioned, because their presence augments both the royal and monastic nature of the site and indicates how thoroughly the entire pictorial scheme was planned. For instance, *St Leontius*'s brothers were *SS Cosmas* and *Damian*, on whose feast-day the Sicilian monarchy was established. They are just around the corner from *Leontius*[137] facing one another on the piers which separate the Peter vestibule from the presbytery. The pendant pair on the opposite side of the transept corridor, close to the royal throne, is *SS Sergius* and *Bacchus*, a pair much revered by Byzantine emperors as army saints.[138]

*Pl. 57*

*Pl. 33*

All the female saints are on the outer face of the sanctuary wall, looking into the arms of the transept. Those on the north side include several royal figures (three out of six). Behind the throne half of the arch are *Agatha*, *Catherine*, and *Benua* [*sic*; Venera], who are also represented in the northern chapel of the Palatina. The group on the other half of the same arch are *Margarita* (beheaded at Antioch), *Queen Radegonda* of France (who became a Benedictine nun), and *Quirica* and *Julitta* (also of Antioch). Facing into the southern arm of the transept are (at the eastern end): *Dominica*, with *Susannah* and *Thecla*, both of whom were martyred at Salerno. Their pendants (on the western half of the same arch) are: *Scholastica* (St Benedict's sister), *Sabina*, and *Giustina* (who was also connected with the Benedictines).

*The Narrative Scenes*

*Pls. 100–2*

*Fig. 5*

*Pl. 100*

*Pl. 101*

*Pls. 102–3*

Scenes from the early lives of the Baptist and the Saviour occupy three sides of the crossing; a double tier circulates downwards across the south, west, and north walls. The Baptist's inclusion here was justified not only because he was Christ's precursor but also because his small chapel was situated just outside the sanctuary's south-west corner.[139] Several scenes of Christ's infancy repeat subjects represented in the lost portico mosaics.[140] Beginning on the south wall, there are four episodes separated by three windows: the *Annunciation to Zacharias* and his *Departure from the Temple*, *Annunciation to Mary*, and *Visitation*. Light also enters by three windows on the west wall, presided over by the host of angels—the agents of spiritual illumination—who hover over the *Nativity*, which occupies the entire upper tier. Continuing to the northern wall are: the *Magi on their Way to Bethlehem*, *Epiphany*, *Herod*, and *Massacre of the Innocents*. This sequence of good and evil rulers coincides with the royal side of the crossing with William's throne below.

The story is resumed in the lower tier of the south wall with the *Angel warning the*     *Pl. 100*
*dreaming Joseph*, followed by the *Flight into Egypt*, which leads into the west wall. Here
there are two temple subjects: the *Presentation* and *Christ among the Doctors*. These two     *Pls. 101–2*
events are represented as a cityscape, which continues on the north wall with the *Marriage
at Cana*, followed by the *Baptism of Christ*.[141] The chronological sequence of these two
scenes is reversed, probably so that the *Baptism* would be almost vertically aligned with     *Pl. 103*
the *Christ crowning King William II*—an allusion to the Holy Spirit as the source of the
chrism used to anoint the Norman kings.[142]

### The Throne, William's Coronation, and Donation

Perhaps because it was a royal enclosure, the crossing was raised above the level of the
nave and transept. The throne, situated on the liturgical right, is in a traditional place—     *Pls. 57, 64,*
close to the presbytery.[143] The throne dais is engaged to the north-eastern crossing-pier,     *103*
and is raised five steps above the crossing-floor. Pictorially and thematically, William's
throne—with the *Coronation* mosaic immediately above it—combines the Christ-crowned
king of the Martorana with the arrangement on the west wall of the Cappella Palatina.     *Frontispiece,*
In both the royal palace chapel and the new cathedral, the royal dais was situated     *Pls. 17, 19*
beneath the enthroned Christ. With its marble lions, William's seat is an allusion to     *Col. Pl. VIII*
Solomon's throne,[144] but both the text and the imagery in the mosaic above are entirely
Davidic. The inscription identifies the ruler as 'ʀᴇx ɢᴠʟɪᴇʟᴍᴠs s[ᴇ]ᴄ[ᴠɴ]ᴅ[ᴠs]'.
Above the Saviour's crowning hand and William's bowed head come the words: 'ᴍᴀɴᴠs
ᴇɴɪᴍ ᴍᴇᴀ ᴀᴠxɪʟɪᴀʙɪᴛᴠʀ ᴇɪ', which is from Vulgate Psalm 88: 22. This phrase belongs
to a verse which, when read in its entirety, reveals not only the nature of the Norman
monarchy—its roots and tradition—but also its claim:

Of old thou didst speak in a vision to thy faithful one and say: I have set the crown upon the one
who is mighty, I have exalted one chosen from the people. I have found David, my servant; with
my holy oil I have anointed him; so that *my hand shall ever abide with him*, my arm shall also
strengthen him.[145]

The mosaic faithfully illustrates the text and is a culmination of the series of Judaean
kings represented in the arch soffit overhead. William here becomes the true heir of
David's earthly throne in Jerusalem. Furthermore, the psalm's lines openly associate the
Norman monarchy with the Davidic kingship, where the covenant with God is sealed by
anointment with the holy chrism on which the Frankish kings always based their divine
right to rule as Christ's earthly ministers. Like the Franks, the Normans saw themselves
as God's Chosen People, and their king therefore assumed the role of a new David.[146] In
the mosaic, William is crowned by the Deity while descending angels bring the orb and
sceptre. In the actual coronation ceremonial, the sceptre and the realm were consigned
to the monarch with the words:

'*Accipe virgam virtutis* . . . [followed by the key phrase] . . . *qui est clavis David et sceptrum domus Israel'*.
[Accept this rod of virtue . . . who is the key of David and the sceptre of the house of Israel.[147]]

*Pl. 91*
*Pls. 57, 69*
*Pls. 68, 103*

The last seems a paraphrase of Balaam's prophecy: 'a star shall come forth out of Jacob and a sceptre shall rise out of Israel.' As the mosaic ending the Genesis sequence states, Israel was Jacob's new name, and *Jacob* faces the *Coronation* from a medallion on the opposite wall. He appears again standing on the adjacent arch of the presbytery vestibule—just above and to the right of the king's throne—with a scroll which reiterates: '[The sceptre] shall not depart [from Judah, nor the ruler's staff from between his feet until he comes to whom it belongs . . .].'[148] Standing just below *Jacob* is *Malachi*, with the text used in ceremonials for the acclamation of kings.[149] Although the king could not see these two prophets from his throne, he could, by looking towards the western sanctuary

*Pls. 96, 98–9*

arch, see another figure of *Malachi* with the very same message. Looking east, the king would have seen the *Annunciation*, and, in the context of all these images and phrases, he would have remembered Luke's text (1: 32–3): '. . . and the Lord God will give to him the throne of his father David, and he will reign over the house of Jacob forever; and of his kingdom there will be no end.' The sacred nature of the royal mission, only suggested at Cefalù, La Martorana, and the Cappella Palatina, is declared at last at Monreale by the inscriptions and the magnificently articulated imagery.

*Col. Pl. VIII*

Materially and thematically, William's throne is associated with those in the presbytery and the three apses. The use of imperial porphyry in the dais links it to the succession of porphyry columns which frame the vision of the celestial Jerusalem in the apse. The throne itself is an earthly materialization of sacred rule represented by a hierarchical

*Pls. 66, 103,*
*62, 75, 81*

sequence of mosaic thrones: the *Hetoimasia* (prepared throne) on the presbytery vault, Christ's throne in the *Coronation*, and the thrones of Mary and the Apostles in the three apses. William II was certainly aware of Peter and Paul's invocation of the king's authority as representing God's ministry on earth; like the Apostles, the king was God's servant for the good of mankind (1 Peter 2: 13–17; Romans 13: 1–7).[150] Nevertheless, this equality at Monreale was qualified by a structural fact: the king's throne is raised above the altars of Peter and Paul, as if to establish once and for all that the monarchy's authority came directly from Christ and not through Rome.

*Pls. 104*
*Col. Pl. VIII*
*frontis-*
*piece, 105,*
*106*

This fusion of royal claims with Messianic texts and visions is mitigated by a few pictorial details. In the *Coronation* mosaic, for instance, the king's face is no longer as Christ-like as Roger II's is at La Martorana. In the *Donation* opposite, William bows before the Virgin Queen, presenting her with the gift of Monreale. Finally, as a reminder of the futility of human vanity, the king on his throne was confronted with the *Temptations of Christ*, which in his day would have been visible to him through the southern crossing-arch. The same subject faced the Venetian patriarch at St Mark's, and later, the pope in the Sistine chapel.[151]

*Pls. 106–11*

## THE CHRISTOLOGICAL SEQUENCES IN THE TRANSEPT

The Christological cycle in the crossing is resumed in both arms of the transept, where a triple tier of scenes is deployed across two walls. The east wall in either arm belongs to

*Pls. 74, 78*

the adjacent *Peter* and *Paul* vestibules; each of these 'façade' walls displays the Apostle's martyrdom in Rome.

Starting at the top of the south wall, the Christological sequence begins with the *Temptations of Christ.* The second tier of scenes are all concerned with manifestations of Christ's divinity: *Jesus with the Samaritan Woman at Jacob's Well,* the *Transfiguration,* the *Raising of Lazarus,* and the *Ass brought for Christ's Entry into Jerusalem.* The *Entry* itself comes directly afterwards on the middle tier of the west wall, followed by the *Last Supper.* All the scenes on the lowermost tier of both walls are devoted to the Passion: the *Washing of Feet, Agony in the Garden,* and *Betrayal,* followed on the western side by *Christ before Pilate* and the episode of *Pilate's Wife* (over the door to the southern aisle).

The upper tier on the west wall consists of two scenes which are out of chronological sequence. In fact, both belong to the ministry cycle, which fills both aisles on either side of the nave. These two miracles are the *Paralytic at the Probatic Pool* and the *Healing of the Blind Man at Siloam* (John 5: 2–4, and 9: 1–11). In both the Greek East and Naples, these subjects were sometimes associated with baptism,[152] and the two Monreale mosaics may therefore have alluded to the nearby Baptist's chapel then located just outside the south-western corner of the sanctuary. Another explanation may be that Christ's miracles were contrasted with the magic professed by the devil, who was illustrated on the adjacent tier of the south wall.

No such break in chronological sequence occurs in the northern arm of the transept, where the Passion continues, followed by posthumous miracles and apparitions. The sequence proceeds across both walls from the top downwards. Beginning at the south are the *Preparation of the Cross* and the *Crucifixion,* followed on the north wall by the *Deposition, Entombment,* and *Harrowing of Hell.* In the next tier come the *Noli me tangere* and the three episodes of the *Emmaus* story, ending with the return of the two disciples to rejoin the Apostles in Jerusalem. In the bottom tier are: *Doubting Thomas* (appropriately below *Noli me tangere*), the *Miraculous Draught of Fishes, Ascension,* and *Pentecost.* Mary's final appearance in this Christological cycle of the transept occurs in the *Ascension.* Its central position on the north wall with Mary's figure dominating is an abbreviated version of the Cefalù apse.

All the scenes in the lower two tiers concern acts of apostolic doubt and faith rewarded—always concluding with the return to Jerusalem. As in the Cappella Palatina, the final scenes are *Ascension* and *Pentecost*—the restoration of the heavenly kingdom of Jerusalem and the institution of the apostolic mission, which develops in the adjacent *Peter* and *Paul* areas (in the aisles at the Palatina and in the vestibules at Monreale).

Several royal tombs are situated in the transept. Those of William II and his father are in the southern arm. The porphyry tomb belongs to William I, while his son's is a late sixteenth-century substitute for an earlier one which has not been securely identified. Local legend associates the original tomb with the monumental ancient Roman sarcophagus now located in the courtyard behind the archbishop's palace.[153] In the northern arm of the transept are William II's mother (Queen Margaret of Navarre) and two brothers—Duke Roger of Apulia (d. 1161) and Duke Henry of Capua (d. 1172).[154] Not included in this royal pantheon is Roger II, the founder of the dynasty, who never left Palermo cathedral. Aside from the inclusion of such traditional funereal subjects as the *Raising of Lazarus* (possibly the *Harrowing of Hell*) and *Resurrection,* the arrangement of the

*Pl. 106*

*Pls. 107–8, 106–7*

*Pl. 107*

*Fig. 5*

*Pls. 109–11*

*Pls. 110–11*

*Pl. 3*

*Pl. 111*

*Pls. 16, 57*

*Pl. 74*

*Pls. 106, 10*

transept mosaics makes no special acknowledgement of the royal dead, beyond the fact that they lie within the realm of the topographical Jerusalem represented there. They, like the enthroned king in the crossing, awaited together the Second Coming represented nearby in the apse.

## CHRIST'S MINISTRY IN THE AISLES

*Pls. 82–5, 87–90, 112–17*

Apparently, there were no set conventions, either in the East or the West, for the choice and sequence of monumental cycles of Christ's ministry.[155] However, at Monreale an arrangement was worked out which did conform to an overall plan. For instance, the miracles included in the southern arm of the transept all took place during the Saviour's lifetime, whereas those in the northern arm are posthumous. Because ministry episodes are scattered throughout the transept as well as the aisles, it has been argued that no governing idea lay behind their distribution.[156] The scenes in the transept, however, have their own particular significance—quite apart from a ministry cycle—in the thematic context of their site. As for the continuous ministry sequence in the aisles, there, too, the arrangement was carefully calculated and co-ordinated with the entire pictorial scheme. A chronological sequence has been noted in the twenty episodes situated in the aisles flanking the nave.[157] Despite claims to the contrary, it can be shown that a geographical order was followed there as well.[158]

*Pls. 112–13*

After the Baptist's death, Christ took up his ministry in Tyre, Sidon, and Galilee. The first scene at the head of the southern aisle (abutting the transept), therefore, is that of the *Healing of the Daughter of the Canaanite Woman*. It occupies two walls: the southern face of the sanctuary pier and over the door to the transept. The event took place at Tyre or Sidon (Matthew 15: 21; Mark 7: 24–30). The next scene, the *Healing of the Possessed Man* (Matthew 9: 2, 32–33), occurred in Capernaum, leaving Galilee as the location for the

*Pl. 114*

eight remaining episodes in this aisle.[159] The last scene, the *Feeding of the Five Thousand*, goes around the corner of the adjacent wall.

*Pl. 115*

The series continues on the opposite side at the western end of the north aisle (which again spans the corner) with the *Curing of the Woman bent by the Spirit of Infirmity* (Luke 13: 11–13). The sites for this scene and its neighbour, the *Healing of the Man Sick with the Dropsy* (Luke 14: 1–6), are not specified in the Scriptures; both are Sabbath healings which aroused the wrath of the synagogue and the Pharisees. The next seven scenes are

*Pl. 88*

all connected with named places. The third episode in this aisle, the *Healing of the Ten Lepers*, is described by Luke (17: 11) as taking place on the road to Jerusalem between Samaria and Galilee. The road between Jericho and Jerusalem is the site for the *Healing of the Two Blind Men* (Matthew 20: 29–34). The next five scenes all take place in Jerusalem or its suburbs: the *Expulsion of the Money Changers*, the *Woman taken in Adultery*, the *Healing*

*Pl. 89*

*of the Paralytic*, the *Healing of the Lame and the Blind*, and the *Feast in the House of Simon*. The final episode, at the end of the aisle—on the walls which separate it from the northern

*Pls. 116–17*

arm of the transept—is the only scene which is out of chronological order. The *Healing of the Centurion's Servant* (Matthew 8: 5–13) belongs in Capernaum in the sequence which includes the *Raising of the Widow's Son at Nain* and the *Healing of Peter's Mother-in-law*—

both in the southern aisle. Why is it placed between the scenes in the northern aisle and transept which are devoted to Christ's last days in Jerusalem? It has been noted that this scene, together with the one at the head of the southern aisle, are treated as pendants both pictorially and thematically.[160] The ailing girl and the centurion's servant are each *Pls. 113, 116* reclining upon their respective beds while Jesus addresses their kin on the adjoining wall. Various explanations for the choice and location of these two scenes as a pair have been made—none of them altogether satisfactory.[161] However, the biblical text for the *Centurion's Servant* is eminently appropriate for the inclusion of this subject at just this point in the church, because it unites the themes of the Genesis cycle in the nave with those of Christ's *Pl. 57* ministry in the aisles: 'Truly ... not even in Israel have I found such faith. I tell you, many will come from east and west and sit at table with Abraham, Isaac and Jacob in the kingdom of heaven' (Matthew 8: 10–11). These very Old Testament patriarchs begin and end the sequences on the other side of the wall on which Christ and the centurion meet. Thus, the progress of the patriarchs moves in parallel with Christ's ministry; all are directed towards the heavenly kingdom, where, just as Jesus tells the centurion, they will be reunited at table, which, at Monreale, in fact, occurs in the mosaics of the apse and presbytery above the altar-table. Viewed in terms of the transept, the ministry scenes begin in one arm, run their course through the lands of Israel back to Jerusalem, and terminate with the *Crucifixion* and its aftermath in the northern arm of the transept.

The ministry cycle, together with the other sequences in the crossing and transept, comprise the largest surviving New Testament cycle on a monumental scale in either Byzantium or the Latin West.[162] All these groups of scenes, whether from the Old Testament or the New, are almost miraculously articulated into a cohesive scheme—a scheme which is united by the Pantocrator's repeated exhortation: 'Ego sum lux mundi, qui sequitur me non ambulabit in tenebris [sed habebit lucem vitae].' The phrase had been used before in domes and apses,[163] but nowhere to greater effect than at Monreale, where the vast pictorial scheme was expressed in glittering mosaic. Because of its light-reflecting qualities, mosaic is extremely susceptible to all nuances of brightness and shade, and therefore the inherent message is entirely dependent upon the revealing power of light. Within the anagogical reasoning which permeates all the Sicilian mosaics, it can indeed be said that here the medium *is* the message.[164] The situation of Christ's ministry in the relative shade of the aisles accords beautifully with the gospel passage: 'he who follows me will not walk in darkness, but will have the light of life.' Appropriately, the light brightens in the transept where Christ enters Jerusalem, sacrifices himself, and triumphs over death.

## MONREALE AS A VISIONARY JERUSALEM

Christ's public ministry in the aisles of Monreale follows a course which represents a *Pl. 57* return to Jerusalem in the transept. As Christ's appointed witness there,[165] Peter carries on the ministry to the right of the central apse and presbytery where the heavenly Jerusalem of the Second Coming, replete with the celestial court, is brought down to meet its terrestrial counterpart. The point of juncture is near the throne of the Norman king, who, in the Frankish tradition, aspired to a Davidic monarchy which assumed reality through Adelaide d'Hauteville and her son Roger II, who could claim the actual throne of Jerusalem occupied by the French of 'Outremer'. Just as in the Cappella Palatina, the choice of glittering mosaic and precious marble for the execution of these and other royal ideas was intended to create a pictorial equivalent of the visionary Jerusalem, described in the Apocalypse as a city made of 'pure gold, clear as glass' (Revelation 21: 10, 18–21).[166]

According to medieval consecration rites, churches and sanctuaries were generally understood to represent reflections of the heavenly Jerusalem, while the actual ceremonial was based on ancient Roman formulas for the founding of cities.[167] Monreale and the Cappella Palatina, therefore, were neither the first nor the last royal monuments to be created with the heavenly city in mind—but they are the most eloquent surviving examples.[168] At the Cappella Palatina several other motifs were woven into the Jerusalem theme: the commemoration of Roger II's Christmas coronation, and an exaltation of the surrogate apostolic legateship. At Monreale, the idea of the Messianic royal mission was joined to the Marian theme; this was introduced not only because Mary was the titular of the abbey cathedral, but also in her capacity as the protectress of, and intercessor in, what was intended to be a royal mausoleum. Furthermore, Mary may also have been understood here as the personification of Ecclesia.[169]

It has been noted that throughout the twelfth century there was a special interest in the symbolic significance of sacred architecture and in the use of allegorical interpretation of Christian worship.[170] This also accounts for the fascination with the metaphysics of light formulated by the pseudo-Dionysius and his French editors, whose ideas were put into practical use by the Abbot Suger of St Denis and by the Norman kings of Sicily. With this, however, went a well-informed interest in the actual monuments of the Holy Land. The Augustinians who looked after the Holy Sepulchre in Jerusalem were invited to take charge of Cefalù, just as the Cluniac Benedictines who cared for the earlier church of the Assumption at Gethsemane assumed the custody of its namesake at Monreale. The Latin kings and queens of Jerusalem had been occupied with the restoration of the original sites in the Holy Land, while the Normans in Sicily imitated them in their own dynastic burial sites at Cefalù and Monreale.

As a materialization of the heavenly Jerusalem, Monreale's interior was, in its eschatological guise, the perfect setting for the royal dead. Here at last the d'Hautevilles, the

Pl. 118

lords 'of the lofty city', had come to their royal mount—Monreale—which, like Jerusalem, stands upon a hill.[171] However, there were several ironies in the fabrication of this allegorical city; as it approached completion, the actual Jerusalem fell to the infidel on 2 October 1187. An impressive expeditionary force of sixty Norman ships with two hundred knights failed to recapture it.[172] Two years later, William II died while planning a Third Crusade,[173] and with that Norman rule in Sicily came to an end; William died without issue and civil war ensued. Eventually, the realm passed to Henry VI Hohenstaufen, who was crowned in Palermo on Christmas Day 1194. It was his heir, Roger II's grandson, Frederick II, who, in 1228, finally seized the crown of Jerusalem on the basis of the old d'Hauteville claim reinforced by that of his wife Isabelle of Brienne. The Norman kings

V. Palermo, Capella Palatina: *St John Chrysostom*, northern chapel.

VI. Palermo, Capella Palatina: soldier from *St Paul in Damascus*.

VII. Monreale cathedral: *Pantocrator*, vault of St Paul chapel.

VIII. Monreale cathedral: *Christ crowning Roger II* and royal throne.

had used their hereditary claim to Jerusalem as a means of bolstering and exalting a new monarchy. Rather than actively pursuing the claim, the Normans employed it as a propagandistic ploy in which politics and theology were intertwined; the realm was spiritualized and thereby the Norman state assumed a sacred nationality.[174] Although Frederick II had the opportunity at Monreale to unite the earthly with the allegorical Jerusalem, he was buried in porphyry at Palermo instead. His model for monarchy was Augustan rather than Davidic. The visionary Jerusalem at Monreale had been inspired by the hopes of kings whose aim, once achieved, lost its *raison d'être*. Nevertheless, the magic remains in two comprehensive pictorial schemes of near-perfect articulation which commemorate their aspirations in glittering glass.

Because of his independent spirit *vis-à-vis* the constituted authority of the papacy, Roger II has been called the first modern ruler in medieval Europe.[175] The mosaics that he and his heirs commissioned used elements from many different traditions, but they do not follow slavishly the reigning conventions of Rome and Byzantium. Otto Demus has noted that much the same is true of the mosaics of St Mark's in Venice.[176] This emancipation was rare for its time, and has a special appeal for the contemporary observer who takes freedom of choice for granted. In the case of the Sicilian kings, however, it was exercised as a deliberate policy to legitimize and fortify a new monarchy.

[1] F. Chalandon, *Histoire de la domination normande en Italie et en Sicile*, 2 vols. (Paris, 1907), ii. 176 f., 305 ff.

[2] U. Falcando, *La historia o Liber de Regno Sicilie e la Epistola ad Petrum*, ed. G. B. Siragusa (Rome, 1897), 89; Chalandon, *Histoire de la domination normande*, ii. 306; cf. Elze ('Zum Königtum Rogers II. von Sizilien', in *Festschrift Percy Ernst Schramm*, i (Wiesbaden, 1964), 114) who says that the coronation took place in the Cappella Palatina.

[3] E. Jamison, 'Alliance of England and Sicily in the Second Half of the Twelfth Century', *Journal of the Warburg and Courtauld Institutes*, 6 (1943), 22.

[4] Chalandon, *Histoire de la domination normande*, ii. 308 f.; Matthew of Ajello had already been chosen by William I to advise the queen, who, at first, turned to the French instead.

[5] Ibid. 332 ff.

[6] Ibid. 181. The name 'Ophamil' or 'of the Mill' is a corruption of the Greek version of one of Walter's titles ('ho familiarios'): L. J. A. Loewenthal, 'For the Biography of Walter Ophamil, Archbishop of Palermo', *English Historical Review*, 87 (1972), 75–82, kindly brought to my attention by Eileen Roberts. See also G. Di Stefano, *Monumenti della Sicilia normanna*, ed. W. Krönig (2nd edn., Palermo, 1979), 76.

[7] Chalandon, *Histoire de la domination normande*, ii. 348; O. Demus, *The Mosaics of Norman Sicily* (London, 1950), 94 ff.

[8] Chalandon, *Histoire de la domination normande*, ii. 310 ff., 348, 351; L. White, *Latin Monasticism in Norman Sicily* (Cambridge, Mass., 1938), 132, 144; Demus, *The Mosaics of Norman Sicily*, 95 f.

[9] White, loc. cit.; Jamison, 'Alliance of England and Sicily', 28; Demus, *The Mosaics of Norman Sicily*, 94 ff. For Matthew of Ajello's many diplomatic achievements, see H. Enzensberger, *Beiträge zum Kanzlei- und Urkundenwesen der normannischen Herrscher Unteritaliens und Siziliens* (Kallmünz Opf., 1971), 54–65.

[10] Chalandon, *Histoire de la domination normande*, ii. 351 f. n. 8, 620.

[11] White, *Latin Monasticism*, 54; Demus, *The Mosaics of Norman Sicily*, 92, 98.

[12] Demus, *The Mosaics of Norman Sicily*, 91, 98, 149 n. 3; W. Krönig, *Il duomo di Monreale e l'architettura normanna in Sicilia* (Palermo, 1965), 15.

[13] L. Trizzino, 'La basilica bizantina di S. Gregorio Agrigentino nel Tempio della Concordia', *Felix Ravenna*, 1/2 (1980), 186.

[14] Demus, *The Mosaics of Norman Sicily*, 91.

[15] Ibid. 91; White, *Latin Monasticism*, 54, 134, 145 ff.

[16] White, *Latin Monasticism*, 55.

[17] Demus, *The Mosaics of Norman Sicily*, 91, 97.

[18] White, *Latin Monasticism*, 134; Demus, *The Mosaics of Norman Sicily*, 91 f.

[19] Demus, *The Mosaics of Norman Sicily*, 97.

[20] White, *Latin Monasticism*, 134.

[21] Ibid. 59, 64, 142 f.; Jamison, 'Alliance of England and Sicily', 27; Demus, *The Mosaics of Norman Sicily*, 93, 98; Di Stefano, *Monumenti della Sicilia*, 66. This papal bull must have seemed hypocritical to the See of Palermo, because in the text Pope Lucius III claimed that Monreale's new privileges injured no one's rights, when, in fact, various properties formerly belonging to Palermo were ceded to endow the new archdiocese.

[22] Di Stefano, *Monumenti della Sicilia*, 74 f.

[23] White, *Latin Monasticism*, 54 f. These abbeys were: Lipari-Patti (dedicated to SS Bartholomew and the Saviour), St Agatha of Catania, St John of the Hermits in Palermo, and Monreale. In 1183, St Agatha's was subordinated to Monreale.

[24] Ibid. 57; Chalandon, *Histoire de la domination normande*, ii. 59 ff.

[25] White, *Latin Monasticism*, 135 ff.; Demus, *The Mosaics of Norman Sicily*, 150 n. 16, 153 n. 70. Cava was founded *c*.1025. Soon after his coronation, William I confirmed the privileges granted to it by Count Roger I, Robert Guiscard, and Roger II: Chalandon, *Histoire de la domination normande*, ii. 11 n. 1, 185 n. 1.

[26] J. Deér, *The Dynastic Porphyry Tombs of the Norman Period in Sicily* (Cambridge, Mass., 1959), 3. Although Bertaux dated the motto's inscription to the late 13th century, it has been noted that the epigraphy could, in fact, be much earlier: G. Fiengo and F. Strazzullo (eds.), *La Badia di Cava* (Cava dei Tirreni, 1985), i.

12, 134, 150 n. 67, pl. xx.3, xc. Evidently Roger II gave funds for a structure of some kind at Cava. A royal donation to Cava is recorded in 1131; Enzensberger, *Beiträge zum Kanzlei-und Urkundwesen der normannischen Herrscher*, 52.

[27] White, *Latin Monasticism*, 136; Demus, *The Mosaics of Norman Sicily*, 92 f.

[28] White, loc. cit., Demus, *The Mosaics of Norman Sicily*, 92 ff., 100.

[29] Demus, *The Mosaics of Norman Sicily*, 92 ff.

[30] White, *Latin Monasticism*, 142.

[31] Ibid. 145 ff.; Di Stefano, *Monumenti della Sicilia*, 38.

[32] White, *Latin Monasticism*, 139 f.; Demus, *The Mosaics of Norman Sicily*, 92 ff.

[33] Demus, *The Mosaics of Norman Sicily*, 98; Di Stefano, *Monumenti della Sicilia*, 76 f.

[34] Di Stefano, *Monumenti della Sicilia*, 67; cf. Demus, *The Mosaics of Norman Sicily*, 99.

[35] Although Mary's corporeal assumption was already a belief in the 6th century, Bernard of Clairvaux did not accept the notion, while Peter of Cluny encouraged the cult: H. Graef, *Mary: A History of Doctrine and Devotion* (New York, 1963), 136, 161, 236. By the 12th century, Torcello cathedral had already been dedicated to the Assumption. See also L. M. Smith, *Cluny in the Eleventh and Twelfth Centuries* (London, 1930), 297; P. Wilhelm, 'Die Marienkrönung am Westportal der Kathedrale von Senlis', Ph.D. diss. (Hamburg, 1941), 5, 9 f.; H. van Os, *Marias Demut und Verherrlichung in der sienesischen Malerei 1300–1450* (The Hague, 1969), 152, 153 n. 20; P. Verdier, *Le Couronnement de la Vierge* (Montreal and Paris, 1980), 17–79. For celebration of the Assumption in medieval Rome, see P. Jounel, *Le Culte des saints dans les basiliques du Latran et du Vatican au douzième siècle* (École française de Rome, 1977), 275 f.

[36] J. B. Chatain, in l'Abbé Broussolle (ed.), *L'Assomption de la Sainte Vierge* (Paris, 1918), i. 13 f.; White (*Latin Monasticism*, 207, 216 f.) mentions that monks from Cava may already have been in Jerusalem at St Mary of the Latins *c*.1070; H. Vincent and F. M. Abel, *Jérusalem: Recherches de topographie, d'archéologie et d'histoire* (Paris, 1922), ii. 813 f. For Cava, the Holy Land, and North Africa, see also M. Rotili, 'La miniatura nella Badia di Cava: Bilancio di uno studio', in *La miniatura italiana in età romanica e gotica: Atti del I° Congresso di storia della miniatura italiana, Cortona, 26–28 maggio 1978*, ed. G. Vailati Schoenburg Waldenburg (Florence, 1979), 161. The Augustinians were also at Gethsemane: see ch. 2 n. 18 above. For the Cluniac prior of the Virgin's church there *c*.1122, see Smith, *Cluny in the Eleventh and Twelfth Centuries*, 267 n. For the controversial history of the site of Mary's tomb, see M. Warner, *Alone of all her Sex: The Myth and Cult of the Virgin Mary* (London, 1976), 86–8.

[37] Early in the 12th century the ruins of the church were described by the Russian pilgrim Daniel in the *Palestine Pilgrims' Text Society*, iv, AD 1047–1106 (London 1895), 23 f.: 'Formerly a large church, with a wooden roof, consecrated to the Assumption of the Holy Virgin was raised above her tomb …'. See also B. Hamilton, 'Rebuilding Zion: The Holy Places of Jerusalem in the Twelfth Century', in *Renaissance and Renewal in Christian History* (Studies in Church History, 14; Oxford, 1977), 108. A later pilgrim's account associates this church with an 'abbey of Black monks', and adds that it was built on the ruins of a Byzantine structure: *Palestine Pilgrims' Text Society*, vi, AD 1220 (London, 1896), 3, 26 f. For frescos in the crypt and a mosaic near the altar, see Verdier, *Le Couronnement de la Vierge*, 89 f. The reconstruction of the church had already begun by 1112 under Arnulf, the patriarch of Jerusalem: White, *Latin Monasticism*, 207. Several royal tombs were located there: Vincent and Abel, *Jérusalem*, ii. 815.

[38] Deér, *Dynastic Porphyry Tombs*, 15 f., for the burial of Queen Margaret and other members of the royal family.

[39] The royal burial chapel adjoining Palermo cathedral was dedicated to the Magdalene. It had been donated by Roger II's first wife Elvira, and was served by two canons from the Cappella Palatina: ibid. 2; cf. Di Stefano, *Monumenti della Sicilia*, 86 f. In Mar. 1187, the archbishop of Palermo asked William II's permission to demolish the chapel to make way for the new cathedral: B. Rocco, 'Il tabulario della Cappella Palatina di Palermo e il martirologio di epoca ruggeriana', *Ho Theologos*, 14 (1977), 137; id., 'L'archivio della Cappella Palatina di Palermo', *Beni culturali ambientali: Sicilia*, 2/3–4 (1981), 183; Demus, *The Mosaics of Norman Sicily*, 191 n. 19.

[40] John of Würzburg, 'Description of the Holy Land (AD 1160–70)', in *Palestine Pilgrims' Text Society*, v (London, 1896), 51 f.

[41] M. Andaloro, G. Naselli-Flores, *et al.*, *I mosaici di Monreale: Restauri e scoperte 1965–1982* (XIII° Catalogo di opere d'arte restaurate, *Beni culturali ambientali: Sicilia* 4, Palermo, 1986), 7, 33; F. d'Angelo and G. Naselli, 'L'impiego della ceramica nei mosaici della cattedrale di Monreale', *Faenza*, 70 (1984), 178, give the figure as '8,000 metri quadri circa'.

[42] White, *Latin Monasticism*, 142; Demus, *The Mosaics of Norman Sicily*, 93, 154 n. 87 (5 Feb. 1183), citing Pope Lucius III: '… simile opus per aliquem regem factum non fuerit a diebus antiquis'; Di Stefano, *Monumenti della Sicilia*, 65 ff.

[43] Jamison, 'Alliance of England and Sicily', 27 ff.; Demus, *The Mosaics of Norman Sicily*, 148. It has been said that the mosaics were left incomplete at William II's death and a period of civil disorder followed: V. Pace, 'Pittura bizantina nell'Italia meridionale (secoli XI–XIV)', in *I bizantini in Italia* (Milan, 1982), 436, 453. E. Kitzinger (*The Art of Byzantium and the Medieval West: Selected Studies*, ed. W. E. Kleinbauer (Bloomington and London, 1976), 369) attributes the mosaics to Greeks working chiefly between *c*.1180 and 1190. In conversation, B. Brenk pointed out that the mosaics must have been finished before the arrival of Frederick II, who would have had no interest in completing them. It is frequently stated that Monreale was only consecrated in 1267, but perhaps this may have been a reconsecration following the change of its title in this year; see n. 34 above.

[44] In conversation with B. Brenk, who observed that the Benedictine monks would not have used the nave or aisles for liturgical purposes and that the lay public had no access to the area.

[45] Demus, *The Mosaics of Norman Sicily*, 100; Di Stefano, *Monumenti della Sicilia*, 66.

[46] Deér, *Dynastic Porphyry Tombs*, 1–15; see also the articles by C. Valenziano, 'La basilica cattedrale di Cefalù nel periodo normanno', *Ho Theologos*, 19 (1978), and M. and C. Valenziano, 'La Supplique des chanoines de la cathédrale de Cefalù pour la sépulture du roi Roger', *Cahiers de civilisation médiévale*, 21 (1978). For an early fifteenth-century account of the tombs, see Appendix, pp. 82 f., 84 f.

[47] T. Thieme and I. Beck, *La cattedrale normanna di Cefalù* (Analecta Romana Instituti Danici, Supplementum 8; Odense, 1977), 29 ff.

[48] Di Stefano, *Monumenti della Sicilia*, pls. iv, lxxvi; Krönig, *Il duomo di Monreale*, 146 ff.

[49] Pointed out to me by B. Brenk; Di Stefano, *Monumenti della Sicilia*, pls. vii, lxxiii, ciii.

[50] Krönig, *Il duomo di Monreale*, 39–42; L. Trizzino, 'Die Kathedrale von Monreale: Was für eine Collage!', *Daidalos*, 16 (15 June 1985), 67.

[51] E. Panofsky, *Abbot Suger on the Abbey Church of St. Denis and its Treasures*, 2nd edn. (Princeton, 1979), 91; B. Brenk, 'Sugers Spolien', *Arte medievale*, 1 (1983), 101–7.

[52] Trizzino, 'Die Kathedrale von Monreale', 74, 80 n. 9. The barrier consisted of a wall with three doors: Krönig, *Il duomo di Monreale*, 54 f.; Demus, *The Mosaics of Norman Sicily*, 106.

[53] Krönig, *Il duomo di Monreale*, 55, 255, citing G. L. Lello, *Historia della chiesa di Monreale* (Rome, 1596; reprinted Bologna, 1967), 29. For an early description, see Appendix, pp. 82–3, 84–6.

[54] K. J. Conant, *Cluny: Les Églises et la maison du chef d'ordre* (Maçon, 1968), 57, 121, pl. LXIV, fig. 123.

[55] Krönig, *Il duomo di Monreale*, 254 ff.; D. B. Gravina, *Il duomo di Monreale* (Palermo, 1859–69), 65.

[56] Demus, *The Mosaics of Norman Sicily*, 106.

[57] It was damaged by a fire in 1811 and subsequently repaired: Krönig, *Il duomo di Monreale*, 47 f.

[58] Ibid. 54 f.

[59] Ibid.; Demus, *The Mosaics of Norman Sicily*, 106. Cf. Nompar de Caumont's early 15th-century description, pp. 82, 84 below; and Lello, *Historia*, 2 f., 27, 29.

[60] Demus, *The Mosaics of Norman Sicily*, 103.

[61] G. Naselli-Flores, 'I mosaici di Monreale: Stato di conservazione e restauro (1960–1982)', typescript (Palermo, 1983), 302, 319, fig. 26; Andaloro and Naselli-Flores, *I mosaici di Monreale*, pp. 10 f., 47 ff., pls. I, III–IV, 34–6, 38–40. Messina cathedral still has some windows with such ornamental stucco screens.

[62] Krönig, *Il duomo di Monreale*, 52 citing Lello (1596); see n. 53 above.

[63] Krönig, *Il duomo di Monreale*, 44 ff.; Trizzino, 'Die Kathedrale von Monreale', 71 ff.

[64] Demus, *The Mosaics of Norman Sicily*, 107; Trizzino, 'Die Kathedrale von Monreale', 74: up to 1514 probably only the chancel was paved. Cf. de Caumont, pp. 82–5 below; and Gravina, *Il duomo di Monreale*, 21 n. 2.

[65] The inscription in the south-west corner of the crossing-pavement reads: 'ANNO DOMINI MCMXV A . QUINQUE VIRIS . TEMPLO . INSTAURANDO / DOMINICO . GASPARE . LANCEA ARCHIEP . / OPUS . MUSIVUM . EX . INTEGRO . FACTUM .' And in the north-west corner: 'IOS . MATRANGA . ET . PETR . REGINELLA . MARMOMARIIS / .'

[66] Demus, *The Mosaics of Norman Sicily*, 107, 110 f.; Trizzino, 'Die Kathedrale von Monreale', 74 ff. At one time the aisle may have been paved only with stone slabs.

[67] Demus, *The Mosaics of Norman Sicily*, 105 f.

[68] Cited by G. Bandmann, 'Kirche, Kirchenbau', *Lexikon der christlichen Ikonographie* (Rome, Freiburg, Basle, and Vienna, 1970), i, col. 523.

[69] These are very difficult to see from the ground. Starting at the eastern end of the southern aisle are: *Metrodora, Cristina, Justice, Faith, Hope, Eulalia*, and *Regina* (cf. Demus, *The Mosaics of Norman Sicily*, 120 f.). In the northern aisle, starting at the eastern end (ibid. 121), are: *Potentiana, Marina, Odilia, Charitas, Fides, Theodora*, and *Ninfodora*. Three smaller medallions occupy the soffits of each arch. Starting at the eastern end of the southern aisle are: *Alexander, Bivianus, Melitus; Cyprius, Helianus, Flavianus; Sissinius, Nicallianus, Priscus; Smaragdus, Angias, Esichius; Eunoicus, Chydius, Eraclius; Valerianus, Gaius, Hicander; Donatus, Savinianus, Satorus; Candedus, Onoratus, Fortunatianus*. Starting at the eastern end of the northern aisle are: *Theophilus, Diometianus, Euthitius; Santhius, Symmacus* (Demus gives this as *Lysimacus*), *Gorgonianus; Claudius, Iohannes, Leontius; Filocthimus, Angias, Iohannes; Acatus, Helias, Valerius; Etius, Domnus, Quirianus; Edigius, Sacerdon, Theodolus; Aurontius, Reositus, Septimianus* (ibid.). See also: Lello, *Historia*, 11 f.

[70] Demus, *The Mosaics of Norman Sicily*, 126 ff., 171 n. 471, 300. Curiously, although Lucius III's bull of 5 Feb. 1183 listed 32 feasts to be celebrated at Monreale, that of Castrensis is not among them. Cf. G. Kaftal, *Iconography of the Saints in Central and South Italian Schools of Painting* (Florence, 1965), col. 252, gives the date of the translation of his relics to Monreale as *c*.1167, about a decade before the wedding.

[71] Ch. 3 n. 127 above, and Anselm of Canterbury (d. 1109), cited by Graef, *Mary*, 212–17.

[72] Demus, *The Mosaics of Norman Sicily*, 122 f.

[73] Ibid. 170 n. 460.

[74] Ibid. 170 n. 461.

[75] Ibid. 122 f.; Krönig, *Il duomo di Monreale*, 137. Cf. Lello, *Historia*, 23

[76] Demus, *The Mosaics of Norman Sicily*, 170 n. 457. For the history of the term 'Theotokos' for Mary, see R. L. Freytag, *Die autonome Theotokosdarstellung der frühen Jahrhunderte* (Augsburg, 1985), i. 63 ff.

[77] Demus, *The Mosaics of Norman Sicily*, 170 n. 457.

[78] Ibid. 310.

[79] e.g. the *Coronation* tympanum at Senlis cathedral (*c*.1153), and the mid-12th-century [?] mosaic of S. Maria in Trastevere, Rome.

[80] Demus, *The Mosaics of Norman Sicily*, 148, 310.

[81] F. Wormald, 'The Throne of Solomon and St. Edward's Chair', *De artibus opuscula*, xl: *Essays in Honor of Erwin Panofsky* (New York, 1961), i. 532–9; I. W. Forsyth, *The Throne of Wisdom: Wood Sculptures of the Madonna in Romanesque France* (Princeton, 1972), 1 ff.; and C. J. Purtle, *The Marian Paintings of Jan van Eyck* (Princeton, 1982), 113.

[82] Demus, *The Mosaics of Norman Sicily*, 310. The Hagia Sophia mosaic has been dated in the late 8th century: N. Oikomidès, 'Some Remarks on the Apse Mosaic of St. Sophia', *Dumbarton Oaks Papers*, 39 (1985), 114 f. The same image already appears in the mid-6th-century apse mosaic at Parenzo, and in the 11th-century apse mosaic of S. Giusto in Trieste, which was originally made for another church dedicated to the Assumption: C. Rizzardi, *Mosaici altoadriatici: Il rapporto artistico Venezia Bisanzio–Ravenna in età medievale* (Ravenna, 1985), 151 ff.

[83] For the iconography of *Sapientia Dei*, see J. Meyendorff, 'L'Iconographie de la sagesse divine dans la tradition byzantine', *Cahiers archéologiques*, 10 (1959), 259–77; U. Mielke, 'Sapientia', *Lexikon der christlichen Ikonographie*, iv (Rome, Freiburg, Basle, Vienna, 1972), cols. 39–43. The concept of *Sapientia Dei* was variously associated with Mary, the Church, and the Trinity. See also Oikomidès, 'Some Remarks', 235; W. Paeseler, 'Gedanken zu Monreale und zur Monrealeser Bauplastik', in *Festschrift für Wolfgang Krönig: Aachener Kunstblätter*, 41 (1971), 49.

[84] Rupert of Deutz's (died *c*.1135) idea of Mary: Graef, *Mary*, 227; for Rupert's visit to southern Italy, see M. L. Arduini, 'Contributo alla biografia di Ruperto di Deutz', *Studi medievali*, 3rd ser., 16/2 (1975), 578 nn. 234, 235; H. de Lubac, *Esegesi medievale: I quattro sensi della scrittura*, i (Rome 1972), 391–425.

[85] *Isaiah* (Isaiah 7: 14):
ECCE VIRGO CO[N]CIPIET.
(Behold the virgin shall conceive.)

*Habakkuk* (Habakkuk 3: 2–10):
DOMINE AVDIVI AVDITU[M] TVV[M].
(O Lord I have heard the report of thee.)

*Jeremiah* (Jeremiah 17: 7):
BENEDICT[US] VIR Q[UI] CONFIDIT.
(Blessed is the man who trusts [in the Lord].)

*Amos* (Amos 9: 13):
ECCE DIES VENIVNT ET CO[M]P[RE]HEND[ET].
(Behold the days are coming when he [the ploughman] shall overtake [the reaper].)

*Obadiah* (Obadiah 1: 2):
ECCE PARVULU[M]; TE DEDI IN GE[N]TIBUS.
(Behold I will make you small among the nations.)

*Joel* (Joel 2: 12):
CONV[ER]TIMINI AD ME IN TOTO CORDE V[EST]RO.
(Return to me with all your heart.)

[86] *Jacob* (Genesis 49: 10):
NEC AVFERETVR.
([The sceptre] shall not depart [from Judah, nor the ruler's staff from between his feet, until he comes to whom it belongs . . .])

*Zechariah* (Luke 1: 79):
ILLVMINARE HIS QVI IN TEN[EBRIS].
(To give light to those who sit in darkness.)

*Malachi* (Malachi 3: 1):
ECCE EGO MITTO ANGELVM MEVM.
(Behold I send my messenger.)

*Jonah* (Jonah 4: 2):
TV DEVS CLEME[N]S ET MISERICORS ES.
(Thou art a gracious God and merciful.)

*Ezekiel* (Isaiah 6: 1):
VIDI DOMINVM SEDENTE[M] SVP[ER SOLIVM].
(I saw the Lord sitting upon a throne [high and lifted up].)

*Moses* (Deuteronomy 18: 15):
SUSCITAVIT D[OMINU]S P[RO]PH[ET]AM DE
F[RA]TRIB[US] [?].
(The Lord [your God] raised up [for you] a prophet from your brethren.)

[87] A. Diemand, *Das Ceremoniell der Kaiserkrönungen von Otto I. bis Friedrich II.* (Munich, 1894), 53; E. Kantorowicz, 'The King's Advent and the Enigmatic Panels in the Doors of Santa Sabina', *Art Bulletin*, 26 (1944), repr. in *Selected Studies* (Locust Valley, 1965), 52 ff.; Kitzinger, *I Mosaici di Monreale* (Palermo, 1960), 32, 126 nn. 29, 40.

[88] Restored at least three times. The most recent repairs inserted the dove of the Holy Spirit, which earlier writers believed belonged there: D. B. Gravina, *Il Duomo di Monreale* (Palermo, 1859–69), 96 n. 3; M. Dixitdomino, G. Naselli-Flores, and S. Cassisa, 'Fabbriceria del Duomo, Monreale: L'intervento di restauro nell'Etimasia', typescript (1979), 1 f., pls. 4–8.

[89] During repairs, a sinopia fragment for such an angel on the left side of the arch was discovered on the base plaster: Andaloro and Naselli-Flores, *I mosaici di Monreale*, 57 ff., pls. 62–3.

[90] *Nathan* (2 Samuel 12: 7):
EGO DEVS TVVS VNXI TE.
(I your God anointed you.)

*Daniel* (Daniel 10: 16):
ECCE QVASI SIMILITUDO.
(Behold [one in the] likeness [of the sons of men touched my lips].)
A reference to the Incarnation?

*Elijah* (1 Kings 18: 15):
VIVIT DOMINVS.
([As the] Lord [of hosts] lives [before whom I stand].)

*David* (Psalm 44: 3, according to the Vulgate translation of the Septuagint):
SPECIOSUS FORMA.
(Fair in form [or 'beauty'].)

*Emmanuel*:
ΙΣ ΧΣ ΕΜΜΑΝΟΥΗΛ
(J[esu]s Ch[risto]s Immanoula.)
For the theological concept of Christ Emmanuel and Matthew's use of the name, see O. Demus, *The Mosaics of San Marco in Venice*, 4 vols. (Chicago and London, 1984), i. 160.

*Solomon* (Vulgate Book of Wisdom 2: 13):
FILIV[M] DEI SE NOMINAT.
(He calls himself [the] Son of God.)

*Samuel* (Psalm 2: 11 or 1 Samuel 12: 20):
SERVITE DOMINO.
(Serve ye the Lord).

*Gideon* (Judges 6: 22):
VIDI ANGELUM DOMINI.
(I have seen the angel of the Lord.)

*Elisha* (2 Kings 7: 1):
H[A]EC DICIT DOMINVS.
(The Lord says this.)

[91] *John* (John 1: 1):
ΟΑᴦ ΙΩ Ο ΘΕΟΛΟΓΟΣ.
(St John the Theologian.)
*and on the scroll:*
ΕΝ Α[Ρ]ΧΗ
(In the beginning [was the word].)

*Matthew* (Matthew 1: 1):
Ο Αᴦ ΜΑΤ ΘΕΟΣ.
(St Matthew)
*and on the open book:*
ΒΙΒΛΟ[Σ].
(Book.)
From the opening words of Matthew's Gospel: 'The book of the genealogy of Jesus Christ, the son of David, the son of Abraham' (Matthew 1: 1).

[92] Demus, *The Mosaics of Norman Sicily*, 129.

[93] White, *Latin Monasticism*, 54 f., 116 f., 137–40, 158; Demus, *The Mosaics of Norman Sicily*, 128–31, 173 nn. 501, 502.

[94] Graef, *Mary*, 3, 46, 55; cf. Demus, *The Mosaics of Norman Sicily*, 128 f.

[95] Demus, *The Mosaics of Norman Sicily*, 129 f. William II's wife Joan was the youngest daughter of the English king Henry II, who was responsible for Becket's assassination.

[96] Information from Professor G. Naselli-Flores, who reported that the northern angel was completely reset in the 15th century. The Veronica veil looks much later.

[97] Information from Professor Naselli-Flores, who reported the discovery of the column bases during recent repair work.

[98] F. Mütherich, in *Das Mittelalter I*, ed. H. Fillitz, Propyläen Kunstgeschichte, V (Berlin, 1969), 273.

[99] White, *Latin Monasticism*, 55, 138, 144. The archbishop of Monreale was then the only monastic prelate in Sicily to be directly subject to the pope.

[100] Chalandon, *Histoire de la domination normande*, ii. 355 ff., 362, 367–84; E. Curtis, *Roger of Sicily and the Normans in Lower Italy 1016–1154* (New York and London, 1912), 433; Jamison, 'Alliance of England and Sicily', 22, 27.

[101] Chalandon, *Histoire de la domination normande*, ii. 376–9.

[102] A. Weis, 'Ein Petruszyklus des 7. Jahrhunderts im Querschiff der Vatikanischen Basilika', *Römisches Quartalschrift für christliche Altertumskunde und Kirchengeschichte*, 58 (1963), 230 ff., 243.

[103] Side chapels devoted to saints with scenes from their lives also existed in post-iconoclastic Byzantium: Demus, *The Mosaics of San Marco*, i. 246 f., 251.

[104] C. A. Mango, *Materials for the Study of the Mosaics at St. Sophia at Istanbul* (Washington, DC, 1962), 36 f., fig. 29; V. Lazarev, *Old Russian Murals and Mosaics* (London, 1966), figs. 11, 60.

[105] A. Carucci, *I mosaici salernitani nella storia e nell'arte* (Cava dei Tirreni, 1983), 111 ff., pl. XLI. For the dating of the Salerno mosaic, see F. Bologna, *La pittura italiana dalle origini* (Rome 1962), 81 ff., 254; id., *I pittori alla corte angioina di Napoli* (Rome, 1969), 23. For Apostles enthroned on *separate* thrones in Pentecost scenes, see Hosios Lukas in Greece and San Marco in Venice; Mango, *Materials for the Study of the Mosaics at St. Sophia*, 37.

[106] W. Braunfels, 'Petus Apostel, Bischof von Rom', in *Lexikon der christlichen Ikonographie*, viii (1976), cols. 164–5; R. Kahsnitz,

'*Imagines et signa*: Romanische Siegel aus Köln', in *Ornamenta Ecclesiae: Kunst und Künstler der Romanik in Köln* (Cologne, 1985), ii. 21–60, figs. D 36, D 58.

[107] P. Testini, 'Osservazioni sull'iconografia del Cristo in trono fra gli apostoli', *Rivista dell'Istituto nazionale d'archeologia e storia dell'arte*, NS, 11–12 (1963), 263; Y. Christe, *La Vision de Matthieu (Matt. XXIV–XXV): Origines et développement d'une image de la Seconde Parousie* (Paris, 1973), 68. On the roles of Peter and Paul as founders of the Roman Church, see R. Krautheimer, 'Intorno alla fondazione di San Paolo fuori le mura', *Rendiconti della Pontificia accademia romana di archaeologia*, 53–4 (1980–1, 1981–2), 215.

[108] Testini, 'Osservazioni sull'iconografia', 263, and Christe, *La Vision de Matthieu*, 89.

[109] Demus, *The Mosaics of Norman Sicily*, 118 f., 299.

[110] Ibid. 136, 299; cf. E. Kitzinger, *I mosaici di Monreale* (Palermo, 1960), 13, 36, who describes the Monreale sequence as a repetition of the mosaics in the Cappella Palatina. However, only two episodes are very alike: *Peter and John healing the Lame Man at the Temple Gate* and the *Disputation with Simon Magus before Nero*.

[111] Demus, *The Mosaics of Norman Sicily*, 261, 418 f.

[112] Ibid. 246.

[113] Graef, *Mary*, 227; E. Guldan, *Eva und Maria* (Graz and Cologne, 1966).

[114] P. A. Underwood, 'The Fountain of Life in Manuscripts of the Gospels', *Dumbarton Oaks Papers*, 5 (1950), 100 f.

[115] Demus, *The Mosaics of Norman Sicily*, 250, 252 f.; Kitzinger, *I mosaici di Monreale*, 13, 36; Demus, *The Mosaics of San Marco*, i. 41.

[115a] S. Der Nersessian, 'The Illustration of the Homilies of Gregory of Nazianzus, Paris Gr. 510', *Dumbarton Oaks Papers*, 16 (1962), 210 repr. in *Études byzantines et armenienne* (Louvain, 1973), i. 90.

[116] The inscription on the mosaic in which Jacob is renamed Israel as a kind of token for the Promised Land is a variation on the Vulgate text.

[117] Graef, *Mary*, 10; Purtle, *The Marian Paintings*, 6 f.

[118] See Rupert of Deutz cited by de Lubac, *Esegesi medievale*, i. 417 f.; S. Der Nersessian, 'Program and Iconography of the Frescoes of the Parecclesion', in *The Kariye Djami*, iv (Princeton, 1975), 334 ff. The inscription for *Jacob wrestling with the Angel* is interesting, because it departs from the Vulgate text—as in the Palatina inscription it specifies that Jacob's antagonist is not a man but an angel. The inscription is:

IACOB LVCTAVIT CU[M] ANGELO | ANGEL[US]
BENEDIC[IT] EI DICE[N]S NEQ[U]AQUA[M]
VOCAB[ER]IS IACOB S[ED] ISR[AEL] ERIT
NOM[EN] TUU[M]

[Jacob wrestled with an angel. The angel blesses him saying 'No more shall you be called Jacob but Israel shall be your name.']

This is a conflation of Genesis 32: 24, 28: 'Ecce vir luctabatur cum eo ... at ille nequaquam inquit Jacob appellabitur nomen tuum sed Israhel.' Much the same occurs with the inscription for *Jacob's Dream* based on Genesis 28: 12, 18:

VIDIT IACOB SCALA[M] SUMMITAS EIUS CELOS
TANGEBAT | EREXIT IACOB LAPIDE[M] IN
TITULU[M] FUNDE[N]S OLEU[M] DESUP[ER]

[Jacob saw a ladder; the top of it reached to heaven. Jacob set up the stone in its honour and poured oil on the top of it.]

[119] L. H. Stookey, 'The Gothic Cathedral as the Heavenly Jerusalem: Liturgical and Theological Sources', *Gesta*, 8 (1969), 35 f.; de Lubac, *Esegesi medievale*, i. 417 f.

[120] See n. 86 above. Is it a coincidence that *Jacob wrestling with*

the Angel also appears at the north-western corner of Monreale's cloister?

[121] See SS Ephraim and Ambrose discussed by G. B. Ladner, *The Idea of Reform: Its Impact on Christian Thought and Action in the Age of the Fathers* (Cambridge, Mass., 1959), 78 f., 144, 229, 291.

[122] However, the angel in the gable at the western end of the nave is a modern replacement for what was originally an Arabic window: information from L. Trizzino.

[123] Saint Augustine, *De civitate Dei*, xi. 9; cf. John 1: 9, 8: 12; M.-T. d'Alverny, 'Les Anges et les jours', *Cahiers archéologiques*, 9 (1957), 274 ff.

[124] Demus, *The Mosaics of Norman Sicily*, 247, 253; Kitzinger, *I mosaici di Monreale*, 56; R. P. Bergman, *The Salerno Ivories* (Cambridge, Mass. and London, 1980), 16 f. For another instance of angels representing light's creation, see the late 13th-century example illustrated in Rotili, 'La miniatura nella Badia di Cava', pl. XXXVII, MS 33, fo. 5′—noted by B. Rocco, 'I mosaici delle chiese normanne in Sicilia: Sguardo teologico, biblico, liturgico', *Ho Theologos*, 17 (1978), 12 f. n. 7. Augustine believed that angels belonged to the same category as the sun, moon, and stars (*Enchiridion*, 58) while SS Basil and Ambrose placed the angels' birth before the creation of the visible world and not at the moment of *Fiat lux*: d'Alverny, 'Les Anges et les jours', 277, 282.

[125] De Caumont, pp. 82, 84 below; cf. Krönig, *Il duomo di Monreale*, 54 ff., 255.

[126] Kindly pointed out to me by B. Brenk. Benedict used 'Obsculta' instead of 'Audi'. For comment on this, see B. Linderbauer, *S. Benedicti: Regula monachorum* (Deggendorf, 1922), 93 ff.

[127] A. Esmeijer, *Divina quaternitas: A Preliminary Study in the Method and Application of Visual Exegesis* (Amsterdam, 1978), 48.

[128] Demus, *The Mosaics of Norman Sicily*, 314 f., 350 f. n. 474; Kitzinger, *I mosaici di Monreale*, 16.

[129] For the location of the chapel see pp. 54, 63 and Fig. 5. The phrase in the inscription is also used in the Greek rite for the Eve of Epiphany (Mark 1: 2).

[130] For the eschatological context, see Kantorowicz, 'The King's Advent', 52 ff.; Kitzinger, 'The Mosaics of the Cappella Palatina', 282 f.

[131] Diemand, *Das Ceremoniell der Kaiserkrönungen*, 53; Kantorowicz, 'The King's Advent', 52–6; id., *Laudes regiae: A Study in Liturgical Acclamations and Medieval Ruler Worship*, 2nd edn. (Berkeley and Los Angeles, 1958), 75 ff.; Kitzinger, *I mosaici di Monreale*, 32 f., 126 n. 40.

[132] Kitzinger, *I mosaici di Monreale*, loc. cit.

[133] Demus, *The Mosaics of Norman Sicily*, 222, 234.

[134] See pp. 10, 15 n. 41 above; Kantorowicz, *Laudes regiae*, 29; id., 'Ivories and Litanies', *Journal of the Warburg and Courtauld Institutes*, 5 (1942), 74.

[135] H. Buchtal, 'A School of Miniature Painting in Norman Sicily', in *Late Classical and Medieval Studies in Honor of Albert Mathias Friend, Jr.* (Princeton, 1955), 316 (where Marcianus is referred to as bishop of Messina), 323; V. Pace, 'Untersuchungen zur sizilianischen Buchmalerei', in *Die Zeit der Staufer* (Stuttgart, 1979), v. 443, 466 n. 52.

[136] D. Ambrasi, 'Gennaro', *Biblioteca sanctorum*, vi (1965), 141.

[137] Another pair of physician saints, *Cyrus* (or *Kyros*) and *Iohannes*, are located at the western entrance to the *Peter* vestibule. These two saints are also placed together at the eastern end of the southern aisle at the Cappella Palatina, and again in the southern corner of La Martorana; their cult was connected with that of the Virgin: Demus, *The Mosaics of Norman Sicily*, 81, 89 n. 94.

[138] Around the corner from them (in positions corresponding to *Cyrus* and *Iohannes* at the other end of the transept), are *Pantaleon* and *Hermolaus*, two saints from Nicomedia.

[139] Demus, *The Mosaics of Norman Sicily*, 106; Krönig, *Il duomo di Monreale*, 55 f.

[140] See p. 57 above.

[141] Demus (*The Mosaics of Norman Sicily*, 234, 273 f.) notes that all the subjects on this wall (except for the *Herod* episodes), were celebrated in the Greek rite on the same day (6 Jan.); see also J. Lafontaine-Dosogne, 'The Cycle of the Infancy of Christ', in *The Kariye Djami*, iv (Princeton, 1975), 237.

[142] There is a similar correspondence of themes between *Pentecost* and *Baptism* in the south chapel of the Cappella Palatina.

[143] F. J. Dölger, *Antike und Christentum: Kultur- und religionsgeschichtliche Studien*, i (Münster, 1929), 62 f.

[144] Krönig, *Il duomo di Monreale*, 48; A. Grabar, 'Trônes épiscopaux du xi^ème et xii^ème siècle en Italie méridionale', *Wallraf-Richartz Jahrbuch*, 16 (1954), 44 ff.; Deér, *Dynastic Porphyry Tombs*, 116; Wormald, 'The Throne of Solomon', 532–9.

[145] The Vulgate text for Psalm 88: 20–2 reads: 'tunc locutus es in visione sanctis tuis et dixisti, posui adiutorium in potentem, exaltavi electum de plebe mea, inveni David servum meum, in oleo sancto meo linui eum *manus enim mea auxiliabitur ei*, et brachium meum confirmabit eum ...' Origen interpreted David in this passage as a figure of Christ: S. Der Nersessian, 'The Illustrations of the Homilies of Gregory of Nazianzus, Paris Gr. 510', *Dumbarton Oaks Papers*, 16 (1962), repr. in *Études byzantines et arméniennes* (Louvain, 1973), i. 84.

[146] See Kantorowicz, *Laudes regiae*, 56 f.; H. Stahl, 'Old Testament Illustration during the reign of St. Louis: The Morgan Picture Book and the New Biblical Cycles', in *Atti del XXIV Congresso Internazionale di Storia dell'Arte* (Bologna, 1982), ii. 88; J. R. Strayer, 'France: The Holy Land, the Chosen People, and the Most Christian King', in T. K. Rabb and J. E. Seigel (eds.), *Action and Conviction in Early Modern Europe: Essays in Memory of E. H. Harbison* (Princeton, 1969), 10. For David and the Byzantine Emperors, see S. S. Alexander, 'Heraclius, Byzantine Imperial Ideology, and the David Plates', *Speculum*, 52/2 (Apr. 1977), 227 ff.; A. Cameron, 'Images of Authority: Élites and Icons in Late Sixth-century Byzantium', *Past and Present*, 5/4 (Aug. 1979), 21. For an illustration of a Frankish prince crowned by the hand of God, see Paris, Bib. Nat. Cod. lat. 1141, fo. 2^v; E. Kantorowicz, 'The Carolingian King in the Bible of San Paolo fuori le mura', in *Studies in Honor of Albert Mathias Friend, Jr.*, 299, pl. xliii, fig. 3, reproduced in *Selected Studies* (Locust Valley, 1965), pl. 23.

[147] The phrase appears to be based on Isaiah 22: 21–2, which includes Jerusalem and the Judaean kings: '... and I will clothe him with your robe, and will bind your girdle on him, and will commit your authority to his hand; and he shall be a father to the inhabitants of Jerusalem and to the house of Judah. And I will place on his shoulder *the key of the house of David* ...'; see also Revelation 3: 7. The passage from the Norman coronation ceremonial (article 21) is:

*Postea sceptrum et regnum accipiat dicente sibi ordinatore*: Accipe virgam virtutis atque equitatis qua intelligas mulcere pios et terrere reprobos, errantibus viam pandere, lapsis manum porrigere, disperdasque superbos et releves humiles, et aperiat tibi hostium Iesus Christus, dominus noster, qui de se ipso ait: Ego sum hostium, per me si quis introierit, salvabitur; et ipse, *qui est clavis David et sceptrum domus Israel*, qui aperit et nemo claudit, claudit et nemo aperit. Sitque tibi auctor, qui educit vinctum de domo carceris, et umbra mortis, et in omnibus sequi merearis eum, de quo David propheta cecinit: Sedes tua, deus, in seculum seculi, virga equitatis virga regni tui. Et imitando ipsum diligas iusticiam et odio habeas iniquitatem, quia propterea unxit te deus tuus ad exemplum illius quem ante secula unxerat oleo exultacionis pre participibus suis, Iesum Christum dominum nostrum.

This is from R. Elze, 'Tre ordines per l'incoronazione di un re e di una regina del regno normanno di Sicilia', in *Atti del Congresso internazionale di studi sulla Sicilia normanna, Palermo, 4–8 dicembre 1972* (Palermo 1973–4), 443, 449 f. The author suggests that the ceremonial may have been composed for Roger II. Many phrases included in this Norman coronation ceremonial are also to be found in a 10th-century Frankish example published by H. Netzer, *L'Introduction de la Messe romaine en France sous les Carolingiens* (Paris, 1910), 273–4. During the 11th century, the French king was occasionally referred to as 'clavis David': P. E. Schramm, 'Das Alte und das Neue Testament in der Staatslehre und Staatssymbolik des Mittelalters', in *La bibbia nell'alto medioevo: Settimana di studio del Centro Italiano di studi sull'alto medioevo, 26 aprile–2 maggio 1962* 15 (Spoleto, 1963), 242.

[148] For the Latin text of the inscription, see n. 86 above.

[149] See ch. 1 p. 3 and n. 86 above.

[150] Ladner, *The Idea of Reform*, 108 f., 119.

[151] O. Demus, *The Church of San Marco in Venice: History, Architecture, Sculpture* (Washington, DC, 1960), 43, 48 ff.; id., *The Mosaics of San Marco*, i. 94 ff., 171, 266, 272: the S. Marco *Temptation* (located to the south of the central square) is late 12th century; E. D. Howe, 'A Temple Façade reconsidered: Botticelli's Temptation of Christ', in P. A. Ramsey (ed.), *Rome in the Renaissance: The City and the Myth* (Medieval and Renaissance Texts and Studies, 18; Binghamton, 1982), 209–21.

[152] P. A. Underwood, 'Some Problems in Programs and Iconography of Ministry Cycles', in *The Kariye Djami*, iv (Princeton, 1975), 258 f., 260 f., 264.

[153] V. Tusa, *I sarcofagi romani in Sicilia* (Palermo, 1957), 90 f., N. 38, figs. 92–5; M. Paoletti, 'Sicilia e Campania costiera: I sarcofagi nelle chiese cattedrali durante l'età normanna, angioina e aragonese', in *Colloquio sul reimpiego dei sarcofagi romani nel medioevo, Pisa 5–12 September 1982*, ed. B. Andreae and S. Settis (Marburg, 1984), 235. Cf. de Caumont, pp. 82, 84 f. below.

[154] White, *Latin Monasticism*, 144. For William II's tomb, see Deér, *Dynastic Porphyry Tombs*, 15, 89.

[155] Underwood, 'Some Problems in Programs', 245, 255, 302. The Apostoleion in Constantinople probably had several scenes of Christ's ministry in both the north and south transepts: Demus, *The Mosaics of San Marco*, i. 242.

[156] Underwood, 'Some Problems in Programs', 246 n. 4, 247, 253, 258; cf. Demus, *The Mosaics of Norman Sicily*, 233.

[157] Underwood, 'Some Problems in Programs', 253; Demus, *The Mosaics of San Marco*, i. 117.

[158] Cf. Underwood, 'Some Problems in Programs', 252–4, dismissing Millet's observation that the sites of the events were a determing factor in their arrangement. Also Demus (*The Mosaics of San Marco*, i. 117) perceives a geographical as well as a chronological order in the Monreale ministry cycle. In another architectural context, the sequence of the capitals in Monreale's cloister has been seen as 'sacred geography': W. Dynes, 'The Medieval Cloister as Portico of Solomon', *Gesta*, 12 (1973), 66–8.

[159] *Healing of the Leper* (Mark 1: 40; Luke 5: 12); *Healing of the Man with the Withered Hand* (Luke 6: 6; Mark 3: 3); *Walking on the Water* (John 6: 19; Mark 6: 48–59); *Raising of the Widow's Son at Nain* (Luke 7: 11); *Healing of the Woman with the Issue of Blood* (Matthew 9: 20; Mark 5: 25–34); *Healing of Jairus' Daughter* (Mark 5: 21–4, 35–43; Luke 8: 40–2, 49–56; Matthew 9: 18–19, 23–6); *Healing of Peter's Mother-in-law* (Matthew 8: 14–15; Mark 1: 28–31; Luke 4: 38–9); *Feeding of the Five Thousand* (Matthew 14: 15–21; Mark 6: 36–44; John 6: 5–13).

[160] Underwood, 'Some Problems in Programs', 253, 267 f.; H. Maguire, *Art and Eloquence in Byzantium* (Princeton, 1981), 80 ff.

[161] Their significance has been interpreted (Underwood, 'Some Problems in Programs', 253, 262 f. 267 f.) as Christ's impartial treatment of the sexes; as a contrast between resistance to Christ's

ministry and humble acceptance of it (Maguire, *Art and Eloquence*, 80 ff.); while Bernard of Clairvaux associated the centurion's humility before the Lord with Joseph's acceptance of Mary's virginity (Bernardo di Chiaravalle, *Lodi della Vergine Maria*, ed. D. Turco (Rome, 1984), Sermon II: 14, p. 81). V. Pace kindly pointed out to me that the *Centurion's Servant* has a eucharistic significance in the modern liturgy, where the text is used in the Communion rite.

[162] Demus, *The Mosaics of Norman Sicily*, 271.

[163] Ibid. 304–9.

[164] Besides Suger, see also Bernard of Cluny, cited by Stookey, 'The Gothic Cathedral', 38.

[165] Acts 1: 8.

[166] Cf. W. Braunfels, *Nimbus und Goldgrund: Wege zur Kunstgeschichte 1949–1975* (Mäander, 1979), 10, kindly brought to my attention by Dr Christina Fiore. Braunfels refers to the Byzantine understanding of gold grounds as representing Paradise, but claims there were no Western counterparts for this idea. Aside from the oft-quoted text from Revelation, see also the literature on light metaphysics by the pseudo-Dionysius and Suger.

[167] Bandmann, 'Kirche, Kirchenbau', col. 518; Stookey, 'The Gothic Cathedral', 35 ff. Cf. Maximus the Confessor's description of the church as a 'symbol of the entire Cosmos as perceived by sense alone, since it has a sanctuary like the heavens and a beautiful nave like the earth', cited by T. F. Mathews, *The Early Churches of Constantinople: Architecture and Liturgy* (University Park and London, 1971), 170.

[168] Besides Stookey and Bandmann, see, for other examples, A. Stange, *Basiliken, Kuppelkirchen, Kathedralen: Das himmlische Jerusalem in der Sicht der Jahrhunderte* (Regensburg, 1964); id., *Das frühchristliche Kirchengebäude als Bild des Himmels* (Cologne, 1950); O. von Simson, *The Gothic Cathedral* (London, 1956), 10 ff.; B. Nolan, *The Gothic Visionary Perspective* (Princeton, 1977), 51, and *passim*; K. Möseneder, '*Lapides vivi*: Über die Kreuzkapelle der Burg Karlstein', *Wiener Jahrbuch für Kunstgeschichte*, 24 (1981), 39–69; R. G. Ousterhout, 'The Church of Santo Stefano: A "Jerusalem" in Bologna', *Gesta*, 20/2 (1981), 311–21; and M. L. Gatti

Perer (ed.), *La Gerusalemme celeste* (cat. Milan, Università del Sacro Cuore, 1983), 77–134.

[169] G. Schiller, *Ikonographie der christlichen Kunst* (Gütersloh, 1971), iii. 163 f.; A. Grabar, *Christian Iconography: A Study of its Origins* (London and Henley, 1980), 76; cf. U. Nilgen, 'Maria Regina: Ein politischer Kultbildtypus?', *Römisches Jahrbuch für Kunstgeschichte*, 19 (1981), 20 ff.; W. Greisenegger, 'Ecclesia', *Lexikon der christlichen Ikonographie* i (1968), cols. 562 ff.; Graef, *Mary*, 163, 175, citing Rabanus Maurus and Bede.

[170] Von Simson, *The Gothic Cathedral*, 95. J. F. White, 'Durandus and the Interpretation of Christian Worship' in *Contemporary Reflections on the Medieval Christian Tradition: Essays in Honor of Ray C. Petry*, ed. G. H. Shriver (Durham, NC, 1974), 44 f.

[171] Monreale has been compared to the temple mount in Jerusalem by Paeseler, 'Gedanken zu Monreale', 48, and Dynes, 'The Medieval Cloister', 66 ff.

[172] B. Lavagnini, 'I Normanni di Sicilia a Cipro ed a Patmo (1186)', *Bizantino-Sicula*, ii, *Miscellanea di scritti in memoria di Giuseppe Rossi Taibbi* (Palermo, 1975), 332 n. 6.

[173] Chalandon, *Histoire de la domination normande*, ii. 416 f.; Jamison, 'Alliance of England and Sicily', 30.

[174] Cf. the Capetian monarchy: G. M. Spiegel, 'The Cult of St. Denis and Capetian Kingship', *Journal of Medieval History*, 1 (1975), 62 ff.

[175] D. C. Douglas, *The Norman Fate 1100–1154* (Berkeley, 1976), 139.

[176] Demus, *The Mosaics of San Marco*, i. 245, 259: '. . . it might be argued that the Sicilian programs are not really Byzantine in the strict sense of the term. . . . In Sicily as well as Venice the original Byzantine models of the decoration were given a new meaning . . . The course of this history [of mankind] is traced in narrative sequences that follow a linear thread of historic, not symbolic time as in Byzantium (where the scenes are part of the ever-revolving cycle of the feasts of the ecclesiastical year). Thus far San Marco and the Sicilian decorations are related to each other.'

# APPENDIX

## Nompar II de Caumont's Description of the Cappella Palatina and Monreale in 1419–1420

THIS early fifteenth-century account by a French nobleman written on his return journey from the Holy Land was brought to my attention by a generous friend, Ronald Lightbown, Keeper of Metalwork at the Victoria and Albert Museum. This very informative text, completely unknown to modern scholarship, was in fact published over a century ago in *Voyaige d'oultremer en Jhérusalem par le seigneur de Caumont l'an M CCCC XVIII. Publié pour la première fois d'après le manuscrit du Musée britannique par le marquis de La Grange* (Paris, 1858), pp. 105–6, 111–16. Because this volume is now so rare, it was decided to print the relevant passages again after consulting the original manuscript (London, British Library, MS Egerton 890, fos. 79ʳ, 83ʳ–86ʳ). The new transcription, editing, and translation are the work of Dr Leofranc Holford-Strevens of Oxford University Press and Dr Nicholas Mann of Pembroke College, Oxford. My gratitude to them both.

Nompar II, seigneur de Caumont—i.e. Caumont-sur-Garonne (Lot-et-Garonne)—(1391–1446), was a vassal of Guyenne who followed his liege-lord the King of England in the Hundred Years War and died in English exile. He set out for Jerusalem on 27 February 1419 (1418 in France, where the year was reckoned from Easter), and arrived home on 14 April 1420. Because of bad weather he spent the winter in Sicily. He was in Palermo during the last week of November, when he visited the Cappella Palatina, and after a stay at Isnello he saw Monreale on 12 February 1420.

(*Cappella Palatina*, fo. 79ʳ) ... En lequelle cipté ha une tresbelle chapelle et grande dedens le palays que l'on appelle de chappelle de santo Petro, lequelle l'enpereur Fedric fist fere au temps qu'il vivoyt, et dit l'on que c'est une des belles que on aye veues ou monde, et par dedens toute fette de art de musique de menue pierre soubredorees de fin or. Et a trois voutes par dessus et deux renx de pilliers de marbre entre lesquels en ha deux que sont de jaspe que est une pierre precieuze. Et davant le cuer de la chapelle ha une grant pierre carree encloustree¹ ou mur que est si clere que toute le chapelle en puet l'on veoir qui regarde liens et aussi clerement si puet l'en veoir come en ung myroer et nulle poynte de dague n'i puet p⟨r⟩endre car davant moy s'est assayé. En celluy mesme palays a une autre chapelle que l'on dizoit solloit estre aussi belle mes l'ont lessea [*sic*] toute decheoir ...

(*Monreale*, fo. 83ʳ) ... Et quant je fuy arrivé par della je allay tout droit vers leditte eglize et trouvay que les portes d'icelle estoient fermees; et tantost je vi venir ung moyne de ceulx de liens, que encontinent qu'il me vy me ouvry toute le porte que estoit en clef fermee et je entray dedens et allay tout droit au cuer de l'eglize ou le grant autel estoie et là que j'eu fette mon orayson je m'en alay tout autour de le eglize avizer le maniere et condicion d'icelle et coment estoie faite. Si moy sembloit estre moult belle et riche et de estrange maniere ouvree. Car premieremant elle est grande et large par dedens et tout autour de grans pierres de marbre obree à belle rengue sutilmant pousees que ont bien ung aste de lance de longueur et environ .v. palmes d'ample bien gentilles, et sont mizes de chief en amont. Et au cuer de leditte eglize a d'autres pierres belles et moult estranges et roluysans que l'on se puet dedens cleremant veoir, et les appellent porfedo et en y a de trois manieres de couleurs: l'une est vert l'autre est blanc et l'autre de viollé.

Et dedens ceste eglize dehors le dit cuer a une (83ᵛ) petite chapelle ou il a .x. piliers reons de ceste ditte pierre porfedo² toux de couleur viollé assés lonx, et du cuer en bas est leditte eglize à deux rengues de piliers de marbre toux reons bien lonx et assés gros et sont faitz moult soutilmant, et tout les coustés de haut en leditte glize de l'une part et de l'autre est toute faite part [*sic*] dedens de menue pierre come ung dé et la plus greigneur partie soubredourees de fin or et d'autres de diversses couleurs. Et cest ouvratge l'on appelle ouvre de musique et de celle est leditte eglize toute estoriee de belles ystories du fait de Nostre Seigneur et de Nostre Dame et dez sains et saintes de paradis sens autre couleur qu'il n'y a fors que celles que lesdittes pierres ont, lequel ouvratge est moult riche et soutil. Et bas au seul de leditte eglize est tout fait et ouvré de menues pierres carrees à petites piesses de pluseurs manyeres de couleurs et aussi il y a de celles pierres susdittes du porfedo reondes et de carrees que est tresbeau à veoir coment le solle de le glize est treshonestemant et richemant ouvree. Et par dessus hault elle n'est pas de voute de pierre mes autremant elle est couverte des toys de grans (84ʳ) chevirons bien gentemant ouvrés et depyns.

Et liens ha une sepulture de ung roy qui s'appelloit le roy Guilhem que ou tamps qu'il vivoit fut roy de celle ylle de Cecille et de Naples, lequelle sepulture est mot belle et riche voyant lez estranges pierres que en ycelle sont. Leditte sepulture est de une grande pierre toute entiere de celle ditte pierre que l'on appelle porfedo de coleur viollé et par dessus ceste tombe est le couvercle tout d'une autre piesse de celle mesme pierre et couleur et sont si soutilmant joyntes que eschassemant l'on le puet conoistre. Ceste sepulture se soustient hault sur terre soubre piliers de celle pierre et à l'environ ha .vj. piliers reons que aussi sont toux du avant dit porfedo viollé les quels soustienent une couverture de ung porfedo blanc que trespasse toute le sepulture gentemant fait à maniere d'une couverture de chappelle.³ Et davant ceste ditte sepulture ha une tombe de pierre ou le filz de cestuy roy est ensevellis que avoit à nom le roy Guilhem ainssi comme son pere, lequel fist fere ceste ditte eglize.⁴ Lequelle tombe n'est my si belle ne fette si richemant, ne encore quant il trespassa il n'en y voulloit point pour ly car il dizoit sellon qu'il dient que celles ondrances (84ᵛ) ne vayneglories du monde à ssa mort n'avoit il cures. Toutesfoix les moynes de liens y ont faite acelle que je dy à memoyre de ly.

Et de l'autre cousté est le sepulture du roy saint Loys qui fut roy de France ont il fu mis apres qu'il fu trespassé, dont me dizoit le moyne qui le porte de l'eglize m'avoit ouverte qu'il morut os parties de Barberie tenant assigié ung roy sarrazin davant Tonys, et là en cell lieu finit de sa maledie et puis fu pourtés son corps à ceste eglize et mis en ceste ditte sepulture. Et le roy de France qui par le tamps estoit envoya prier au roy Guilhem de Cecille qu'il ly voulsisse envoyer le corps, et qu'il luy trametoit une dez espines de Nostre Seigneur et ung chaperon de Nostre Dame, et le dit roy Guillem resseu le present et ly envoya le corps de saint Loys excepté les ventrailles que demourerent par reliquies en leditte tombe.

Et encore je demanday audit moyne coment il estoit allé du sietge quil tenoit au roy de tonys sarrazin. Il me dit que quant il fut mort sa gent demoura toute audit roy Guilleaume pere d'icelluy que fist leditte eglize, et le roy de Tonys sarrazin qui assigié estoit luy donna une somme d'or par tiel qu'il se levast du (85ʳ) sietge et s'en allast avec toute le gent. Et ainssi il le fist et se departi du sietge et par celle cause le appelloit on depuis en sà le mal Guillem e à sson fill l'on appelloit le bon Guillem parse qu'il avoye fait fere et bastir leditte eglize. Et fist porter le corps de son pere et celluy deu dit saint Loys de France qui aillors estoient sevelis en le eglize susditte lequelle en sen tamps qu'ilx morirent n'estoit mye achevee.

Et les portes de celle sont de boys mes par dessus sont toutes couvertes de metal lequel est toute ouvré et pourtrait de ymatges ystorié honnestemant.[5] Et davant le grant porte de ceste eglize a une plasse assés grande couverte de boys gentemant, et soustiennent leditte couverture .viij. piliers de marbre reons et bien haults et plain fais, et toute celle paroy davant celle entree et les coustés, tant comme tient leditte couverture, que est tout de belles tables de marbre joyntes cousté et cousté mises au lonc le chief en amont moult belles et playnes.[6] Et toute le place de bas est ouvree de belle viollete de pierre et de grandes pierres de porfedo et de marbre et est mot beau à veoir le entree de ceste ditte eglize.

Et au cousté de celle a une claustre carree lequelle ha .lxiij. pas de lonc par chascun caire. En chascun dez (85ᵛ) trois caires a ung griffon par ont gete l'eve fresche nuyt et jour et devert le porte par on l'en entre en leditte claustre n'en ha poynt mes à lautre caire devers celle part à main droite en a deux: l'une saill par ung grant griffon, l'autre par ung petit pillier reont que est de celle pierre d'un porfedo vert et l'eve saut pour le chief d'amont sans cesser.[7] Et tout autour de ceste claustre sont les piliers de deux en deux mot gentemant ouvrés, l'un pareill de marbre tout plain bien ouvré et entrelassé à chascun chief et l'autre pareill tout ouvré de ouvre de musique de celle menue pierre susditte soubredoree et les chiefs soutilmant entrelassés en diversses manieres. Et par dessus la claustre sont lez deux caires couvers de voute de pierre et lez autres deux non ains sont de boys parse qu'il ne fut acheve; et au caire de le claustre où sont les deux griffons de le fonteyne est le porte du reffreteur lequel est bell et gent lonc et large assés, et au mylieu de celluy a ung pillier de marbre fait tout en reont et par le chief de haut saut l'eve et celle que tombe chiet à sson pie et s'en vet par conduys dehors.

Si que l'eglize et tout le monestir me sembloit estre beau et puissant d'ouvratge et de notables hediffiamens, mes il ha si lonc tamps qu'il (86ʳ) fu fait quil se disenys tout et est grant perdre de laixer ainsi decheoir ung tiel ouvratge.

Enquore demanday je au moyne combien il avoit de tamps qu'il fut fait. Il me dist qu'il povoit bien avoir .cclx. ans et souloit estre au comensemant abbaye et y eut deux abbés et depuis fu fait arcevesquez c'or il est au present. Si luy dis s'il povoient savoir ni trouver par livres de celle eglize quant povoyt bien avoir cousté de fere. Il me respondi qu'il ne le trovoient par escripture mes il estoit de ssi grant afere qu'il seroit grant fait à la somer ne estimer toutes celles grans pierres dessus dittes lesquelles dizoit il estoient apourtees de Troye et de Constantinoble[8] et c'estoit grant merveile à trouver tante belle et puissante pierrerie coment il y a, ny d'estre ouvrees par le maniere et si richemant.

Et sus hault en le montaigne ha ung chasteau que l'on appelle le chasteau de Montreal et chiere par chiere de leditte sipté non guieres long a une abbaye que appellent le abbaye de Loparto[9] . . .

*     *     *

(*Cappella Palatina*) . . . In which city (Palermo) there is a very large and beautiful chapel inside the palace, called the Cappella di San Pietro, which the Emperor Frederick had built in his lifetime; it is said to be one of the most beautiful seen in the world, and on the inside consists entirely of mosaic, with tiny stones gilded in fine gold. There are three vaults overhead, and two rows of marble columns; among them are two columns of jasper (a precious stone). In front of the chapel choir a large square stone is fixed in the wall,[1] so clear that anyone looking into it can see the whole chapel in it, and one can see oneself in it as plainly as in a mirror; no dagger-point will stick in it (the experiment was made in my presence). In that same palace there is also another chapel that was said to have been just as beautiful, but it has been allowed to fall into total ruin...

(*Monreale*) ... And on my arrival there I went straight to this church and found its doors shut; I soon saw one of the monks who lived there coming, who on catching sight of me opened the whole locked door for me. I entered and went straight up to the choir of the church, where the great altar stood; after saying my prayers, I walked all round the church to view its design, nature, and construction; I thought it very rich and beautiful, and an extraordinary piece of work. First of all, it is large and wide inside, with great slabs of wrought marble on all sides, artistically placed in beautiful rows; they are a good lance-shaft long and about five spans across, very lovely, and set upright. In the choir of the church there are other stones, beautiful and very unusual and so resplendent that one can plainly see oneself within them; they are called porphyry and come in three colours, green, white, and crimson.

Inside the church, but outside the choir, there is a small chapel with ten round columns in this porphyry,[2] all crimson, and quite tall; below the choir the church has two rows of marble columns, completely round, very tall and quite thick; and wrought with great artistry. The entire upper part of the church, on both sides, is covered on the inside in tiny die-like stones, most of them gilded in fine gold and others in various colours. This device is called mosaic; it is used to adorn the entire church with beautiful narrative pictures of the life of Our Lord and Our Lady and the male and female saints of Paradise, with no other colour but that of the stones; the work is very rich and artistic. Below, the flooring of the church is entirely composed of tiny square stones, in small patches of various colours together with round and square stones in the above-mentioned porphyry; it is a very beautiful sight, the very noble and rich workmanship of the church floor. High above, there is no stone vault; instead, the church is covered with a roof of huge beams beautifully carved and painted.

Inside is the burial-place of a king, William by name, who while he lived was king of this island of Sicily and of Naples; the tomb is very beautiful and rich, in view of the uncommon stones in it. It consists of a great porphyry monolith, crimson in colour; above it, the lid consists of another monolith, also of crimson porphyry, the join being so skilful that one can hardly detect it. This tomb is supported high above the ground by columns of this same stone; it is encircled by six round columns, again all of crimson porphyry, supporting a canopy of white porphyry extending over and beyond the entire tomb, of lovely workmanship, in the style of a chapel ceiling.[3] In front of this tomb is a stone one in which is buried this king's son, also called William like his father, who had this church built.[4] It is nowhere near as beautiful, nor so richly wrought; in fact, when he died he did not want one there for himself, reportedly saying that at his death he had no thought of those worldly honours and vain glories. Nevertheless, the local monks made this tomb there in his memory.

On the other side is the tomb of St Louis, king of France, where he was laid after his death; the monk who had opened the door for me told me that he died in the lands of Barbary while besieging a Saracen king before Tunis; after he had succumbed there to his disease, his body was brought to this church and laid in this tomb. The then king of France sent a request to King William of Sicily to send him the body, handing over to him one of Our Lord's thorns and a hood of Our Lady's. King William accepted the gift and sent him St Louis's body, except for the entrails, which remained as relics in the tomb.

I further asked the monk how it had gone with his siege of the Saracen king of Tunis. He told me that after his death, his entire army passed under the command of the aforesaid King William, the father of the king who built the church; the besieged king of Tunis paid him a sum in gold to raise the siege and depart with all his army. He did so, abandoning the siege; for that reason he was ever after called William the Bad, his son being called William the Good for building the church. The latter had his father's and St Louis of France's bodies, which had been buried elsewhere, brought to the church, which had not been completed when they died.

Its doors are made of wood, but covered all over in bronze, itself all adorned with narrative figures of noble workmanship.[5] In front of the church's main door there is quite a large area with a lovely wooden canopy supported by eight smooth marble columns, round and very tall; and the entire wall in front of that entry and as much of the sides as the canopy covers are made entirely of beautiful slabs of marble joined side to side laid all along upright, very beautiful and smooth.[6] And the entire floor of this area is wrought in beautiful crimson stone and in large porphyry and marble slabs, and the entrance to this church is a very beautiful sight.

And at its side there is a square cloister, each side being 63 paces long. On each of three sides there is a griffin from which fresh water spouts night and day; on the side of the cloister door there is none, but on the other side towards the right there are two; one (fountain) spouts from a large griffin, the other from a small round green porphyry column, the water spouting upwards from the capital without interruption.[7] All round this cloister there are alternating pairs of columns, of lovely workmanship: one pair all in plain marble, finely wrought and with interlaced capitals; and the other pair entirely covered in mosaics of the gilded stones already mentioned, the capitals artistically interlaced in various ways. Two sides of the cloister are covered with stone vaults, but the other two only in wood, since it was not finished, and on the side with the two griffins is the door to the beautiful and imposing, long and wide refectory, in the middle of which there is a marble column, completely round; water spouts from its capital, and the overflow falls at its foot and runs away outside through conduits.

Thus the church and the entire monastery struck me as a beautiful and mighty piece of work and remarkable buildings, but it was put up so long ago that it is all crumbling; it is a great loss to let such a work collapse in this manner.

I further asked the monk how long ago it had been built. He told me it might well be 260 years; it used at first to be an abbey (there were two abbots there) and was later made an archbishopric, as it is at present. I then asked whether they might know, or find out from books, how much it might have cost to build. He replied that they had no written record of the amount, but it was such a major enterprise that it would be a great feat to calculate its costs, or to value all those large stones mentioned above, which he said had been brought from Troy and Constantinople;[8] it was a great wonder to find such beautiful and mighty stonework, or any wrought in that manner and so richly.

At the top of the mountain (Monte Caputo) is a castle called the Castello di Monreale and facing the city, not very far, there is an abbey called the Abbey of Loparto.[9]

---

[1] Although the author describes the inlay as square, its size and position corresponds to the large octagon set into the back of the throne dais at the western end of the nave.

[2] This is the now lost chapel dedicated to the Baptist once located just outside the south-west corner of the crossing; see p. 55 and Fig. 5 above.

[3] The tomb of William I. The canopy and columns were probably destroyed during the great fire of 1811.

[4] The tomb of William II.

[5] Bonanno's bronze doors at the nave entrance.

[6] This and what follows is an account of the portico or narthex at the western end of the church. Nothing survives of the rich marble and porphyry panelling nor of the inlaid pavement. Curiously, Caumont says nothing of the mosaics, some of which were still visible to Lello (see pp. 57, 75 n. 75 above) in the late 16th century.

[7] Evidently, there were several fountains in the cloister, only one of which survives at the south-west corner.

[8] Possibly a reference to the use of spoils in the church or to the grey marble panels used in the dado of the transept and presbytery which looks like marble from the island of Proconnesus in the Sea of Marmara (pointed out to me by Professor Brenk). For the wide use of this marble throughout the Mediterranean, see R. Gnoli, *Marmora romana* (Rome, 1971), 227 f.

[9] Can this refer to the Norman palace and chapel known as 'il Parco'? These are located on a hill facing Monreale in the town of Altofonte; G. Di Stefano, *Monumenti della Sicilia normanna*, 2nd edn. (Palermo, 1979), 97 ff.

# BIBLIOGRAPHY

ABEL, F. M.: *see* VINCENT.

ALEXANDER, JONATHAN J. G., *Norman Illumination at Mont St. Michel, 966–1100* (Oxford, 1970).

ALEXANDER, SUZANNE SPAIN, 'Heraclius, Byzantine Imperial Ideology, and the David Plates', *Speculum*, 52/2 (Apr. 1977), 217–37.

AMARI, MICHELE, *Storia dei musulmani di Sicilia*, iii (Florence, 1868).

AMBRASI, DOMENICO, 'Gennaro, *Bibliotheca Sanctorum*, VI (1965), cols. 135–51.

ANDALORO, MARIA, 'La decorazione del presbiterio prima del Scicento', in *Materiali per la conoscenza storica e il restauro di una cattedrale: Catalogo della Mostra di documenti e testimonianze figurative della basilica ruggeriana di Cefalù* (Cefalù, 1982), 96–101.

—— 'I mosaici di Cefalù dopo il restauro', *III° Colloquio internazionale sul mosaico antico: Ravenna 6–10 settembre 1980* (Ravenna, 1984), 105–16.

—— NASELLI-FLORES, GIROLAMO, *et al.*, *I mosaici di Monreale: Restauri e scoperte 1965–1982* (XIII° Catalogo di opere d'arte restaurate, *Beni culturali ambientali: Sicilia*, 4, Palermo, 1986).

ANDREAE, B. and SETTIS, S. (eds.) *Colloquio sul reimpiego dei sarcofagi romani nel medioevo, Pisa 5–12 settembre 1982* (Marburg, 1984)

ANDREESCU, IRINA, 'Torcello, I: Le Christ inconnu; II: Anastasis et Jugement dernier: Têtes vraies, têtes fausses', *Dumbarton Oaks Papers*, 26 (1972), 183–223.

—— 'Torcello, III: La Chronologie relative des mosaïques pariétales', *Dumbarton Oaks Papers*, 30 (1976), 245–341.

ANONYMOUS PILGRIM: *see Palestine Pilgrims' Text Society*.

ARDUINI, MARIA LODOVICA, 'Contributo alla biografia di Ruperto di Deutz', *Studi medievali*, 3rd ser., 16/2 (Dec. 1975), 537–82.

BALDUCCI, ANTONIO, 'Castrense', *Bibliotheca sanctorum*, iii (Rome, 1963), col. 945.

BANDMANN, G., 'Kirche, Kirchenbau', *Lexikon der christlichen Ikonographie*, ii (Rome, Freiburg, Basle, and Vienna, 1970), 514–29.

BARCLAY LLOYD, JOAN, 'The Trinity amid the Hierarchies of Angels: A Lost Fresco from S. Clemente in Rome and an Iconographic Tradition of the Angelic Choirs', *Arte cristiana*, 708 (1985), 167–80.

BECK, INGAMAJ, 'The First Mosaics of the Cappella Palatina in Palermo', *Byzantion*, 40 (1970), 119–64.

—— *see* THIEME.

BECKWITH, JOHN, *Early Christian and Byzantine Art* (Harmondsworth, 1970).

BELLAFIORE, GIUSEPPE, 'Iconografia della cattedrale di Palermo anteriore al 1781', *Bollettino d'arte*, 57 (1972), 93–112.

BERGMAN, ROBERT P., *The Salerno Ivories* (Cambridge, Mass. and London, 1980).

BERNARDO DI CHIARAVALLE, *Lodi della Vergine Maria*, ed. Domenico Turco (Rome, 1984).

BLOCH, HERBERT, 'Monte Cassino, Byzantium and the West in the Early Middle Ages', *Dumbarton Oaks Papers*, 3 (1946), 163–224.

—— 'The Schism of Anacletus II and the Glanfeuil Forgeries of Peter the Deacon of Montecassino', *Traditio*, 8 (1952), 159–264.

BLOCH, HERBERT, *Monte Cassino in the Middle Ages*, 3 vols. (Rome, 1986).

BLOCH, MARC, *The Royal Touch: Sacred Monarchy and Scrofula in England and France*, trans. J. E. Anderson (London, 1973).

BOGLINO, LUIGI, *Storia della Real Cappella di S. Pietro della reggia di Palermo* (Palermo, 1894).

BÖHMER, HEINRICH, *Kirche und Staat in England und in der Normandie im XI. und XII. Jahrhundert* (Wiesbaden, 1968; repr. of 1899 edn.).

BOLOGNA, FERDINANDO, *La pittura italiana dalle origini* (Rome, 1962).

—— *I pittori alla corte angioina di Napoli 1266–1414 e un riesame dell'arte nell'età fridericiana* (Rome, 1969).

BRAUNFELS, WOLFGANG, *Nimbus und Goldgrund: Wege zur Kunstgeschichte 1949–1975* (Mäander, 1979).

—— 'Petrus Apostel, Bischof von Rom', in *Lexikon der Christlichen Ikonographie*, viii (Rome, Freiburg, Basle, Vienna, 1976), cols. 158–74.

BRENK, BEAT, 'Los primeros mosaicos dorados del arte cristiano', *Paleta*, 38 (n.d.), 16–26.

—— *Tradition und Neuerung in der christlichen Kunst des ersten Jahrtausends: Studien zur Geschichte des Weltgerichtsbildes* (Vienna, 1966).

—— *Die frühchristlichen Mosaiken in Santa Maria Maggiore zu Rom* (Wiesbaden, 1975).

—— 'Sugers Spolien', *Arte medievale*, 1 (1983), 101–7.

BROUSSOLLE, L'ABBÉ, *L'Assomption de la Sainte Vierge*, i (Paris, 1918).

BRÜHL, CARLRICHARD, *Diplomi e cancelleria di Ruggero II* (Palermo, 1983).

BUCHTAL, HUGO, 'A School of Miniature Painting in Norman Sicily', in *Late Classical and Medieval Studies in Honor of Albert Mathias Friend, Jr.* (Princeton, 1955), 312–39.

—— 'Early Fourteenth-century Illuminations from Palermo', *Dumbarton Oaks Papers*, 20 (1966), pp. 103–18.

BULST-THIELE, MARIE LUISE, 'Die Mosaiken der "Auferstehungskirche" in Jerusalem und die Bauten der "Franken" im 12. Jahrhundert', *Frühmittelalterliche Studien*, 13 (1979), 442–71.

CALANDRA, ROBERTO, 'Le trasformazioni interne', in *Materiali per la conoscenza storica e il restauro di una cattedrale: Catalogo della Mostra di documenti e testimonianze figurative della basilica ruggeriana di Cefalù, luglio–settembre 1982* (Palermo, 1982), 128–30.

CAMERON, AVERIL, 'Images of Authority: Elites and Icons in Late Sixth-century Byzantium', *Past and Present*, 84 (Aug. 1979), 3–35.

CAPPELLI, A., *Cronologia, cronografia e calendario perpetuo dal principio dell'era cristiana ai nostri giorni* (Milan, 1930).

CARATA, GIUSEPPE, 'Cataldo', Bibliotheca sanctorum, iii (Rome, 1963) cols. 950–2.

CARUCCI, ARTURO, *I mosaici salernitani nella storia e nell'arte* (Cava dei Tirreni, 1983).

CASPAR, ERICH, *Roger II. (1101–1154) und die Gründung der Normannisch-Sicilischen Monarchie* (Innsbruck, 1904).

CASSISA, S.: *see* DIXITDOMINO.

CAVALLARI, S.: *see* TERZI.

CHALANDON, FERDINAND, *Histoire de la domination normande en Italie et en Sicile*, 2 vols. (Paris, 1907).

CHATAIN, J. B., in L'Abbé Broussolle (ed.), *L'Assomption de la Sainte Vierge*, i (Paris, 1918).

CHENU, M. D., *Nature, Man and Society in the Twelfth Century*, trans. and ed. J. Taylor and L. K. Little (Chicago and London, 1979).

CHRISTE, YVES, *Les Grands Portails romans: Études sur l'iconologie des théophanies romanes* (Geneva, 1969).

—— *La Vision de Matthieu (Matt. XXIV–XXV): Origines et développement d'une image de la Seconde Parousie* (Paris, 1973).

CHRISTERN, JÜRGEN, 'Zum Verhältnis von Palasttriklinium und Kirche', *Istanbuler Mitteilungen*, 13–14 (1963–4), 108–12.

CONANT, KENNETH JOHN, *Cluny: Les Églises et la maison du chef d'ordre* (Mâcon, 1968).

CONSTABLE, GILES, 'Renewal and Reform in Religious Life: Concepts and Realities', in R. L. Benson, G. Constable, and C. D. Lanham (eds.), *Renaissance and Renewal in the Twelfth Century* (Cambridge, Mass., 1982), 37–67.

CORRIGAN, KATHLEEN, 'The Ivory Sceptre of Leo VI: A Statement of Post-Iconoclastic Imperial Ideology', *Art Bulletin*, 60 (Sept. 1978), 407–16.

ĆURČIĆ, SLOBADAN, 'Some Palatine Aspects of the Cappella Palatina in Palermo', *Dumbarton Oaks Papers*, 41 (1987), 125–44.

CURTIS, EDMUND, *Roger of Sicily and the Normans in Lower Italy 1016–1154* (New York and London, 1912).

D'ALESSANDRO, VINCENZO, *Storiografia e politica nell'Italia normanna* (Naples, 1978).

D'ALVERNY, MARIE-THÉRÈSE, 'Les Anges et les jours', *Cahiers archéologiques*, 9 (1957), 271–300.

D'ANGELO, FRANCO, and NASELLI, GIROLAMO [*sic*: Naselli-Flores], 'L'impiego della ceramica nei mosaici della cattedrale di Monreale', *Faenza: Bollettino del Museo internazionale delle ceramiche di Faenza*, 70/3–4, (1984), 178–82.

DANIEL (Russian pilgrim), 'Pilgrimage of the Russian Abbot Daniel in the Holy Land, ca.1106–1107', in *Palestine Pilgrims' Text Society*, iv (AD 1047–1106) (London, 1895), 1–82.

DANIÉLOU, JEAN, *Bibbia e liturgia: La teologia biblica dei sacramenti e delle feste secondo i padri della chiesa* (Milan, 1965).

DE CAUMONT, Nompar II, *Voyaige d'oultremer en Jhérusalem par le seigneur de Caumont l'an M CCCC XVIII. Publié pour la première fois d'après le manuscrit du Musée britannique par le marquis de La Grange* (Paris, 1858).

DEÉR, JOSEF, *The Dynastic Porphyry Tombs of the Norman Period in Sicily* (Cambridge, Mass., 1959).

—— 'Das Grab Friedrichs II.', in J. Fleckenstein (ed.), *Probleme um Friedrich II.* (Sigmaringen, 1974), 361–83.

DEICHMANN, F. W., 'Cella trichora', in *Reallexikon für Antike und Christentum*, ii (Stuttgart, 1954), cols. 944–54.

DELOGU, R. and SCUDERI, V., *La reggia dei normanni e la Cappella Palatina*, I tesori no. 25 (Florence, Sadea–Sansoni, 1969).

DE LUBAC, HENRI, *Esegesi medievale: I quattro sensi della scrittura*, i (Rome, 1972).

DELVOYE, CHARLES, 'Empore', *Reallexikon zur byzantinischen Kunst*, ii (Stuttgart, 1967), cols. 129–44.

DEMUS, OTTO, *Die Mosaiken von San Marco in Venedig 1100–1300* (Vienna, 1935).

—— *Byzantine Mosaic Decoration* (London, 1947).

—— *The Mosaics of Norman Sicily* (London, 1950).

—— *The Church of San Marco in Venice: History, Architecture, Sculpture* (Washington, DC, 1960).

—— *Romanische Wandmalerei* (Munich, 1968).

—— *The Mosaics of San Marco in Venice*, 4 vols. (Chicago and London, 1984).

—— *see* DIEZ.

DER NERSESSIAN, SIRARPIE, 'Two Images of the Virgin in the Dumbarton Oaks Collection', *Dumbarton Oaks Papers*, 14 (1960), 71–86, repr. in *Études byzantines et arméniennes* (Louvain, 1973), i. 61–76.

DER NERSESSIAN, SIRARPIE, 'The Illustrations of the Homilies of Gregory of Nazianzus, Paris Gr. 510', *Dumbarton Oaks Papers*, 16 (1962), 197–228, repr. in *Études byzantines et arméniennes* (Louvain, 1973), i. 77–107.

——'Program and Iconography of the Frescoes of the Parecclesion', in *The Kariye Djami*, iv (Princeton, 1975), 305–49.

DIEMAND, ANTON, *Das Ceremoniell der Kaiserkrönungen von Otto I. bis Friedrich II.* (Munich, 1894).

DIEZ, ERNST, and DEMUS, OTTO, *Byzantine Mosaics in Greece: Daphni and Hosios Lucas* (Cambridge, Mass., 1931).

DI MARZO, GIOCCHINO, *Delle belle arti in Sicilia*, i (Palermo, 1858).

DIONIGI L'AREOPAGITA, *Tutte le opere*, ed. and trans. Piero Scazzoso and Enzo Bellini (Milan, 1981).

DI STEFANO, GUIDO, *Monumenti della Sicilia normanna*, ed. W. Krönig (2nd edn., Palermo, 1979).

DIXITDOMINO, M., NASELLI-FLORES, G., and CASSISA, S., 'Fabbriceria del duomo di Monreale: L'intervento di restauro nell'Etimasia', typescript (1979).

DÖLGER, FRANZ JOSEPH, *Antike und Christentum: Kultur und Religionsgeschichtliche Studien*, i (Münster, 1929); v (Münster, 1936); vi (Münster, 1950).

D'ONOFRIO, MARIO, and PACE, VALENTINO, *Italia romanica: La Campania* (Milan, 1981).

DOUGLAS, DAVID C., *The Norman Fate 1100–1154* (Berkeley and Los Angeles, 1976).

DVORNIK, FRANCIS, *The Idea of Apostolicity in Byzantium and the Legend of the Apostle Andrew* (Cambridge, Mass., 1958).

——*Early Christian and Byzantine Political Philosophy: Origins and Background*, 2 vols. (Washington, DC, 1966).

DYGGVE, EJNAR, 'Le Type architectural de la *Cāmera Santa* d'Oviedo et l'architecture asturienne', *Cahiers archéologiques*, 6 (1952), 125–33.

DYNES, WAYNE, 'The Medieval Cloister as Portico of Solomon', *Gesta*, 12 (1973), 61–9.

ELEEN, LUBA, 'Acts Illustrations in Italy and Byzantium', *Dumbarton Oaks Papers*, 31 (1977), 255–78.

ELZE, REINHARD, 'Zum Königtum Rogers II. von Sizilien', *Festschrift Percy Ernst Schramm*, i (Wiesbaden, 1964), 102–16.

——'Tre ordines per l'incoronazione di un re e di una regina del regno normanno di Sicilia', in *Atti del Congresso internazionale di studi sulla Sicilia normanna, Palermo, 4–8 dicembre 1972* (Palermo, 1973–4), 438–59.

——'Ruggero II e i papi del suo tempo', in *Società, potere e popolo nell'età di Ruggero II* (Atti delle terze giornate normanno-sveve, Bari, 23–5 May 1977; Bari, 1979), 27–39.

ENZENSBERGER, HORST, *Beiträge zum Kanzlei- und Urkundwesen der normannischen Herrscher Unteritaliens und Siziliens* (Kallmünz, Opf., 1971).

——'Basileus', *Lexikon des Mittelalters*, i (Munich and Zurich, 1980), cols. 1523 f.

ESCH, ARNOLD, 'Spolien: Zur Wiederverwendung antiker Baustücke und Skulpturen im mittelalterlichen Italien', *Archiv für Kulturgeschichte*, 51 (1969), 1–64.

ESMEIJER, ANNA C., Divina quaternitas: *A Preliminary Study in the Method and Application of Visual Exegesis* (Amsterdam, 1978).

EVANS, JOAN, *Monastic Life at Cluny 910–1157* (Oxford, 1931).

FAEDO, LUCIA, review of G. Occhiato, 'La SS. Trinità di Mileto e l'architettura normanna meridionale', in *Prospettiva*, 19 (1979), 69–71.

——'La sepoltura di Ruggero, Conte di Calabria', *Aparchai: Nuove ricerche e studi sulla Magna Grecia e la Sicilia antica in onore di Paolo Enrico Arias* (Pisa, 1982), ii. 691–706.

FALCANDO, UGO, *Storia di Ugone Falcando*, ed. G. del Re, *Cronisti e scrittori sincroni napoletani dalla fondazione della monarchia fino alla venuta di Carlo I Borbone* (Naples, 1845).

——*La* historia *o* Liber de Regno Sicilie *e la* Epistola ad Petrum Panormitane Ecclesie Thessaurarium, ed. G. B. Siragusa (Rome, 1897).

FAZELLO, T., *De rebus siculis decadi secundae* (Catania, 1751).

FERRANTE, NICOLA, *Santi italo-greci in Calabria* (Reggio Calabria, 1981).

*Festal Menaion*, trans. Mother Mary and Kallistos Ware (London and Boston, 1984).

FICHTENAU, HEINRICH, 'Byzanz und die Pfalz zu Aachen', *Mitteilungen des Instituts für österreichische Geschichtsforschung*, 59 (1951), 1–54.

FIENGO, GIUSEPPE, and STRAZZULLO, FRANCO, *La Badia di Cava*, i (Cava dei Tirreni, 1985).

FINK, HAROLD S., 'The Foundation of the Latin States, 1099–1118', in K. M. Setton and M. W. Baldwin (eds.), *A History of the Crusades: The First Hundred Years* (Madison, Milwaukee, and London, 1969), i. 368–409.

FORSYTH, GEORGE H., and WEITZMANN, KURT, *The Monastery of St. Catherine at Mt. Sinai: The Church and Fortress of Justinian*, ii (Ann Arbor, 1973).

FORSYTH, ILENE H., *The Throne of Wisdom: Wood Sculptures of the Madonna in Romanesque France* (Princeton, 1972).

FRAZER, M. E., 'Church Doors and the Gates of Paradise: Byzantine Bronze Doors in Italy', *Dumbarton Oaks Papers*, 27 (1973), 147–62.

FREYTAG, RICHARD LUKAS, *Die autonome Theotokosdarstellung der frühen Jahrhunderte*, 2 vols. (Augsburg, 1985).

FRIEND, A. M., 'Carolingian Art in the Abbey of St. Denis', *Art Studies*, 1 (1923), 67–75.

FRUGONI, CHIARA SETTIS, 'Il mosaico di Otranto: Modelli culturali e scelte iconografiche', *Bullettino dell'Istituto storico italiano per il medio evo e archivio Muratoriano*, 82 (1970), 243–70.

——'*Historia Alexandri elevati per griphos ad aerem*: Origine, iconografia e fortuna di una tema', *Istituto storico per il medio evo: Studi storici*, 80–2 (Rome, 1973).

FUIANO, MICHELE, 'La fondazione del *Regnum Siciliae* nella versione di Alessandro di Telese', *Papers of the British School at Rome*, 24 (1956), 65–77.

GAGE, JOHN, 'Gothic Glass: Two Aspects of a Dionysian Esthetic', *Art History*, 51 (1982), 36–58.

GANDOLFO, FRANCESCO, 'Scultori e lapicidi nell'architettura normanno-sveva della chiesa e del chiostro', in *Materiali per la conoscenza storica e il restauro di una cattedrale: Catalogo della Mostra di documenti e testimonianze figurative della basilica ruggeriana di Cefalù* (Palermo, 1982), 73–89.

GATTI PERER, M. L. (ed.), *La Gerusalemme celeste* (cat., Milan, Università del Sacro Cuore, 20 maggio–5 giugno 1983).

GEANAKOPLOS, DENO J., *Byzantine East and Latin West: Two Worlds of Christendom in Middle Ages and Renaissance* (New York, 1966).

GELFER-JØRGENSEN, MIRJAM, *Medieval Islamic Symbolism and the Paintings in the Cefalù Cathedral* (Leiden, 1986).

GIGANTE, MARCELLO, 'La civiltà letteraria', in *I bizantini in Italia* (Milan, 1982), 615–51.

GNOLI, RANIERO, *Marmora romana* (Rome, 1971).

GODEFROY, T., and D., *Le Cérémonial françois* (Paris, 1649), i.

GOUSSET, MARIE-THÉRÈSE, 'Un aspect du symbolisme des encensoirs romans: La Jérusalem céleste', *Cahiers archéologiques*, 30 (1982), 81–106.

GRABAR, ANDRÉ, *L'Empereur dans l'art byzantin* (Paris, 1936).

GRABAR, ANDRÉ, 'Trônes épiscopaux du XI^ème et XII^ème siècle en Italie méridionale', *Wallraf–Richartz Jahrbuch*, 16 (1954), 7–52.

——*Christian Iconography: A Study of its Origins* (Princeton, 1968).

GRAEF, HILDA, *Mary: A History of Doctrine and Devotion*, i (New York, 1963).

GRAMIT, DAVID, 'I dipinti musicali della Cappella Palatina di Palermo', *Schede medievali*, 10 (1986), 5–55.

GRAVINA, DOMENICO B., *Il duomo di Monreale* (Palermo, 1859–69).

GREISENEGGER, W., 'Ecclesia', *Lexikon der christlichen Ikonographie*, i (Rome, Freiburg, Basle, and Vienna, 1968), cols. 562–9.

GRISAR, H., *Analecta romana*, i (Rome, 1899).

——*Das Missale im Lichte römischer Stadtgeschichte* (Freiburg, 1925).

GULDAN, ERNST, *Eva und Maria* (Graz and Cologne, 1966).

GUTBERLET, HELENA, *Die Himmelfahrt Christi in der bildenden Kunst von den Anfängen bis ins hohe Mittelalter*, 2nd edn. (Strassburg, 1935).

HAMILTON, BERNARD, 'Rebuilding Zion: The Holy Places of Jerusalem in the Twelfth Century', in *Renaissance and Renewal in Christian History* (Studies in Church History, 14; Oxford, 1977).

HAMILTON, R. W., *The Church of the Nativity, Bethlehem: A Guide* (Jerusalem, 1968).

HEISENBERG, AUGUST, *Grabeskirche und Apostelkirche: Zwei Basiliken Konstantins, Untersuchungen zur Kunst und Literatur des ausgehenden Altertums*, 2 vols. (Leipzig, 1908).

HERKLOTZ, INGO, '*Sepulcra*' e '*Monumenta*' del medioevo: studi sull' arte sepolcrale in Italia (Rome, 1985).

HEUSER, MARY L., review of B. Brenk, 'Die frühchristlichen Mosaiken in S. Maria Maggiore zu Rom', in *Art Bulletin*, 61 (1979), 473–7.

HILEY, DAVID, 'The Norman Chant Traditions: Normandy, Britain, Sicily', *Proceedings of the Royal Musical Association*, 107 (1980–1), 1–33.

HOLLOWAY, H., *A Study of the Byzantine Liturgy* (London, n.d.).

HOPPER, VINCENT FOSTER, *Medieval Number Symbolism* (New York, 1938).

HOWE, EUNICE D., 'A Temple Façade reconsidered: Botticelli's Temptation of Christ', in P. A. Ramsey (ed.), *Rome in the Renaissance: The City and the Myth* (Medieval and Renaissance Texts and Studies, 18; Binghamton, 1982), 209–21.

IHM, CHRISTA, *Die Programme der christlichen Apsismalerei vom vierten Jahrhundert bis zur Mitte des achten Jahrhunderts* (Wiesbaden, 1960).

JAMES, E. O., *Christian Myth and Ritual* (London, 1933).

JAMISON, EVELYN, *The Sicilian Norman Kingdom in the Mind of Anglo-Norman Contemporaries* (Annual Italian Lecture of the British Academy; London, 1938).

——'Alliance of England and Sicily in the Second Half of the Twelfth Century', *Journal of the Warburg and Courtauld Institutes*, 6 (1943), 20–32.

——*Admiral Eugenius of Sicily: His Life and Work* (London, 1957).

JANIN, RAYMOND, 'Parasceve Vergine', *Bibliotheca sanctorum* (Rome, 1968), x, cols. 327–32.

JENKINS, R.J.H., and MANGO, C.A., 'The Date and Significance of the Tenth Homily of Photius', *Dumbarton Oaks Papers*, 9–10 (1956), 125–40.

JOHN OF WÜRZBURG, 'Description of the Holy Land (AD 1160–1170)', *Palestine Pilgrims' Text Society*, v (London, 1896).

JOHNSON, MARK J., 'The Royal View at Cefalù: A Note on the Choice of Subjects and their Arrangement in the Mosaics of Norman Sicily', Abstract from the Ninth Byzantine Studies Conference, 4–6 Nov. 1983, held at Duke University, North Carolina, 112–13.

JONES, CHARLES W., *San Nicola: Biografia di una leggenda* (Bari, 1983).

JOUNEL, PIERRE, *Le Culte des saints dans les basiliques du Latran et du Vatican au douzième siècle* (École française de Rome, 1977).

JUNGMANN, J. A., *Missarum sollemnia*, 4th edn. (Vienna, 1958).

KAFTAL, GEORGE, *Iconography of the Saints in Central and South Italian Schools of Painting* (Florence, 1965).

KAHSNITZ, RAINER, '*Imagines et signa*: Romanische Siegel aus Köln', in Ornamenta Ecclesiae: *Kunst und Künstler der Romanik in Köln* (Cologne, 1985), ii. 21–60.

KANTOROWICZ, ERNST, 'Ivories and Litanies', *Journal of the Warburg and Courtauld Institutes*, 5 (1942), 56–81.

—— 'The King's Advent and the Enigmatic Panels in the Doors of Santa Sabina', *Art Bulletin*, 26 (1944), 207–31, repr. in *Selected Studies* (Locust Valley, 1965), 37–75.

—— 'The Carolingian King in the Bible of San Paolo fuori le mura', in *Late Classical and Medieval Studies in Honor of Albert Mathias Friend*, ed. K. Weitzmann *et al.* (Princeton, 1955), 287–300, repr. in Selected Studies (Locust Valley, 1965), 82–94.

—— Laudes regiae: *A Study in Liturgical Acclamations and Medieval Ruler Worship*, 2nd edn. (Berkeley and Los Angeles, 1958).

—— '*Puer exoriens*: On the Hypapante in the Mosaics of S. Maria Maggiore', *Beiträge zur Geschichte des alten Mönchtums und des Benediktiner Ordens*, Supplementband 2 (Münster, 1963), 118–35, repr. in *Selected Studies* (Locust Valley, 1965), 25–36.

—— *Selected Studies* (Locust Valley, 1965).

KARPP, HEINRICH, *Die frühchristlichen und mittelalterlichen Mosaiken in Santa Maria Maggiore zu Rom* (Baden-Baden, 1966).

KATZENELLENBOGEN, ADOLF, *Allegories of the Virtues and Vices in Medieval Art from Early Christian Times to the Thirteenth Century* (London, 1939).

KAUFFMANN, C. M., 'JAKOB', in *Lexikon der christlichen Ikonographie*, ii (Rome, Freiburg, Basle, Vienna), cols. 370–83.

KEHR, KARL ANDREAS, *Die Urkunden der Normannisch-Sicilischen Könige* (Innsbruck, 1902).

KEHR, P., 'Die Belehnungen der süditalienischen Normannenfürsten durch die Päpste (1059–1192)', *Abhandlungen der preussischen Akademie der Wissenschaften*, Phil.-hist. Klasse (1934), 3–52.

KENAAN-KEDAR, NURITH, 'Symbolic Meaning in Crusader Architecture: The Twelfth-century Dome of the Holy Sepulchre Church in Jerusalem', *Cahiers archéologiques*, 34 (1986), 109–17.

KIDSON, PETER, 'Panofsky, Suger and St. Denis', *Journal of the Warburg and Courtauld Institutes*, 50 (1987) 1–17.

KIRSCHBAUM, ENGELBERT, 'Der Prophet Balaam und die Anbetung der Weisen', *Römische Quartalschrift für christliche Altertumskunde und Kirchengeschichte*, 49 (1954), 129–71.

KITZINGER, ERNST, 'The Mosaics of the Cappella Palatina in Palermo: An Essay on the Choice and Arrangement of the Subjects', *Art Bulletin*, 31 (1949), 269–92.

—— 'On the Portrait of Roger II in the Martorana in Palermo', *Proporzioni*, 2 (1950), 30–40.

—— review of O. Demus, *The Mosaics of Norman Sicily*, in *Speculum*, 28/1 (1953), 143–50.

—— 'The Cult of Images in the Age before Iconoclasm', *Dumbarton Oaks Papers*, 8 (1954), 83–150.

—— *I Mosaici di Monreale* (Palermo, 1960).

—— 'The First Mosaic Decoration of Salerno Cathedral', *Jahrbuch der österreichischen Byzantinistik*, 21 (1972), 149–62.

KITZINGER, ERNST, 'The Date of Philagathos' Homily for the Feast of Sts. Peter and Paul', in *Byzantino-Sicula*, ii: *Miscellanea di scritti in memoria di G. Rossi Taibbi* (Palermo, 1975), 301–6.

—— *The Art of Byzantium and the Medieval West: Selected Studies*, ed. W. E. Kleinbauer (Bloomington and London, 1976).

—— 'Art in Norman Sicily: Report on the Dumbarton Oaks Symposium of 1981', *Dumbarton Oaks Papers*, 37 (1983), 167–70.

—— 'Two Mosaic Ateliers in Palermo in the 1140's', in *Artistes, artisans, et production artistique au Moyen Âge (Colloque international, Université de Rennes, 2–6 mai 1983)*, i (Paris, 1986), 277–94.

KLAPISCH-ZUBER, CHRISTIANE, *Les Maîtres du marbre: Carrare, 1300–1600* (Paris, 1969).

KLEINBAUER, W. EUGENE, 'Charlemagne's Palace Chapel at Aachen and it Copies', *Gesta*, 4 (1965), 2–11.

—— 'The Orants in the Mosaic Decoration of the Rotunda at Thessaloniki: Martyr Saints or Donors?', *Cahiers archéologiques*, 30 (1982), 25–45.

KOLLWITZ, J., review of A. Stange, *Das frühchristliche Kirchengebäude als Bild des Himmels*, in *Byzantinische Zeitschrift*, 47 (1954), 169–71.

KÖTTING, BERNHARD, Peregrinatio religiosa: *Wallfahrten in der Antike und das Pilgerwesen in der alten Kirche* (Regensburg and Münster, 1950).

KRAUTHEIMER, RICHARD, 'Again Saints Sergius and Bacchus at Constantinople', *Jahrbuch der österreichischen Byzantinistik*, 23 (1974), 251–3.

—— 'Intorno alla fondazione di San Paolo fuori le mura', *Rendiconti della Pontificia accademia romana di archeologia*, 53–4 (1980–1, 1981–2), 207–20.

—— *Architettura paleocristiana e bizantina* (Turin, 1986).

KRÖNIG, WOLFGANG, 'Considerazioni sulla Cappella Palatina di Palermo', in *Atti del Convegno internazionale di studi ruggeriani, 21–25 aprile 1954* (Palermo, 1955), i. 247–68.

—— 'Zur Transfiguration der Cappella Palatina in Palermo', *Zeitschrift für Kunstgeschichte*, 19 (1956), 162–79.

—— *Cefalù: der sizilische normannendom* (Kassel, 1963).

—— *Il Duomo di Monreale e l'architettura normanna in Sicilia* (Palermo, 1965).

—— 'Vecchie e nuove prospettive sull'arte della Sicilia normanna', in *Atti del congresso internazionale di studi sulla Sicilia normanna, Palermo, 4–8 dicembre 1972* (Palermo, 1973–4), 132–45.

—— 'Il Duomo di Cefalù: Osservazioni sulla storia della sua costruzione', *Atti della 'Tavola rotonda sul duomo di Cefalù': Cefalù 30–31 agosto 1977* (Cefalù, 1979), 57–71.

KUCHAREK, CASIMIR, *The Byzantine–Slav Liturgy of St. John Chrysostom: Its Origin and Evolution* (Allendale, NJ, 1971).

LADNER, GERHART B., *The Idea of Reform: Its Impact on Christian Thought and Action in the Age of the Fathers* (Cambridge, Mass., 1959).

LAFONTAINE-DOSOGNE, JACQUELINE, 'The Cycle of the Infancy of Christ', in *The Kariye Djami*, iv (Princeton, 1975), 195–241.

LA LUMIA, ISIDORO, *Storie siciliane*, i (Palermo, 1881).

LA MONTE, JOHN, *Feudal Monarchy in the Latin Kingdom of Jerusalem 1100 to 1291* (Cambridge, Mass., 1932).

LAVAGNINI, B., 'I normanni di Sicilia a Cipro e a Patmo (1186)', *Byzantino-Sicula*, ii: *Miscellanea di scritti in memoria di Giuseppe Rossi Taibbi* (Palermo, 1975), 321–34.

LAVIN, IRVING, 'The House of the Lord: Aspects of the Role of Palace Triclinia in the Architecture of Late Antiquity and the Early Middle Ages', *Art Bulletin*, 44 (1962), 1–27.

LAZAREFF, VICTOR, 'The Mosaics of Cefalù', *Art Bulletin*, 17 (1935), 184–232.

Lazarev, Victor, *Old Russian Murals and Mosaics* (London, 1966).

—— *Storia della pittura bizantina* (Turin, 1967).

Lecoy de la Marche, A., *Œuvres complètes de Suger* (Paris, 1867).

Lello, Giovanni Luigi, *Historia della chiesa di Monreale* (Rome, 1596; repr. Bologna, 1967).

Linderbauer, Benno, *S. Benedicti: Regula monachorum* (Deggendorf, 1922).

Lipinski, Angelo, 'Le insegne regali dei sovrani di Sicilia e la scuola orafa Palermitana', in *Atti del Congresso internazionale di studi sulla Sicilia normanna, Palermo, 4–8 dicembre 1972* (Palermo, 1973–4), 162–94.

Loewenthal, L. J. A., 'For the Biography of Walter Ophamil, Archbishop of Palermo', *English Historical Review*, 87 (1972), 75–82.

Longo, Augusta Acconcia, 'Gli epitaffi Giambici per Giorgio di Antiochia per la madre e per la moglie', *Quellen und Forschungen aus italienischen Archiven und Bibliotheken*, 61 (1981), 25–59.

Loomis, Laura Hibbard, 'The Holy Relics of Charlemagne and King Athelstan: The Lances of Longinus and St Mauricius', *Speculum*, 25 (1950), 437–56.

—— 'The Oriflamme of France and the War-cry "Monjoie" in the Twelfth Century', in *Studies in Art and Literature for Belle da Costa Greene* (Princeton, 1954), 67–82.

L'Orange, H. P., *Studies on the Iconography of Cosmic Kingship in the Ancient World* (Oslo, 1953; repr. New Rochelle, 1982).

Maccarone, Michele, 'Il pellegrinaggio a San Pietro e il giubileo del 1300', *Rivista di storia della chiesa in Italia*, 34/2 (July–Dec. 1980), 363–429.

MacCormack, Sabine G., *Art and Ceremony in Late Antiquity* (Berkeley, 1981).

—— 'Christ and Empire, Time and Ceremonial in Sixth Century Byzantium and Beyond', *Byzantion*, 52 (1982), 287–309.

Maguire, Henry, *Art and Eloquence in Byzantium* (Princeton, 1981).

Mâle, Emile, *L'Art religieux du xiie siècle en France*, 2nd edn. (Paris, 1924).

Mango, Cyril A., *The Homilies of Photius, Patriarch of Constantinople* (Cambridge, Mass., 1958).

—— *The Brazen House: A Study of the Vestibule of the Imperial Palace of Constantinople* (Arkaeologisk-kunsthistoriske Meddeleser det kongelige Danske Videnskabernes Selskab, 4/4; Copenhagen, 1959).

—— *Materials for the Study of the Mosaics at St. Sophia at Istanbul* (Washington, DC, 1962).

—— 'The Church of Saints Sergius and Bacchus at Constantinople and the Alleged Tradition of Octagonal Palatine Churches', *Jahrbuch der österreichischen Byzantinistik*, 21 (1972), 189–93.

—— *see* Jenkins.

Manselli, Raoul, 'Anacleto II, papa', *Dizionario biografico degli Italiani*, iii (1961), 17–19.

Marongiu, Antonio, 'Concezione della sovranità di Ruggerio II', in *Atti del Convegno internazionale di studi ruggeriani, 21–25 aprile 1954* (Palermo, 1955), i. 213–33.

Mathews, Thomas F., *The Early Churches of Constantinople: Architecture and Liturgy* (University Park and London, 1971).

Matthiae, Guglielmo, *Mosaici medioevali delle chiese di Roma*, 2 vols. (Rome, 1967).

May, H. G., and Metzger, B. M., *The New Oxford Annotated Bible: The Holy Bible*, 2nd edn. (New York and Oxford, 1971).

Mayer, Hans Eberhard, 'Das Pontifikale von Tyrus und die Krönung der lateinischen Könige von Jerusalem', *Dumbarton Oaks Papers*, 21 (1967), 141–232.

Ménager, Léon Robert, 'L'institution monarchique dans les États normands d'Italie: Contribution à l'étude du pouvoir royal dans les principautés occidentales, aux xie–xiie siècles', *Cahiers de civilisation médiévale*, 2/2, 4 (1959), 303–31, 445–68.

MERCENIER, E., and PARIS, FRANÇOIS, *La Prière des églises de rite byzantin*, ii (Amary sur Meuse, 1939).

METZGER, B. W.: *see* MAY.

MEYENDORFF, JEAN, 'L'Iconographie de la sagesse divine dans la tradition byzantine', *Cahiers archéologiques*, 10 (1959), 259–77.

MIELKE, U., 'Sapientia', *Lexikon der christlichen Ikonographie*, iv (Rome, Freiburg, Basle, and Vienna, 1972), cols. 39–43.

*La miniatura italiana in età romanica e gotica: Atti del I° Congresso di storia della miniatura italiana, Cortona, 26–28 maggio 1978*, ed. G. Vailati Schoenburg Waldenburg (Florence, 1979).

MÖSENEDER, KARL, '*Lapides vivi*: Über die Kreuzkapelle der Burg Karlstein', *Wiener Jahrbuch für Kunstgeschichte*, 24 (1981), 39–69.

MÜTHERICH, FLORENTINE, in *Das Mittelalter I*, ed. H. Fillitz, Propyläen Kunstgeschichte V (Berlin, 1969), 273.

NASELLI-FLORES, GIROLAMO, 'I mosaici di Monreale: Stato di conservazione e restauro (1960–1982)', typescript (Palermo, 1983), 295–321.

—— *see* ANDALORO.

—— *see* D'ANGELO.

—— *see* DIXITDOMINO.

NERSESSIAN, NORA N., 'The Cappella Palatina of Roger II: The Relationship of its Imagery to its Political Function', Ph.D. diss. (University of California at Los Angeles, 1981).

NETZER, H., *L'Introduction de la Messe romaine en France sous les Carolingiens* (Paris, 1910).

NILGEN, URSULA, '*Maria regina*: Ein politischer Kultbildtypus?', *Römisches Jahrbuch für Kunstgeschichte*, 19 (1981), 1–33.

NOLAN, BARBARA, *The Gothic Visionary Perspective* (Princeton, 1977).

NORRIS, HERBERT, *Church Vestments: Their Origin and Development* (London, 1949).

OCCHIATO, GUISEPPE, 'L'Abbatiale détruite de la Sainte-Trinité de Mileto (Calabre)', *Cahiers de civilisation médiévale*, 21 (1978), 231–46.

ODO OF DEUIL, *De profectione Ludovici VII in orientem*, ed. (with English trans.) Virginia Gingerick Berry (New York, 1948).

OIKOMIDÈS, NICOLAS, 'Some Remarks on the Apse Mosaic of St. Sophia', *Dumbarton Oaks Papers*, 39 (1985), 111–15.

OSBORNE, JOHN, 'The Christological Scenes in the Nave of the Lower Church of San Clemente, Rome', in *Medieval Lazio: Studies in Architecture, Painting, and Ceramics* (Papers in Italian Archaeology 3; British Archaeological Reports; International Series, 125 (1982)), 237–85.

OUSTERHOUT, ROBERT G., 'The Church of Santo Stefano: A "Jerusalem" in Bologna', *Gesta*, 20/2 (1981), 311–21.

*The Oxford Dictionary of the Christian Church* (London, 1961).

PACE, VALENTINO, 'Le componenti inglesi dell'architettura normanna di Sicilia nella storia della critica', *Studi medievali*, 3rd ser., 16 (1975), 395–406.

—— 'Le componenti inglesi nell'architettura e nella miniatura siciliana fra XII e XIII secolo', in *Ruggero il gran conte e l'inizio dello stato normanno: Relazioni e communicazioni nelle seconde giornate normanno-sveve, Bari, maggio 1975* (Rome, 1977), 175–81.

—— 'Untersuchungen zur sizilianischen Buchmalerei', in *Die Zeit der Staufer* (Stuttgart, 1979), v. 431–76.

—— 'Pittura bizantina nell'Italia meridionale (secoli XI–XIV)', in *I bizantini in Italia* (Milan, 1982), 429–94.

——*see* D'ONOFRIO.

PAESELER, W., 'Gedanken zu Monreale und zur Monrealeser Bauplastik', *Aachener Kunstblätter*, 41 (1971), 48–59.

*Palestine Pilgrims' Text Society*, vi, AD 1220 (London, 1896).

PANOFSKY, ERWIN, *Abbot Suger on the Abbey Church of St. Denis and its Treasures*, 2nd edn. (Princeton, 1979).

PAOLETTI, M., 'Sicilia e Campania costiera: I sarcofagi nelle chiese cattedrali durante l'età normanna, angioina e aragonese', in *Colloquio sul reimpiego dei sarcofagi romani nel medioevo, Pisa, 5–12 settembre 1982*, ed. B. Andreae and S. Settis (Marburg, 1984), 229–44.

PARIS, FRANÇOIS: *see* MERCENIER.

PASCA, CESARE, *Descrizione della imperiale e regal Cappella Palatina di Palermo* (Palermo, 1841).

PATERA, BENEDETTO, *L'arte della Sicilia normanna nelle fonti medievali* (Palermo, 1980).

PERTUSI, AGOSTINO, 'Insigne del potere sovrano e delegato a Bisanzio e nei paesi di influenza bizantina', in *Simboli e simbolismo nell' alto medioevo, 3–9 Aprile 1957* (Atti: Settimane di Studio del Centro Italiano di studi sull' alto medioevo XXIII), ii (Spoleto, 1976), 481–568.

PHOCAS, JOANNES, 'A Brief Description ... of the Holy Places in Palestine [AD 1185]', *Palestine Pilgrims' Text Society*, 5 (London, 1896).

PIERCE, HAYFORD, and TYLER, ROYALL, 'Three Byzantine Works of Art', *Dumbarton Oaks Papers*, 2 (1941), 1–26.

PIETRO DA EBOLI, *Liber ad honorem Augusti*, ed. G. B. Siragusa, 2 vols. (Rome, 1906).

PODALE, SALVATORE, 'Il gran conte e la sede apostolica', in *Ruggero il gran conte e l'inizio dello stato normanno* (Relazioni e communicazioni nelle seconde giornate normanno-sveve, Bari, May 1975; Rome, 1977), 25–42.

PONTIERI, ERNESTO, 'La madre di re Ruggero: Adelaide del Vasto, contessa di Sicilia, regina di Gerusalemme (?–1118)', in *Atti del Convegno internazionale di studi ruggeriani, 21–25 aprile 1954* (Palermo, 1955), ii. 327–432; repr. in *Tra i normanni nell'Italia meridionale*, 2nd edn. (Naples, 1964), 409–509.

——'Adelaide del Vasto', *Dizionario biografico degli italiani*, i (Rome, 1960), 253–5.

—— 'I normanni d'Italia e la prima crociata', in *Tra i normanni nell'Italia meridionale*, 2nd edn. (Naples, 1964), 361–408.

POTTINO, FILIPPO, 'Le vesti regali normanne dette dell'incoronazione', in *Atti del Convegno internazionale di studi ruggeriani, 21–25 aprile 1954* (Palermo, 1955), i. 277–94.

—— *La Cappella Palatina di Palermo*, trans. A. Oliver (Palermo, 1976).

PRATESI, LORENZA COCHETTI, 'In margine ad alcuni recenti studi sulla scultura medievale dell'Italia meridionale', *Commentari*, 16 (1965), 186–203.

PRAWER, JOSHUA, *Colonialismo medievale: Il regno latino di Gerusalemme*, trans. F. Cardini (Rome, 1982).

PURTLE, CAROL J., *The Marian Paintings of Jan van Eyck* (Princeton, 1982).

QUASTEN, JOHANNES, 'Oriental Influence in the Gallican Liturgy', *Traditio*, 1 (1943), 55–78.

REICHENMILLER, MARGRIT, 'Bisher unbekannte Traumerzählungen Alexanders von Telese', *Deutsches Archiv für Erforschung des Mittelalters*, 19 (1963), 339–52.

RIDDLE, MARGARET, 'Illustration of the "Triumph" of Joseph the Patriarch', in E. and M. Jeffreys, *et al.* (eds.), *Byzantine Papers: Proceedings of the First Australian Byzantine Studies Conference, Canberra, 17–19 May 1978* (Canberra, 1981), 69–81.

RIZZARDI, CLEMENTINA, *Mosaici altoadriatici: Il rapporto artistico Venezia–Bisanzio–Ravenna in età medievale* (Ravenna, 1985).

ROCCO, BENEDETTO, 'I mosaici delle chiese normanne in Sicilia: Sguardo teologico, biblico, liturgico. II. La Cappella Palatina', *Ho Theologos: Cultura cristiana di Sicilia*, 11–12 (1976), 121–212; id. (III), ibid. 17 (1978), 9–108; 20 (1978), 79–110.

—— Il tabulario della Cappella Palatina di Palermo e il martirologio di epoca ruggeriana', *Ho Theologos*, 14 (1977), 131–44.

—— 'L'archivio della Cappella Palatina di Palermo', *Beni culturali ambientali: Sicilia*, 2/3–4 (1981), 179–93.

—— 'La Cappella Palatina di Palermo: Lettura teologica', *Beni culturali ambientali: Sicilia*, 4 (1983, pub. 1985), 21–74.

—— 'La Cappella Palatina di Palermo. Lettura teologica (Parte seconda)', *Beni culturali ambientali: Sicilia*, 5 (3–4, 1984, pub. 1987), 31–100.

ROSENAU, HELEN, *Vision of the Temple: The Image of the Temple of Jerusalem in Judaism and Christianity* (London, 1979).

ROTILI, MARIO, 'La miniatura nella Badia di Cava: Bilancio di uno studio', *La miniatura italiana in età romanica e gotica: Atti del Iº Congresso di storia della miniatura italiana, Cortona, 26–28 maggio 1978*, ed. G. Vailati Schoenburg Waldenburg (Florence, 1979), 159–86.

RUNCIMAN, STEVEN, 'The Holy Lance found at Antioch', *Analecta bollandiana*, 68 (1950), 197–209.

—— *A History of the Crusades: The Kingdom of Jerusalem and the Frankish East 1100–1187*, ii (Cambridge, 1952).

RYCCARDI DE S. GERMANO, 'Chronica', in *Rerum italicarum scriptores*, 7 (1725), 967–1052, part ii.

SALVO DI PIETRAGANZILI, ROSARIO, *Cefalù: La sua origine e i suoi monumenti* (Palermo, 1888).

SALZER, ANSELM, *Die Sinnbilder und Beiworte Mariens in der deutschen Literatur und lateinischen Hymnenpoesie des Mittelalters* (Darmstadt, 1967).

SAMMAN, TARIF AL, 'Arabische Inschriften auf den Krönungsgewändern des Heiligen Römischen Reiches', *Jahrbuch der kunsthistorischen Sammlungen in Wien*, 78 (1982), 7–34.

SCHEFOLD, KARL, 'Altchristliche Bilderzyklen: Bassussarkophag und S. Maria Maggiore', *Rivista di archeologia cristiana*, 16 (1939), 289–316.

SCHILLER, GERTRUD, *Ikonographie der christlichen Kunst*, i, iii (Gütersloh, 1966, 1971).

SCHMID, A. A., 'Himmelfahrt Christi', *Lexikon der christlichen Ikonographie*, ii (Rome, Freiburg, Basle, and Vienna, 1970), cols. 268–75.

SCHNITZLER, HERMANN, 'Das Kuppelmosaik der Aachener Pfalzkapelle', *Aachener Kunstblätter*, 29 (1964), 17–44.

SCHÖNE, WOLFGANG, 'Die künstlerische und liturgische Gestalt der Pfalzkirche Karls der Grossen in Aachen', *Zeitschrift für Kunstwissenschaft*, 15 (1961), 97–148.

SCHRAMM, PERCY ERNST, 'Die geistliche und die weltliche Mitra mit Seitenblicken auf die Geschichte der päpstlichen Tiara', in *Herrschaftszeichen und Staatssymbolik: Beiträge zu ihrer Geschichte vom dritten bis zum sechzehnten Jahrhundert*, i (Stuttgart, 1954), 51–98.

—— 'Von der Trabea Triumphalis des römischen Kaisers über das byzantinische Lorum zur Stola der abendländischen Herrscher', ibid. 25–50.

—— 'Das Alte und das Neue Testament in der Staatslehre und Staatssymbolik des Mittelalters', in *La bibbia nell'alto medioevo: Settimana di studio del Centro italiano di studi sull'alto medioevo*, 10, 26 Apr.–2 May 1962 (Spoleto, 1963), 229–55; reprd. in *Beiträge zur allgemeinen Geschichte*, 4/1 (Stuttgart, 1970), 123–40.

—— '*Sacerdotium* und *Regnum* in Austausch ihre Vorrechte: "imitatio imperii" und "imitatio sacerdotii"', in *Beiträge zur allgemeinen Geschichte*, 4/1 (Stuttgart, 1970), 57–102.

SCHUSTER, ILDEFONSO, *The Sacramentary*, i (London, 1924).

SCHWARZ, HEINRICH M., 'Die Baukunst Kalabriens und Siziliens im Zeitalter der Normannen, I: Die lateinischen Kirchengründungen des 11. Jahrhunderts und der Dom in Cefalù', *Römisches Jahrbuch für Kunstgeschichte*, 6 (1942–4), 3–112.

SCUDERI, V.: *see* DELOGU.

SETTIS FRUGONI, C.: *see* FRUGONI.

SETTIS, S.: *see* ANDREAE.

SETTON, KENNETH M., and BALDWIN, MARSHALL W. (eds.), *History of the Crusades: The First Hundred Years*, i (Madison, Milwaukee, and London, 1969).

SIRAGUSA, G. B., *Il regno di Guglielmo I° in Sicilia* (Palermo, 1929).

SMITH, L. M., *The Early History of the Monastery of Cluny* (Oxford, 1920).

—— *Cluny in the Eleventh and Twelfth Centuries* (London, 1930).

SPAIN, SUZANNE, 'The Promised Blessing: The Iconography of the Mosaics of S. Maria Maggiore', *Art Bulletin*, 61 (1979), 518–40.

—— *see* ALEXANDER.

SPIEGEL, GABRIELLE M., 'The Cult of St. Denis and Capetian Kingship', *Journal of Medieval History*, 1 (1975), 43–69.

STAHL, HARVEY, 'Old Testament Illustration during the Reign of St. Louis: The Morgan Picture Book and the New Biblical Cycles', in *Atti del XXIV Congresso Internazionale di storia dell' Arte, 10 al 18 settembre 1979*, ii (Bologna, 1982), 79–93.

STANGE, A., *Das frühchristliche Kirchengebäude als Bild des Himmels* (Cologne, 1950).

—— *Basiliken, Kuppelkirchen, Kathedralen: Das himmlische Jerusalem in der Sicht der Jahrhunderte* (Regensburg, 1964).

STEGER, HUGO, David Rex et propheta: *König David als vorbildliche Verkörperung des Herrschers und Dichters im Mittelalter, nach Bilddarstellungen des achten bis zwölften Jahrhunderts* (Nuremberg, 1961).

STEINBERG, SIGFRID H., 'I ritratti dei re normanni di Sicilia', *Bibliofilia*, 39 (1937), 29–57.

STOOKEY, LAWRENCE HULL, 'The Gothic Cathedral as the Heavenly Jerusalem: Liturgical and Theological Sources', *Gesta*, 8 (1969), 35–41.

STRAYER, J. R., 'France: The Holy Land, the Chosen People, and the Most Christian King', in T. K. Rabb and J. E. Seigel (eds.), *Action and Conviction in Early Modern Europe: Essays in Memory of E. H. Harbison* (Princeton, 1969), 3–16.

STRUBE, CHRISTINE, *Die westliche Eingangsseite der Kirchen von Konstantinopel in Justinianischer Zeit* (Wiesbaden, 1973).

SUMPTION, JONATHAN, *Monaci, santuari, pellegrini: La religione nel medioevo* (Rome, 1981).

SWOBODA, KARL M., 'The Problem of the Iconography of Late Antique and Early Medieval Palaces', *Journal of the Society of Architectural Historians*, 20/2 (1961), 78–89.

TERZI, A., CAVALLARI, S., *et al.*, *La cappella di S. Pietro nella reggia di Palermo* (Palermo, 1873–85).

TESTINI, PASQUALE, 'Osservazioni sull'iconografia del Cristo in trono fra gli apostoli', *Rivista dell'istituto nazionale d'archeologia e storia dell'arte*, NS, 11–12 (1963), 230–300.

THIEME, THOMAS, and BECK, INGAMAJ, *La cattedrale normanna di Cefalù* (Analecta Romana Instituti Danici, Supplementum 8; Odense, 1977).

TOPPING, E. CATAFYGIOTU, 'Romanos, on the Entry into Jerusalem: A *Basilikos Logos*', *Byzantion*, 47 (1977), 65–91.

TOUBERT, HÉLÈNE, 'Le Renouveau paléochrétien à Rome au début du XIIe siècle', *Cahiers archéologiques*, 20 (1970), 99–154.

TRAMONTANA, SALVATORE, *La monarchia normanna e sveva* (Turin, 1986).

TREITINGER, OTTO, *Die oströmische Kaiser und Reichsidee: Nach ihrer Gestaltung im höfischen Zeremoniell* (Jena, 1938).

TRIZZINO, LUCIO, 'La basilica bizantina di S. Gregorio Agrigentino nel Tempio della Concordia', *Felix Ravenna*, 1/2 (1980), 172–88.

—— 'Die Kathedrale von Monreale: Was für eine Collage!', *Daidalos*, 16 (15 June 1985), 65–80.

—— 'Cappella Palatina: Dissesti e restauri', typescript (Soprintendenza beni culturali e artistici; Palermo, 1979).*

TRONZO, WILLIAM, 'The Prestige of St. Peter's: Observations on the Function of Monumental Narrative Cycles in Italy', in *Pictorial Narrative in Antiquity and the Middle Ages* (Studies in the History of Art, 16; National Gallery of Art, Washington, 1985), 93–112.

TUSA, VINCENZO, *I sarcofagi romani in Sicilia* (Palermo, 1957).

TYLER, ROYALL: *see* PIERCE.

ULLMANN, WALTER, *The Carolingian Renaissance and the Idea of Kingship* (London, 1969).

—— *Principles of Government and Politics in the Middle Ages* (London and New York, 1974).

UNDERWOOD, PAUL A., 'The Fountain of Life in Manuscripts of the Gospels', *Dumbarton Oaks Papers*, 5 (1950), 43–138.

—— 'Some Problems in Programs and Iconography of Ministry Cycles', in *The Kariye Djami*, iv (Princeton, 1975), 243–302.

VALENZIANO, CRISPINO, 'La basilica cattedrale di Cefalù nel periodo normanno', *Ho Theologos*, 19 (1978), 85–140.

—— 'Reliquario della croce e frammenti di abiti ruggeriani', in *Materiale per la conoscenza storica e il restauro di una carredrale: Mostra di documenti e testimonianze figurative della Basilica Ruggeriana di Cefalù* (Palermo, 1982), 159–61.

VALENZIANO, MARIA, and CRISPINO, 'La Supplique des chanoines de la cathédrale de Cefalù pour la sépulture du roi Roger', *Cahiers de civilisation médiévale*, 21 (1978), 3–30; 137–50.

VAN MILLINGEN, ALEXANDER, *Byzantine Churches in Constantinople: Their History and Architecture* (London, 1912).

VAN OS, HENRIK, *Marias Demut und Verherrlichung in der sienesischen Malerei 1300–1450* (The Hague, 1969).

VECCHI, MAURIZIA, *Torcello: Ricerche e contributi* and *Torcello: nuove ricerche* (Studia archaeologica, 25 and 34; Rome, 1979 and 1982).

VERDIER, PHILIPPE, *Le Couronnement de la Vierge: Les Origines et les premiers développements d'un thème iconographique* (Montreal and Paris, 1980).

VINCENT, HUGUES, and ABEL, F. M., *Jérusalem: Recherches de topographie, d'archéologie et d'histoire*, ii (Paris, 1922).

VITALIS, ORDERICUS, *The Ecclesiastical History of England and Normandy*, trans. and annot. Thomas Forester, i (London, 1853).

—— *The Ecclesiastical History of Orderic Vitalis*, ed. Marjorie Chibnall, 6 vols. (Oxford, 1969–80).

VON SIMSON, OTTO, *Sacred Fortress: Byzantine Art and Statecraft in Ravenna* (Chicago, 1948).

—— *The Gothic Cathedral* (London, 1956).

WADDELL, CHRYSOGONUS, 'The Reform of the Liturgy from a Renaissance Perspective', in R. L. Benson, *et al.*, *Renaissance and Renewal in the Twelfth Century* (Oxford, 1982), 88–109.

WAETZOLDT, STEPHAN, *Die Kopien des 17. Jahrhunderts nach Mosaiken und Wandmalereien in Rom* (Vienna and Munich, 1964).

WALLACE-HADRILL, J. M., *The Frankish Church* (Oxford, 1983).

WALTER, CHRISTOPHER, *Art and Ritual of the Byzantine Church* (London, 1982).

WARNER, MARINA, *Alone of all her Sex: The Myth and the Cult of the Virgin Mary* (London, 1976).

WATT, JOHN A., *The Theory of Papal Monarchy in the Thirteenth Century: The Contribution of the Canonists* (London, 1965).

WEIS, ADOLF, 'Ein Petruszyklus des 7. Jahrhunderts im Querschiff der Vatikanischen Basilika', *Römisches Quartalschrift für christliche Altertumskunde und Kirchengeschichte*, 58 (1963), 230–70.

WEITZMANN, KURT, *Studies in Classical and Byzantine Manuscript Illumination* (Chicago and London, 1971).

WEITZMANN, K.: *see* FORSYTH, G.

WELLEN, G. A., *Theotokos: Eine ikonographische Abhandlung über das Gottesmutterbild in frühchristlicher Zeit* (Utrecht, 1960).

WEYER-DAVIS, CÄCELIA, 'Das Traditio-Legis-Bild und seine Nachfolge', *Münchner Jahrbuch der bildenden Kunst*, 3rd ser. 12 (1961), 7–45.

WHITE, J. F., 'Durandus and the Interpretation of Christian Worship', in G. H. Shriver (ed.), *Contemporary Reflections on the Medieval Christian Tradition: Essays in Honor of Ray C. Petry* (Durham, NC, 1974), 41–52.

WHITE, LYNNE T., *Latin Monasticism in Norman Sicily* (Cambridge, Mass., 1938).

WIERUSZOWSKI, HELENE, 'The Norman Kingdom of Sicily and the Crusades', in K. M. Setton, R. L. Wolff, and H. W. Hazard (eds.), *A History of the Crusades*, ii (Madison, Milwaukee, and London, 1969), 3–42.

WILHELM, P., 'Die Marienkrönung am Westportal der Kathedrale von Senlis', Ph.D. diss. (Hamburg, 1941).

WORMALD, FRANCIS, 'The Throne of Solomon and St. Edward's Chair', *De artibus opuscula*, xl: *Essays in Honor of Erwin Panofsky* (New York, 1961) i, 532–9.

\* *Addendum*: All the references to Lucio Trizzino's typescript entitled 'Cappella Palatina: Dissesti e restauri' are now superseded by its publication as *La Palatina di Palermo: dalle opere funzionali al restauro, dal ripristino alla tutela* printed in Palermo in 1983 but only released in May 1989. Cf. our pp. 43 n. 13; 44 nn. 27–30, 32, 37, 39; 45 n. 53, 47 n. 100.

# PHOTOGRAPHIC CREDITS

# INDEX

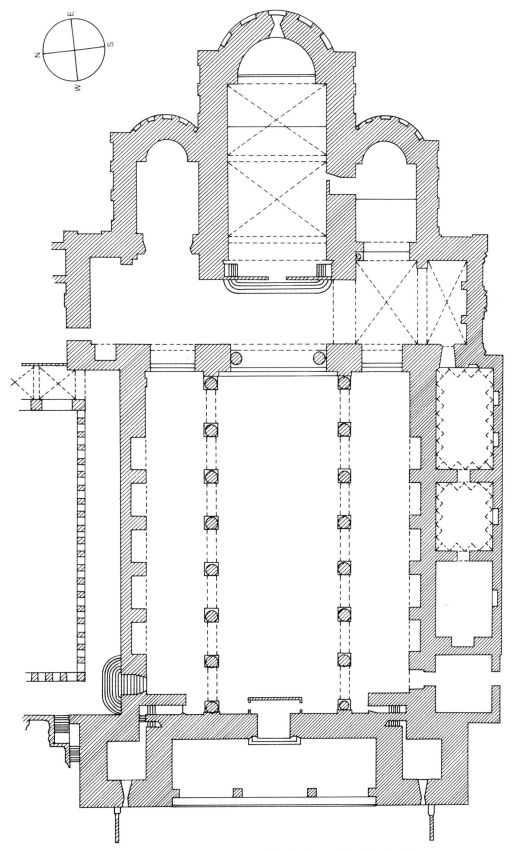

1. Plan of Cefalù cathedral (after Samonà and Krönig).

2. View of Cefalù and its cathedral.

3. Cefalù cathedral: general view of apse and presbytery.

4. Cefalù cathedral, *Pantocrator*, apse conch, 1148.

5. Detail of Plate 4.

6. Cefalù cathedral: presbytery vault adjacent to apse.

7. Detail of Plate 6.

8. Cefalù cathedral, left wall of presbytery: *Prophets, Deacon Martyrs,* and *Latin Bishop Saints*.

9. Cefalù cathedral, right wall of presbytery: *Prophets*, *Warrior Saints*, and *Greek Patriarchs* and *Theologians*.

Within the mosaic:

SCS MELCHIS EDECH

OSEE PROPHETA.    PROPHETA. MOYSES

VIVIFICABIT NOS DNS DS PST DVOS DI ES IN DIE TER CIA SVSCABIT NOS ET VENI

IN PRINCIPIO CREAVIT DS CELVM ET TERRAM TERRA AVT EM ERAT INANIS

R. RIOLO. 1862

10. Cefalù cathedral, lunette of left presbytery wall: *Hosea*, *Melchizedek*, and *Moses*.

11. Cefalù cathedral, lunette of right presbytery wall: *David*, *Abraham*, and *Solomon*.

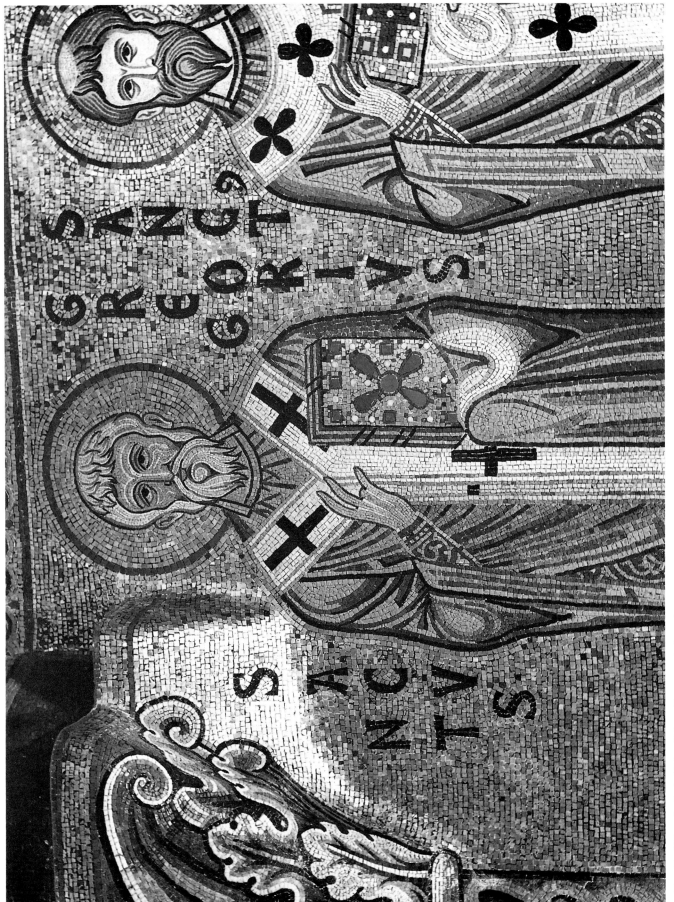

12. Detail of Plate 8: *Latin Bishop Saints: Gregory and Augustine*.

13. Detail of Plate 9: *SS John Chrysostom and Gregory Nazianzenus.*

14. Cefalù cathedral: view of presbytery with royal throne (dismantled in 1985) at entrance.

15. Cefalù cathedral: view of presbytery with bishop's throne (dismantled in 1985) at entrance.

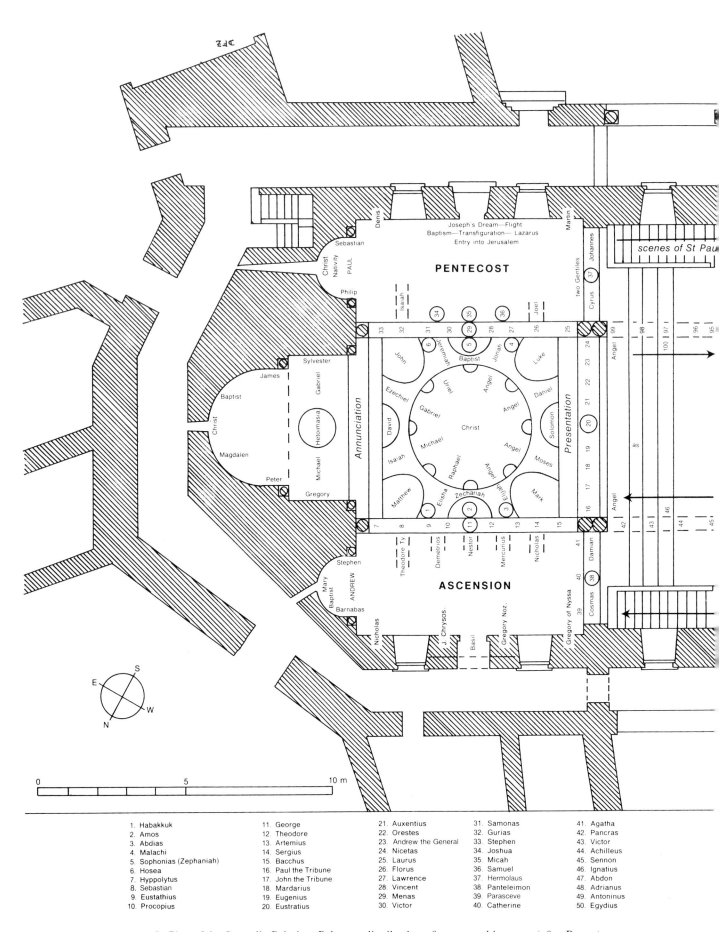

Plan of the Cappella Palatina, Palermo, with labelled scenes and imagery:

Top chamber:
Joseph's Dream—Flight
Baptism—Transfiguration—Lazarus
Entry into Jerusalem

**PENTECOST**

Denis, Sebastian, Christ Nativity, PAUL, Philip, Martin, two Gentiles, Cyrus, Johannes, scenes of St Pau[l]

Isaiah · Joel

34 · 35 · 36

33 · 32 · 31 · 30 · 6 · 29 · 28 · 27 · 26 · 25 · 24 · 99 · 98 · 100 · 97 · 96 · 95

Sylvester, James, Baptist, Christ, Magdalen, Michael (Hetoimasia), Gabriel, Peter, Gregory

Annunciation

John · Jeremiah · 5 · Jonah · 4 · Luke
Ezechiel · Uriel · Baptist · Daniel
David · Gabriel · Angel · Angel · Solomon
Isaiah · Michael · Christ · Moses
Matthew · Elisha · Raphael · Zechariah · Angel · Elijah · Mark
Angel

Presentation

Angel · as · Angel

1 · 2
7 · 8 · 9 · 10 · 11 · 12 · 13 · 14 · 15 · 16 · Damian · 41 · 42 · 43 · 46 · 44 · 45

Theodore Ty · Demetrios · Nestor · Mercurius · Nicholas

Stephen, Mary Baptist, ANDREW, Barnabas

**ASCENSION**

Cosmos, Gregory of Nyssa, Paraceve, Catherine

Nicholas · J. Chrysos. · Basil · Gregory Noz. · Gregory of Nyssa

Compass rose: S, E, W, N

Scale: 0 — 5 — 10 m

1. Habakkuk
2. Amos
3. Abdias
4. Malachi
5. Sophonias (Zephaniah)
6. Hosea
7. Hyppolytus
8. Sebastian
9. Eustathius
10. Procopius
11. George
12. Theodore
13. Artemius
14. Sergius
15. Bacchus
16. Paul the Tribune
17. John the Tribune
18. Mardarius
19. Eugenius
20. Eustratius
21. Auxentius
22. Orestes
23. Andrew the General
24. Nicetas
25. Laurus
26. Florus
27. Lawrence
28. Vincent
29. Menas
30. Victor
31. Samonas
32. Gurias
33. Stephen
34. Micah
35. Micah
36. Samuel
37. Hermolaus
38. Panteleimon
39. Parasceve
40. Catherine
41. Agatha
42. Pancras
43. Victor
44. Achilleus
45. Sennon
46. Ignatius
47. Abdon
48. Adrianus
49. Antoninus
50. Egydius

16. Plan of the Cappella Palatina, Palermo: distribution of scenes and imagery (after Rocco).

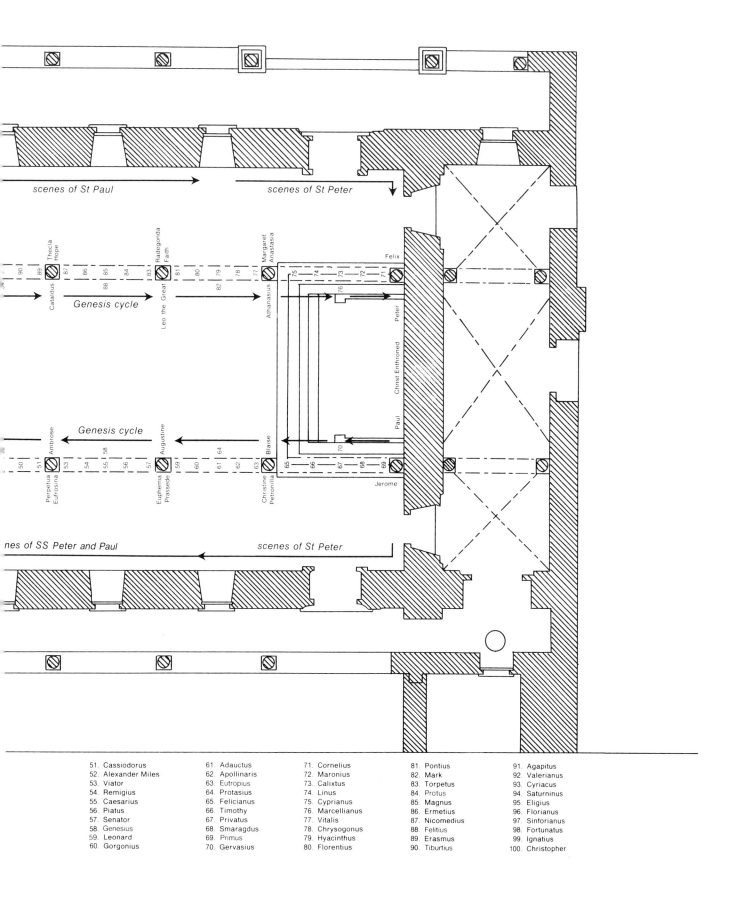

scenes of St Paul

scenes of St Peter

Genesis cycle

Genesis cycle

scenes of SS Peter and Paul

scenes of St Peter

Thecla Hope
Radegonda Faith
Margaret Anastasia
Felix
Cataldus
Leo the Great
Athanasius
Peter
Christ Enthroned
Paul
Ambrose
Euphemia Prassede
Christine Petronilla
Blaise
Jerome
Perpetua Eutrosina

| 51. Cassiodorus | 61. Adauctus | 71. Cornelius | 81. Pontius | 91. Agapitus |
| 52. Alexander Miles | 62. Apollinaris | 72. Maronius | 82. Mark | 92. Valerianus |
| 53. Viator | 63. Eutropius | 73. Calixtus | 83. Torpetus | 93. Cyriacus |
| 54. Remigius | 64. Protasius | 74. Linus | 84. Protus | 94. Saturninus |
| 55. Caesarius | 65. Felicianus | 75. Cyprianus | 85. Magnus | 95. Eligius |
| 56. Piatus | 66. Timothy | 76. Marcellianus | 86. Ermetius | 96. Florianus |
| 57. Senator | 67. Privatus | 77. Vitalis | 87. Nicomedius | 97. Sinforianus |
| 58. Genesius | 68. Smaragdus | 78. Chrysogonus | 88. Felitius | 98. Fortunatus |
| 59. Leonard | 69. Primus | 79. Hyacinthus | 89. Erasmus | 99. Ignatius |
| 60. Gorgonius | 70. Gervasius | 80. Florentius | 90. Tiburtius | 100. Christopher |

17. Palermo, Cappella Palatina: view of crossing and nave looking west, towards entrance.

18. Palermo, Cappella Palatina: view of apse and sanctuary from nave looking east.

19.  Palermo, Cappella Palatina: royal dais at west end of nave with *Christ Enthroned between SS Peter and Paul*.

20. Palermo, Cappella Palatina: view of apse with *SS Gregory, Peter, Mary Magdalen, and the Virgin Mary*.

21. Palermo, Cappella Palatina: *Pantocrator*, apse conch.

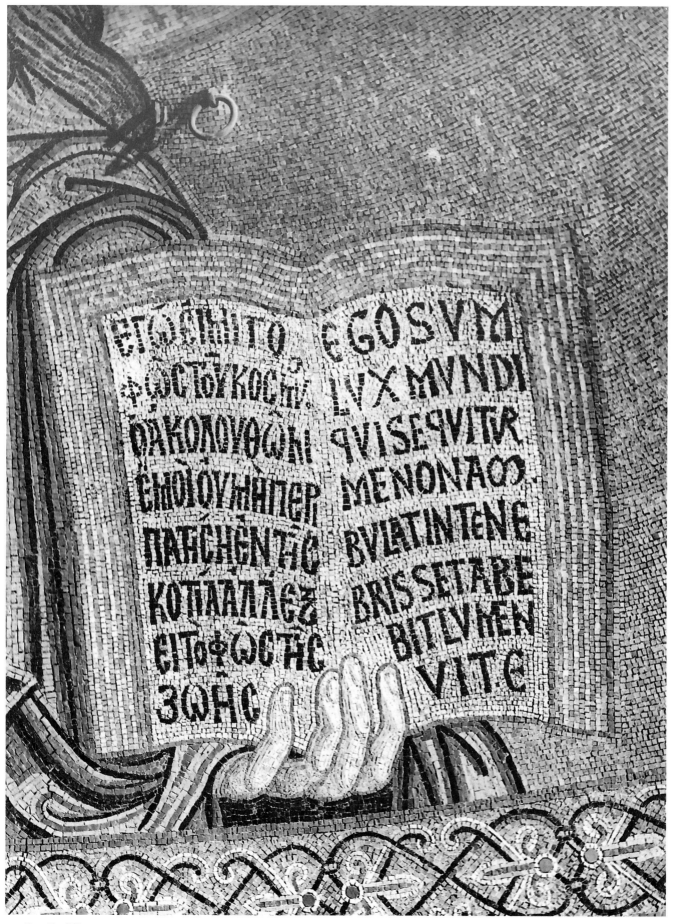

22. Detail of Plate 21.

23. Detail of Plate 21.

24. Palermo, Cappella Palatina: *St James as Patriarch of Jerusalem*, right side of apse.

25. Palermo, Cappella Palatina: view of crossing-vault and arches.

26. Palermo, Cappella Palatina, western arch of crossing: *Presentation in the Temple*.

27. Palermo, Cappella Palatina, south-west corner of crossing.

28.  Palermo, Cappella Palatina: view of northern chapel from the crossing.

HÍC
PRÆCEPTO
PETRI ORATIONE PAULI.
SIMON MAGUS CECIDIT
IN TERRAM.

29. Palermo, Cappella Palatina: view of aisle entrance to northern chapel with the *Fall of Simon Magus* (left), *St Cosmas* (on arch), and *St Gregory of Nyssa* inside the chapel.

30.  Palermo, Cappella Palatina: *St Damian* on entrance arch between northern aisle and northern chapel.

31. Palermo, Cappella Palatina: *Ascension* vault, northern chapel.

32. Palermo, Cappella Palatina: detail of *Ascension*, northern chapel.

33. Palermo, Cappella Palatina: view of western end of northern chapel with *SS Agatha*, *Catherine*, and *Parasceve* [?].

34. Palermo, Cappella Palatina: view of eastern end of northern chapel, with the *Baptist* and the *Hodegetria* above and *St Andrew* below.

35. Palermo, Cappella Palatina, northern chapel: *SS Theodore Tyro*, *Demetrios*, and *Nestor*, southern arch wall.

36. Palermo, Cappella Palatina, northern chapel: *SS Nestor*, *Mercurios*, and *Nicholas*, southern arch wall.

37. Palermo, Cappella Palatina: view of crossing and southern chapel from the north.

38. Palermo, Cappella Palatina: view of southern chapel from apse.

39. Palermo, Cappella Palatina: view of apse and southern chapel looking east.

40. Palermo, Cappella Palatina: western end of southern chapel, with *Personifications of the still Unconverted Tribes* above and *Egypt* below.

41. Palermo, Cappella Palatina, southern chapel: *Joel*, northern arch wall.

42. Palermo, Cappella Palatina, southern chapel: *Isaiah* and *Nativity*, eastern end.

43. Palermo, Cappella Palatina, southern chapel: *Samuel, Micah,* and *Joshua,* northern arch wall.

44. Palermo, Cappella Palatina, southern chapel: *Pentecost* vault.

45. Palermo, Cappella Palatina: *St Martin of Tours* (left) and *St Johannes* on arch between southern chapel and aisle.

46.  Palermo, Cappella Palatina: *St Cyrus* (Kyros) on arch between southern chapel and aisle.

47.  Palermo, Cappella Palatina: *Genesis* scenes on southern nave arcade, and Pauline sequence in aisle.

48. Palermo, Cappella Palatina: sanctuary arch and *Genesis* scenes on southern nave arcade.

49. Palermo, Cappella Palatina: *Genesis* scenes on southern nave arcade and Pauline sequence in aisle.

50. Palermo, Cappella Palatina: *Genesis* scenes on southern nave arcade and apostolic sequence in aisle.

51. Palermo, Cappella Palatina: *Liberation of Peter* in south-west corner of southern aisle, with *St Felix of Nola* to right of window.

52. Palermo, Cappella Palatina: western end of northern aisle with *St Jerome* and *SS John and Peter healing the Cripple at the Temple Gate.*

53. Palermo, Cappella Palatina: *Genesis* scenes on wall of northern nave arcade, and apostolic sequence in aisle.

54. Palermo, Cappella Palatina: *Genesis* scenes on wall of northern nave arcade, and scenes of *SS Peter* and *Paul* in aisle.

55. Palermo, Cappella Palatina: *Genesis* scenes on northern nave arcade, and scenes of *SS Peter* and *Paul* in aisle.

56. Palermo, Cappella Palatina: view of north-eastern end of aisle and nave arcade with sanctuary arch.

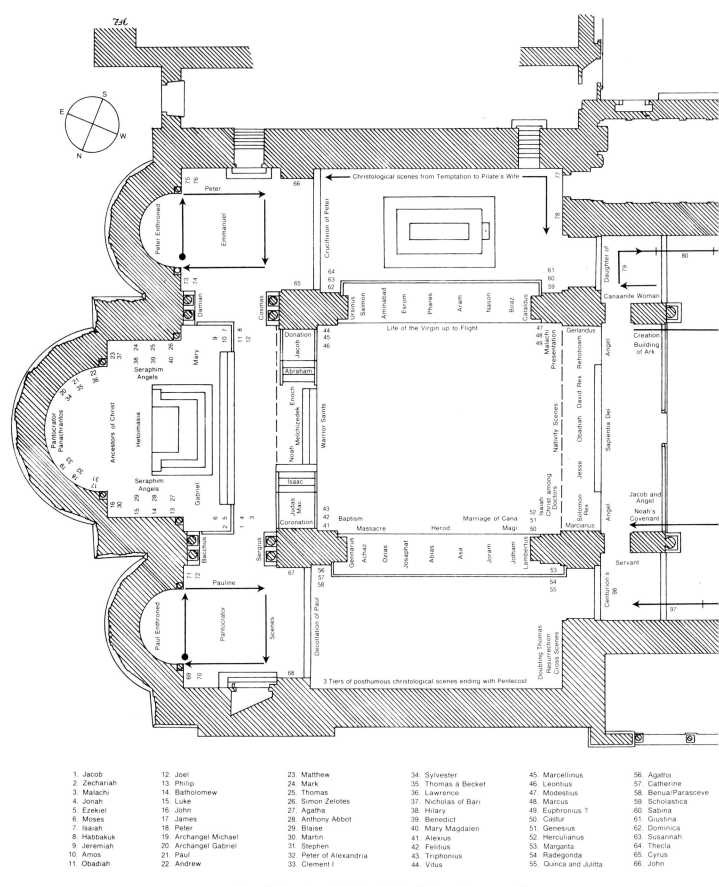

57. Plan of Monreale cathedral with distribution of scenes and imagery.

The following labels appear within the plan:

Compass: S, E, W, N (with 2F2 rotated at top)

Peter Enthroned — Peter — Emmanuel
75 76 73 74
66
Christological scenes from Temptation to Pilate's Wife 77
78
Crucifixion of Peter
64 63 62
65
Ursinus — Salmon — Aminabad — Esrom — Phares — Aram — Nason — Boaz — Cataldus
61 60 59
Daughter of
79 80
Canaanite Woman
Damian
9 10 7 11 8 12
23 37 24 38 25 39 26 40
Mary
Seraphim Angels
20 34 21 35 22 36
Pantocrator Panachrantos
Ancestors of Christ
Hetoimasia
18 32 19 33
17 31
16 30 15 29 14 28 13 27
Gabriel
Seraphim Angels
6 2 5 1 4 3
Cosmas
Donation
44 45 46
Jacob
Abraham
Noah
Melchizedek
Enoch
Warrior Saints
Isaac
Judas Mac.
Coronation
43 42 41
Life of the Virgin up to Flight
Malachi
Presentation
47 48 49
Gerlandus
Nativity Scenes
Rehoboam
David Rex
Obadiah
Jesse
Solomon Rex
Marcianus
Isaiah Christ among Doctors
52 51 50
Angel
Sapientia Dei
Angel
Creation Building of Ark
Jacob and Angel
Noah's Covenant
Servant
Baptism
Massacre
Herod
Marriage of Cana
Magi
Gennarus — Achaz — Ozias — Josaphat — Abias — Asa — Joram — Jotham — Lambertus
53 54 55
Sergius
67
56 57 58
Paul Enthroned — Pauline — Pantocrator
71 72 69 70
Scenes
68
Decollation of Paul
Decollation of Paul
Centurion's 98
97
Doubting Thomas
Resurrection
Cross Scenes
3 Tiers of posthumous christological scenes ending with Pentecost
Bacchus

1. Jacob
2. Zechariah
3. Malachi
4. Jonah
5. Ezekiel
6. Moses
7. Isaiah
8. Habbakuk
9. Jeremiah
10. Amos
11. Obadiah

12. Joel
13. Philip
14. Batholomew
15. Luke
16. John
17. James
18. Peter
19. Archangel Michael
20. Archangel Gabriel
21. Paul
22. Andrew

23. Matthew
24. Mark
25. Thomas
26. Simon Zelotes
27. Agatha
28. Anthony Abbot
29. Blaise
30. Martin
31. Stephen
32. Peter of Alexandria
33. Clement I

34. Sylvester
35. Thomas à Becket
36. Lawrence
37. Nicholas of Bari
38. Hilary
39. Benedict
40. Mary Magdalen
41. Alexius
42. Felitius
43. Triphonius
44. Vitus

45. Marcellinus
46. Leontius
47. Modestius
48. Marcus
49. Euphronius ?
50. Castur
51. Genesius
52. Herculianus
53. Margarita
54. Radegonda
55. Quirica and Julitta

56. Agatha
57. Catherine
58. Benua/Parasceve
59. Scholastica
60. Sabina
61. Giustina
62. Dominica
63. Susannah
64. Thecla
65. Cyrus
66. John

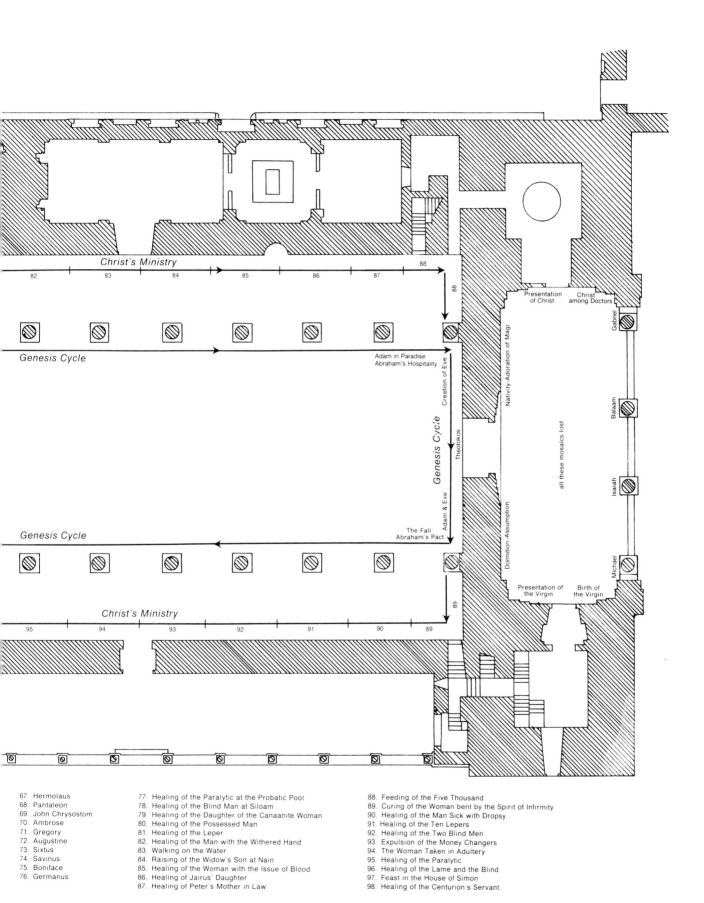

Christ's Ministry

| 82 | 83 | 84 | 85 | 86 | 87 | 88 |

Genesis Cycle

Adam in Paradise
Abraham's Hospitality

*Genesis Cycle*

Creation of Eve

Theotokos

Adam & Eve

*Genesis Cycle*

The Fall
Abraham's Pact

Christ's Ministry

| 95 | 94 | 93 | 92 | 91 | 90 | 89 |

Presentation
of Christ

Christ
among Doctors

Nativity-Adoration of Magi

all these mosaics lost

Gabriel

Balaam

Isaiah

Michael

Dormition-Assumption

Presentation of
the Virgin

Birth of
the Virgin

67. Hermolaus
68. Pantaleon
69. John Chrysostom
70. Ambrose
71. Gregory
72. Augustine
73. Sixtus
74. Savinus
75. Boniface
76. Germanus

77. Healing of the Paralytic at the Probatic Pool
78. Healing of the Blind Man at Siloam
79. Healing of the Daughter of the Canaanite Woman
80. Healing of the Possessed Man
81. Healing of the Leper
82. Healing of the Man with the Withered Hand
83. Walking on the Water
84. Raising of the Widow's Son at Nain
85. Healing of the Woman with the Issue of Blood
86. Healing of Jairus' Daughter
87. Healing of Peter's Mother in Law

88. Feeding of the Five Thousand
89. Curing of the Woman bent by the Spirit of Infirmity
90. Healing of the Man Sick with Dropsy
91. Healing of the Ten Lepers
92. Healing of the Two Blind Men
93. Expulsion of the Money Changers
94. The Woman Taken in Adultery
95. Healing of the Paralytic
96. Healing of the Lame and the Blind
97. Feast in the House of Simon
98. Healing of the Centurion's Servant.

58. Monreale cathedral: left valve of main portal in bronze by Bonanno di Pisa, 1186, with the *Assumption of the Virgin* in upper panel.

59. Monreale cathedral: right valve of main portal in bronze by Bonanno di Pisa, 1186, with *Christ in Majesty* in upper panel.

60. Monreale cathedral: *Mary as Theotokos* (Mother of God), tympanum over main portal inside church.

61. Monreale cathedral: view down nave from the west.

62. Monreale cathedral: central apse.

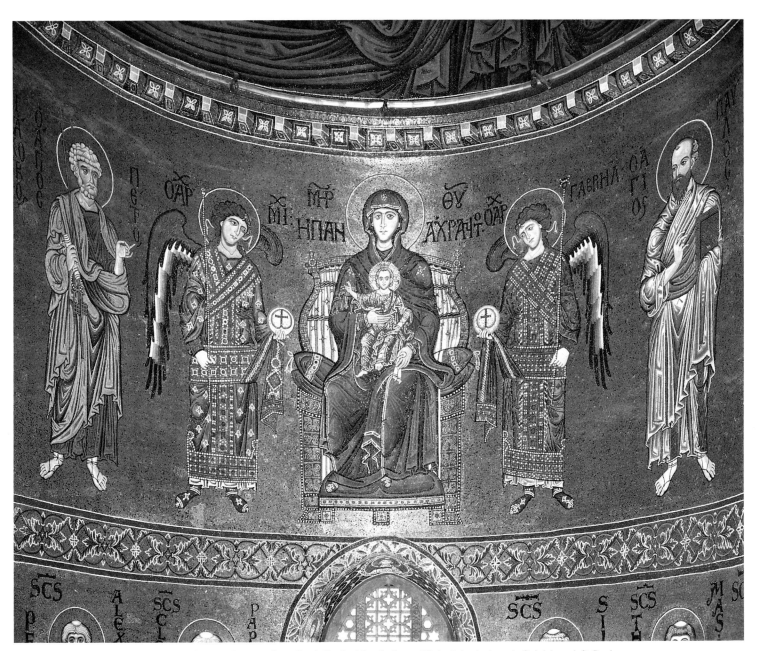

63. Detail of Plate 62: *Mary as Panachrantos* (Immaculate One) flanked by *St Peter*, *Michael the Archangel*, *Gabriel*, and *St Paul*.

64. Monreale cathedral: view of sanctuary area from nave.

65. Detail of Plate 64: *Sapientia Dei* in gable of sanctuary arch.

66. Monreale cathedral: view of presbytery arch with *Hetoimasia*, *Seraphim*, and *Archangels*.

67. Monreale cathedral: detail of apse conch.

68. Monreale cathedral: view north between crossing and apse.

69. Monreale cathedral: view south between crossing and apse.

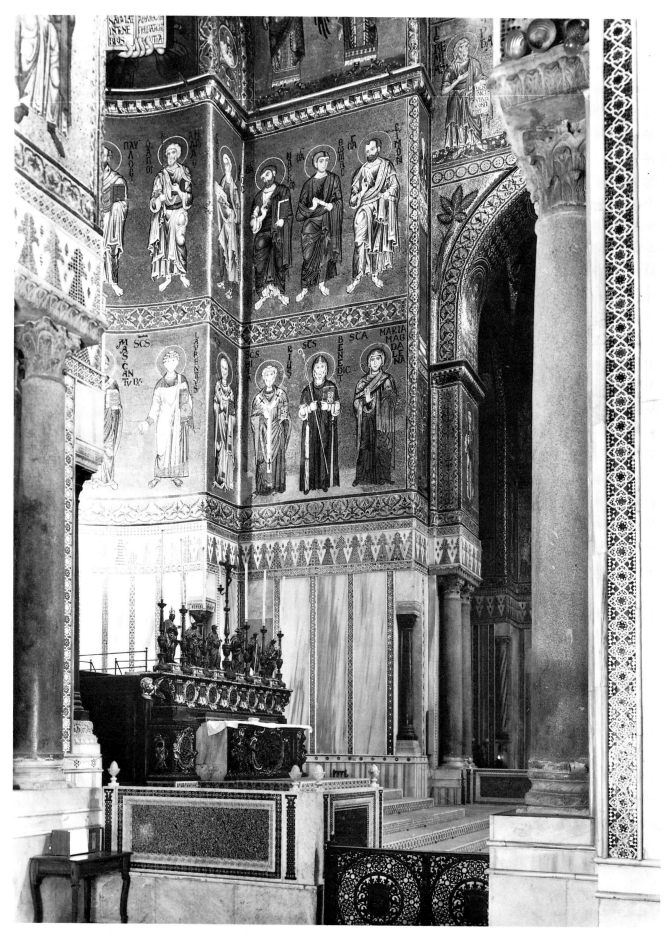

70.  Monreale cathedral: view of southern side of presbytery and apse.

71. Detail of Plate 69: *Isaiah* and *Habbakuk* (above), *Jeremiah, Amos, Obadiah,* and *Joel* (below).

72. Monreale cathedral: northern side of presbytery arch and apse with *SS Philip, Bartholomew, Luke, John, James,* and *Peter* above; and *SS Agatha, Anthony Abbot, Blaise, Martin, Stephen,* and *Peter of Alexandria* below.

73. Monreale cathedral: southern side of presbytery arch and apse with *SS Andrew, Matthew, Mark, Thomas,* and *Simon Zelotes* above: and *SS Lawrence, Nicholas of Bari, Hilary, Benedict,* and *Mary Magdalen* below.

74. Monreale cathedral: view of St Peter chapel from southern aisle.

75. Monreale cathedral: view of St Peter chapel from door to archbishop's palace.

76. Monreale cathedral: south wall of St Peter chapel.

77. Monreale cathedral: *Emmanuel*, vault of St Peter chapel.

78. Monreale cathedral: view of St Paul chapel from northern aisle.

DECOLA
S PAVLI
3 IO. ROMA
S̅ PAVS

79. Monreale cathedral: *Martyrdom of St Paul*, detail of Plate 78.

80. Monreale cathedral: view of St Paul chapel looking north.

81. Monreale cathedral: apse of St Paul chapel.

82. Monreale cathedral: *Genesis* scenes on southern nave arcade and scenes of *Christ's Ministry* in aisle.

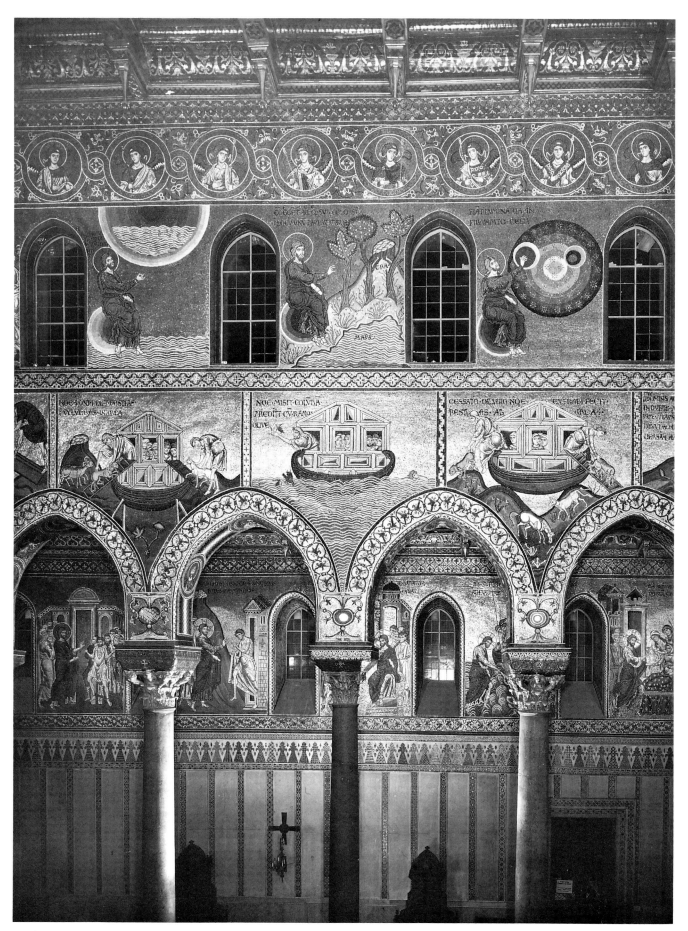

83. Monreale cathedral: *Genesis* scenes on southern nave arcade and scenes of *Christ's Ministry* in aisle.

84. Monreale cathedral: *Genesis* scenes on southern nave arcade and scenes of *Christ's Ministry* in aisle.

85. Monreale cathedral: *Genesis* scenes on southern nave arcade and scenes of *Christ's Ministry* in aisle.

86. Monreale cathedral: west end of nave with *Genesis* scenes and three episodes from the lives of *SS Castus*, *Cassius*, and *Castrensis*.

87. Monreale cathedral: *Genesis* scenes on northern nave arcade, and scenes of *Christ's Ministry* in aisle.

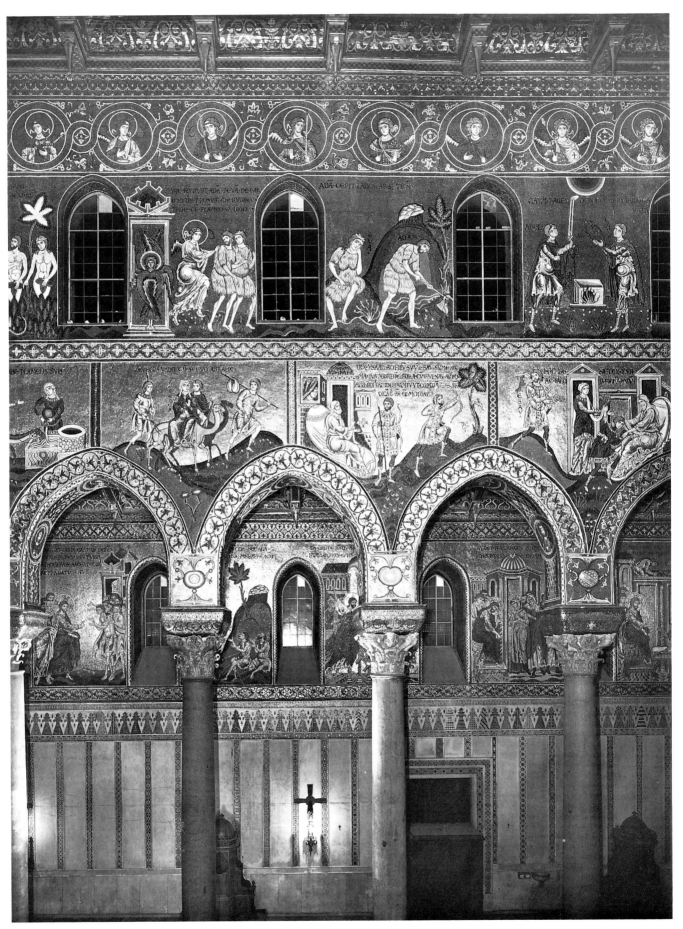

88. Monreale cathedral: *Genesis* scenes on northern nave arcade and scenes of *Christ's Ministry* in aisle.

89. Monreale cathedral: *Genesis* scenes on northern nave arcade and scenes of *Christ's Ministry* in aisle.

90. Monreale cathedral: *Genesis* scenes on northern nave arcade and scenes of *Christ's Ministry* in aisle.

91. Monreale cathedral: view of north-eastern corner of nave with sanctuary arch.

92. Monreale cathedral: view of nothern side of sanctuary arch with *Jesse, Solomon*, and *SS Genesius, Marcianus*, and *Herculianus*.

93. Monreale cathedral: soffit of western arch between nave and sanctuary with *Jesse*, *Obadiah*, and *David*.

94. Monreale cathedral: *St Gerlandus*, southern pier of sanctuary arch, north face.

95. Monreale cathedral: *Warrior Saints* on eastern arch of crossing facing west.

96. Monreale cathedral: *Malachi*, spandrel of sanctuary arch looking west from within crossing.

97. Monreale cathedral: *Isaiah*, spandrel of sanctuary arch looking west from within crossing.

98. Monreale cathedral: view of arches at north-eastern corner of crossing with three medallions of *Kings of Judea* on the left.

99. Monreale cathedral: view of arches at south-eastern corner of crossing with medallions of *Salmon*, *Aminabad*, and *Esrom* on the right.

100. Monreale cathedral: scenes of the *Life of the Virgin* and *Christ's Infancy* on southern arch wall of crossing.

101. Monreale cathedral: view of western arch wall of crossing with the *Nativity*, *Presentation in the Temple*, *Christ among the Doctors*, and the prophets *Malachi* and *Isaiah*.

102. Monreale cathedral: view of northern arch wall of crossing with scenes of *Christ's Infancy* above, and the *Marriage at Cana* and *Christ's Baptism* below.

103. Monreale cathedral: *St Cosmas* and view of throne and northern side of crossing and presbytery.

104. Monreale cathedral: *Christ crowning King William II*, north-eastern corner of crossing.

105.  Monreale cathedral: *William II presenting Monreale Cathedral to the Enthroned Virgin*, south-east corner of crossing.

106. Monreale cathedral: Christological scenes in southern arm of transept.

107. Monreale cathedral: Christological scenes on south-west wall of transept.

108. Monreale cathedral: Christological scenes in south-west corner of transept.

109. Monreale cathedral: Christological scenes on north-west wall of transept.

110.  Monreale cathedral: posthumous events from the *Life of Christ*, north wall of transept.

111. Detail of Plate 110.

112. Monreale cathedral: left half of *Christ curing the Daughter of the Canaanite Woman*, eastern end of south aisle.

113. Monreale cathedral: view of *Christ curing the Daughter of the Canaanite Woman*, eastern end of south aisle.

114. Monreale cathedral: *Christ feeding the Five Thousand*, western end of south aisle.

115. Monreale cathedral: *Christ curing the Woman with the Spirit of Infirmity*, western end of north aisle.

116. Monreale cathedral: view of *Christ curing the Centurion's Servant*, eastern end of north aisle.

DNE FILI MEVS IACET
IN LECTO PARALITIC?
ET MALE TORQVET

117. Monreale cathedral: right half of *Christ curing the Centurion's Servant*, eastern end of north aisle.

118. View of Monreale overlooking the Conca d'Oro of Palermo.